The Dvořák Society
For Czech and Slovak Music

Occasional Publications No.6

Vilém Tauský CBE FGSM

1910-2004

A celebration of his life and achievements published with affectionate remembrance in his centenary year

Foreword by the late Sir Charles Mackerras CH AC CBE

Compiled and edited by Richard Beith

Newcastle-under-Lyme: The Dvořák Society

The Dvořák Society is a Registered Charity, No.267336

Published by

The Dvořák Society
For Czech and Slovak Music

13 Church Lane
Knutton
Newcastle-under-Lyme
Staffordshire ST5 6DU

First Published: 2010

ISBN: 978-0-9532769-8-1 (pbk)
ISBN: 978-0-9532769-9-8 (hbk)

Front Cover illustration:

Vilém Tauský with his WWII medals, the Czechoslovak Military Cross and the Czechoslovak Military Medal of Merit, second class, at his London flat, 21 October, 1997
[Photo: K. Janovický]

Rear cover illustration: [Collection R. Beith]

Printed by:

Greenhouse Graphics, Bramley, Hampshire RG26 5DL

The Dvořák Society is grateful to the Czech Ministry of Foreign Affairs, Department of Cultural Affairs for Czechs Living Abroad (MZV-OKKV) for financial assistance with the production of its various publications.

FOREWORD

What an inspired idea to honour the memory of Vilém Tauský!

I had known Vilém for many a long year because of our common interest in Czech music and the fact that we had both been the Chief Conductor of the BBC Concert Orchestra. I heard his famous broadcast performance of Janáček's *Osud (Fate)* and, of course, he was related to the Fall family of operetta composers, so I always respected him as a musician of extremely wide tastes and experience.

On hearing of his death, it suddenly dawned on me that the last musician who had known Janáček had left us and that from now on there are no more living links with the great composer. Apart from having commenced his studies at the Brno Conservatoire in the last year of Janáček's life, he participated in the editing of *Z mrtvého domu (The House of the Dead)* after the composer's death and also *Výlety páně Broučkovy (The Excursions of Mr Brouček)*, when the Brno Opera staged a nearly complete cycle of Janáček's operas in 1934.

Tauský's musical career was long and distinguished and the present publication presents a magnificent overview of the achievements, interests and personality of this great Moravian musician.

Sir Charles Mackerras

22 August 2007

PREFACE

Vilém Tauský was one of the founder members of the Dvořák Society of Great Britain with the accession number '60'. He was made an Honorary Vice-President in 1993 and from then on was a regular attendee at events in the London area, including Annual General Meetings and Annual Dinners. Many members and guests will remember with pleasure his informative talks in London and at Czech music weekends at Leamington Spa.

This tribute volume originated at a committee meeting in the autumn of 2004 with the very simple idea that the Society should publish a Tauský discography, probably in our journal *Czech Music*. This final volume is somewhat longer and more varied than that original three page list of record numbers.

It opens by reprinting three of Tauský's own essays and continues with personal memories from two younger conductors who were greatly influenced by working with him. It is interesting to note the comments from these professional musicians as to the importance of Tauský as a composer as well as a conductor and teacher. Such comments usually refer to his Meditation *Coventry*. Karel Janovický and I have attempted to summarise Tauský's 'Life and Times' with particular reference to his early days in Czechoslovakia and his wartime experiences between 1939 and 1945. The variety and importance of his work in Brno up to 1939 is quite amazing.

Graham Melville-Mason has contributed two articles, firstly a short piece on letters from Osvald Chlubna and Bohuslav Martinů to Tauský dating from the mid-1950s and, secondly, has provided a detailed discussion of Tauský's repertoire. In particular, the list of all of the works conducted by Tauský during his Manchester years, 1952-1956, taken from his *Little Black Book*, gives a fascinating insight into his activities.

Peter Herbert has written a major essay on the early performance history of Dvořák's *Rusalka* in Great Britain, with particular reference to the first professional production at Sadler's Wells in 1959, conducted by Tauský.

There is some slight duplication between the main texts by Peter Herbert and Graham Melville-Mason and the accounts in the 'Life and Times' section, but all have been left as stand-alone essays.

The volume concludes with a description of the commemorations of his life in 2005, the discography, a listing of Tauský material held by the National Sound Archive and a list of compositions.

Photographic illustrations of Tauský's early life are hard to find, especially of a quality suitable for reproduction. However, one has been located to go with the photographs from his later life. Two family portraits and some Second World War photographs can be found in the biography *Vilem Tausky tells his story* written by his wife Margaret, and Tauský conducting the Czechoslovak Army Band at Aston Abbotts in 1942, can be seen in Neil Rees's study *The Czech Connection.* [1,2]

Every attempt has been made to include the correct Czech diacriticals in the text, but where direct quotations are given from contemporary sources, no attempt has been made to add missing diacriticals, unless so noted. The usage of diacriticals in the 1979 biography of Tauský was inconsistent.

The name Czechoslovakia with a hyphen, *Czecho-Slovakia*, is only correctly used in the context of the Second Czechoslovak Republic, October 1938 - March 1939. Again, no attempt has been made to remove hyphens from direct quotations.

Richard Beith

Blackford, Perth & Kinross

---

[1] Tauský, M., *Vilem Tausky tells his story*, (London: Stainer and Bell, 1979). As the title page of that volume states 'Recounted by Margaret Tausky', I have classified it as a biography rather than an autobiography throughout the present volume. It must be said that the chronology in that volume is not always 100% correct, and that Tauský omitted some fascinating memories in the mistaken assumption that they would not interest the reader! A number of contributors have referred to that volume. To avoid confusion with other texts, after the first appearance in each chapter, the text is referred to as '*his story*', rather than use the formal abbreviations *op. cit.* or *ibid.*

[2] Rees, N., *The Czech Connection, The Czechoslovak Government in Exile in London and Buckinghamshire*, (Chesham: the author, 2005).

ACKNOWLEDGEMENTS

Firstly, we remember our late President, Sir Charles Mackerras CH AC CBE (1925-2010) for kindly contributing the Foreword. From the Dvořák Society, my grateful thanks go to Bob Batey, Margaret Beith, Ronald Corp, Peter Herbert, Karel Janovický, Patrick Lambert, Ray Latham, Bill and Vera Marsden, Tim Marshall, Alex and Graham Melville-Mason, Annette Percy, Pat and Shawn Pullman, Brenda Rayson, Bernard Reynolds (†), David Roberts, Sylva Šimsová, Greg Terian, Haig Utidjian, Heinz Vogel and Eva Wilkinson for their contributions, encouragement, information, proof reading, suggestions and translations.

Special thanks to Fraser Goulding and Philip Hesketh for contributing their memories of Tauský, to the publishers Kahn and Averill for permission to reprint Tauský's text on conducting, to the publishers of the magazine *Opera* for reprinting Tauský's article on *Rusalka*, to Jan Janíček of Brno for supplying photocopies of Free Czechoslovak Forces' ephemera in his archive, to the BBC Written Archives Centre at Caversham for permission to reproduce both the Second World War programme information submitted by Greg Terian and the many Caversham references in Peter Herbert's study of *Rusalka*. Thanks to Pavla Škachová, Press, Politics and Culture, Embassy of the Czech Republic, London. Thanks to all those who helped with photographs and illustrations. These are individually acknowledged.

Grateful thanks to Martin Anderson; Geraldine Auerbach MBE, Director, Jewish Music Institute, London; Julia Creed, Archivist, Royal Opera House Collections, London; Robert Elias, Executive Director, The Orel Foundation, Stevenson Ranch, California; Michael Goold, Historian of WWII musical life in Great Britain; Michael Haas, Producer of the *Entartete Musik* series of CDs; Georg Hamann, violist of the Aron Quartet, Vienna; Derek Katz, Associate Professor Music History, University of California, Santa Barbara; Edmund Pirouet, Archivist of the London Philharmonic Orchestra and the helpful staff of the Central Library, Edinburgh.

Additional thanks to my friends and correspondents Robert Kingsley, Stanley Klar, Eric D. Smith, and Fred Stubens.

CONTENTS

A Tauský family group from the early 1930s probably taken at their home in Přerov

Back row, left to right: Vilém Tauský, his mother Josefina, his father, Dr Emil Tauský, his bother's wife, Anna and his brother Charles. In front: His younger sister Julia and her husband Arnold, with 'Arco'

[Photo: courtesy B. Rayson and Mrs H. Wolff]

Vilém Tauský, outside his WWII billet on The Parade, Leamington Spa, taken during the May 1995 Warwick & Leamington Czech Music Weekend

[Photo: P. Herbert]

Vilém Tauský and Sir Charles Mackerras
at the Czech Embassy, London, in 2000,
on the occasion of Tauský's 90th birthday party

[Photo: S. Pullman]

Vilém Tauský thanks members of the Martinů Quartet following their performance of Tauský's 'Coventry' at the May 2001 Leamington Czech Music Festival Shown: Petr Matěják (Second Violin), Jan Jiša (Viola) and Jitka Vlašánková (Violoncello)

[Photo: S. Pullman]

1

LEOŠ JANÁČEK: A RECOLLECTION

by Vilém Tauský

LEOŠ JANÁČEK: A RECOLLECTION

by Vilém Tauský

He was born in 1854, the son of a Moravian school master and christened Leoš Janáček. The name was well chosen, for throughout his life he was to prove himself lionhearted, as I shall hope to show. He possessed however another quality which I feel lay even deeper than his courage and which he was always trying to express through his inborn musicality. I am speaking of the sense of wonder with which we are all born but which most of us throw aside so easily and so early in our lives. Throughout his life he felt wonder and enjoyment in the life around him in nature, in animals, in flowers and birds, and above all in the everyday life of the people around him. Janáček could echo the Psalmist: 'The heavens declare the glory of God and the firmament sheweth His handiwork'.

These qualities filtered through to me as a student under his direction. Very shy and self-conscious I felt as I walked up the pleasant tree-lined Smetana Street to become a student at the Brno Conservatoire. It was the month of September 1927 and I was one of the youngest students, only seventeen and a bit. I was one of 200 students, all of whom felt grateful and proud as well as shy, as they passed Janáček's little house within the grounds of the Conservatoire. We all knew that we owed our chance of becoming musicians to the courage and perseverance of one man. I also know that I was fortunate enough to be joining an establishment with avant-garde ideas on the teaching of music but just what the new outlook was I had no very clear idea. However I did know what Janáček had achieved in a practical sense. In 1882 he had founded an organ school with nine pupils and three teachers. When the new Republic of Czechoslovakia was established in 1918, the school was ready to become a State Conservatoire with 186 pupils, thirteen teachers and its own buildings.

My first impression of him confirmed my feelings of nervousness and shyness, although he himself would have laughed at the idea that he was frightening. He was a stocky, rather tubby figure, full of energy, surmounted by an abnormaly large head of bristling silver hair and blazing blue eyes, which lent force to all he said. His speech was very characteristic and most alarming. His words came out in staccato patterns like a cross between a machine-gun and a typewriter. All his life he spoke with a Lachian accent. He often gave his operatic characters speech rhythms typical of his own way of talking, as in *Káťa Kabanová*, where the matriarch says: 'You must learn better manners .. better manners ... better ... manners'. If one of his pupils had shown a lack of originality in composition, a favourite rebuke was to rap out, 'What's in your head, boy? Straw?'.

When I knew him he had already gained acceptance of his new ideas in the musical world around him and was beginning to be a world name in music. In his sixties and during the last ten years of his life he wrote *Káťa Kabanová, The Cunning Little Vixen* and *The Macropulos Case*, all of which gained an immediate success. Perhaps he summarised his life in his triumphant second String Quartet which expresses his failures and also the ultimate breakthough to happiness. Before this there were many bitter years, when his great opera *Jenůfa* lay unacknowledged for nearly twenty years after its first production in 1904. Recognition, when it did come, came from Vienna and Germany rather than from Prague.

I have spoken already of his great interest in the world of nature. In the last year of his life, in the spring of 1928, I saw him often sitting in his garden. He loved flowers as he loved animals. Cowslips, snowdrops, violets gave him great pleasure and birdsong was his special delight. Two hens he had trained to jump on the garden table to say good night to him before they went to roost. His two dogs Čipera (Lively one) and Čert (Devil) were constantly with him. He made notes of their speech patterns, even including the change of intonation in Čipera's voice when he changed from a puppy to a dog. I cannot help feeling that as he sat there in the sunshine he was compensating with these simple things for the dark thoughts of his last opera, *The House of the Dead.* Before he left the world he wanted to record the misery of man in chains and his belief in redemption through that spark of divinity in every character, however depraved, which will eventually lead mankind to light and freedom. The score is headed 'In every man there is a spark of God'.

He was an acute observer of life, especially in the sphere of sound; his interest in speech rhythms extended to those of human beings and it is here that his revolutionary ideas about opera began. He listened to the sounds of the human voice made in different situations and instead of expressing emotion through unrelated melodic line he tried to convey it through actual sounds the human voice uttered in this situation. This is his most original contribution to the form of opera, an idea which today has gained worldwide recognition among operatic composers. As students he often told us how he constantly listened to the speech of people going about their normal occupation and noted their intonations. 'I don't need to understand the words', he said, 'I can tell by the tempo and modulation of speech how a man feels, if he is excited, if he lies, or if this is just a conventional conversation. I have been collecting these speech rhythms for over fifty years and I have an immense dictionary. These are my windows into the soul of man and when I need to find a dramatic expression I have recourse to my library'.

At the age of eleven he became a pupil in an Augustinian monastery [in Brno] where the boys were given a general education and a specialised education in church music, so that they could participate in the services and celebrations of the monastery. It was here that he first developed his deep love of Moravia and an enthusiasm for all things Slavonic, which was to colour his music throughout his life. Later he entered a teacher's training college and worked there for some years after his graduation. He also studied at the Organ School in Prague and later in Leipzig and Vienna. With these exceptions Janáček spent his whole life in Brno. He worked extremely hard and acquired a habit of strict discipline in work, which he passed on to his pupils. 'First you must know the rules', he would tell us, 'then sometimes you can afford to break them'. The early years of his life were not happy, because while he worked relentlessly at acquiring a mastery of technique, he was aware within himself that he had something new to say in the world of music, yet he did not know as yet what it was, only that he was dissatisfied with the prison in which conventional musical training fettered his creative spirit.

Perhaps the first happiness that Janáček achieved in music was in his collections of Moravian folksongs, undertaken in collaboration with František Bartoš, the famous Czech philologist. He went first to Hukvaldy, his native region, where he realised that much that he had to say in music was based in the life of this part of the country. The songs reflected the hard life his people led. His famous *Lachian Dances* are a fruit of this experience. From there he went on to Southern Moravia where the songs and dances were much more sparkling and gayer. Wherever he went he made friends with local people, who therefore were 'not shy to sing and dance in front of the gentleman from Brno'.

This is how he felt about folksongs: 'I have lived in it since childhood, in folksong the entire man is enshrined, his body and soul, his milieu, everything. He who is rooted in folksong becomes a complete man'. Even in my day his interest in folksong was undiminished, although he was over seventy. On Sundays he used to walk with some of his students to Moravian festivals in outlying villages, talking of music all the way. The exhausted students used to be glad to climb on a bus for the journey home; not so Janáček who looked forward to the walk back. He was a real father to his students, and took a great interest in their progress and their circumstances. If someone was absent he would sometimes call at his lodgings to see what was the trouble. If the student was merely taking a day off this could be rather embarrassing.

The manner of his death was typical of his life: he died trying to help somebody. He was on holiday at Hukvaldy when a young girl was missing from the village and he insisted on joining the search. He became overheated and exhausted, complications set in and he died in hospital in Ostrava on 12 August 1928. [1]

His death was a grievous shock to the world of music, but especially to the Brno Conservatoire and Opera House. The consolation for us, his students, was that he had formed on his teaching staff a band of colleagues who were deeply imbued with his principles. They were determined that his contribution to music should live on. This was his credo:

> *Grow out of your innermost selves*
> *Never renounce your opinions*
> *Do not toil for recognition*
> *But always do all you can*
> *So that the field allotted to you may prosper.*

---

[1] Tauský was misinformed here. The 'search for a missing child' story is probably a myth, see Tyrrell, J., *Intimate Letters*, (London: Faber and Faber, 1994), especially pp.341-344. It had been suggested that it was Otto Stössel, the eleven-year-old son of Janáček's muse Kamila Stösslová, who was lost on this occasion. Otto and his mother were indeed visiting Janáček at this time, but throughout his long life, Otto Stössel, (1916-2003), always denied being lost on that occasion. (ed.)

These principles he carried out unswervingly in his own life. He counted it a worthwhile task to put Brno and Moravia on the musical map of Europe and in so doing he wrote his own name into the history of music.

In 1974, after an absence of over thirty years, I went back to the little house in the grounds of the old Brno Conservatoire (now the Janáček Museum). All was as formerly, even Paní Janáčeková's mending basket was in its accustomed place. Over all brooded the spirit of the great Janáček. 'What's in your head, boy? Straw?' 'I hope not, Mistře, I hope not'.

Adapted by Vilém Tauský from *Janáček - Leaves from his life,* edited and translated by Vilém and Margaret Tauský, (London: Kahn & Averill, 1982), especially pp.18-23.

Vilém Tauský at Janáček's piano in Janáček's house in Brno, October 1999

[Photo: B. Rayson]

2

DVOŘÁK'S *RUSALKA*

by Vilém Tauský

DVOŘÁK'S *RUSALKA*

by Vilém Tauský

This essay was previously published in the magazine 'Opera' for February 1959. It is reproduced here with the kind permission of the Editor

....

Rusalka is Dvořák's ninth opera (Op.114), and his penultimate work written in the fifty-ninth year of his life at the height of his creative powers. All through his artistic life he was interested in musical dramatic art, but it was not a medium which, in the beginning came easily to him. His great gift for translating atmosphere and situation into exuberant, pure music sometimes obscured the dramatic needs of the story. Although the listener enjoyed floods of beautiful music and melody, he was aware that the dramatic situation had been held up by the composer's over-rich powers of musical inspiration. There was constant conflict between the musician and the dramatist.

Nevertheless, all the early operas were successful in some measure. He began with historic-romantic operas, then came those comic operas in which the national element appears for the first time. After that, the historic operas *Dimitrij* and *The Jacobin*, which were the first highly successful ones from the point of view of the public. It was only after these first seven operas that he found the medium best suited to his operatic genius — the fairy tale. In *The Devil and Kate* and in *Rusalka* he found the material which really fitted the contribution he could make to opera. The stories suited the lyrical quality of his music, the settings were enriched by the national melodies and rhythms which he used, and, perhaps most important of all, he was able to match the dramatic movement of the story in the kind of music which came naturally to him.

It seems probable that the symphonic poems that he wrote between 1896 and 1900 — *The Water Goblin, The Noonday Witch, The Golden Spinning Wheel* and *The Wild Dove,* as well as the oratorio *The Spectre's Bride,* all based on ballad poems by Erben, were the preparations for the Czech national fairy tale through which he reached his ultimate success as an operatic composer.

In considering Dvořák as an operatic composer we must always keep in mind Dvořák the man as well as the musician. His was a peasant nature of simple poetic imagination. He loved the Czech people, their songs and their countryside, and he used these subjects in his music not from an intellectual choice but because they arose directly from his life and his interests. He was also well aware of the great respect in which Smetana was held through his operas of Czech national life, and from time to time he did consciously long to excel in the same sphere. This aim he eventually achieved with *Rusalka*, which for the Czech people from the first performance equalled *The Bartered Bride* in popularity.

The libretto of *Rusalka* is the work of Jaroslav Kvapil, a young and gifted poet who was only 31 at the time and who later became Director of the National Theatre in Prague. He offered it to Dvořák when the National Theatre advertised in the newspaper that the composer was looking for a new libretto. The story has elements in common with De la Motte Fouqué's *Undine* and Andersen's *Sea Maiden*. It is the tale of a water nymph *Rusalka* who greatly desires the love of a man-prince, but having been disappointed in her love brings about her own destruction and that of her lover.

A little story told me by Kvapil himself during the preparations for his own production at Brno illustrates Dvořák's approach to the whole opera. Kvapil said that when he first finished reading the story to Dvořák, he waited for comment — none came. Respectfully he looked up at the master and saw tears in his eyes. 'Poor Prince', said Dvořák sadly, 'Poor Prince!'. The old man was as lost in the story as any child.

His simplicity and sincerity are also shown in a problem he brought to Kvapil connected with the libretto. The text put into the mouth of the Prince contains the following speech:

> On heaven and earth I lay my curse
> I curse both god and spirits all
> Answer then, answer now my call.

This distressed Dvořák very much. 'Listen, I am a believer; I can't curse God in my music. I won't do it!'. It took Kvapil some time to explain that for the Prince in his madness to curse the gods of the Water World is not at all the same as Dvořák himself cursing the Lord God Almighty.

These stories show how simple Dvořák the man was. The sources of his music were to be found in the songs and dances of his own people, and he himself constantly asserted 'I am, and remain, a simple Czech musician'. On the other hand, it must be remembered that although the melodic and rhythmic material was drawn from the people, Dvořák's music did not take the form of folk art. As a man he may have been identified with the people, but as a musician he was of great stature, not only in craftsmanship but in the artistic individuality which led him to make a distillation of the natural musical elements of his environment. Dvořák might truly be said to have fallen in love with the story *Rusalka* and with the main figures of the opera. This is shown in the fact that he finished the whole opera, including the scoring, in five months. The resulting unity can be felt in the work which is like one great song of love. For the first time he succeeded in incorporating the element of song into the dramatic line of the music, giving it a valid function in the drama. In the same way the fine musical phrases are grafted into the dramatic mood of the scene.

From the opening bar the little prelude, only 54 bars long, is already a title page, a distillation of the story we are going to hear. The motive for each of the main characters is given, and even the moods which link the events of the story are suggested in the music. Dvořák was naturally influenced by Wagner in the structure which he used, and all the main characters can be recognized by their leitmotives. Dvořák, with great sensitivity, varied the form of the leitmotive according to the situation in which the character found himself. Although he developed the operatic tradition of his day in this way, he also borrowed from the past in his use of strophic song, but used it so skilfully that rather than halting the dramatic action it actually heightened the tension, as in the Watersprite's Song, and in Rusalka's 'Song to the moon'. His special love and compassion was for the supernatural characters of the story. Rusalka is a fragile figure of great poetic beauty, pathetic in her longing for human love. As the opera develops, sacrifice becomes the key note of her character. Dvořák chose this simple and beautiful melody to represent her at the start of the opera:

This motive undergoes a number of variations throughout the opera. Here is a haunting one which constantly recurs to express her longing for human love. Rusalka's motive is in the clarinets, in typically Slav sixths and thirds, with an undulating string accompaniment on a pedal B flat.

A typically Dvořák variation of Rusalka's theme occurs in unusual circumstances, in the polonaise of the ballet music.

When towards the end Rusalka becomes resigned to her fate, the motive undergoes a final change which suggests fulfilment through sacrifice. This mood is expressed by the tragic sound in the strings, with brass and timpani accompaniment.

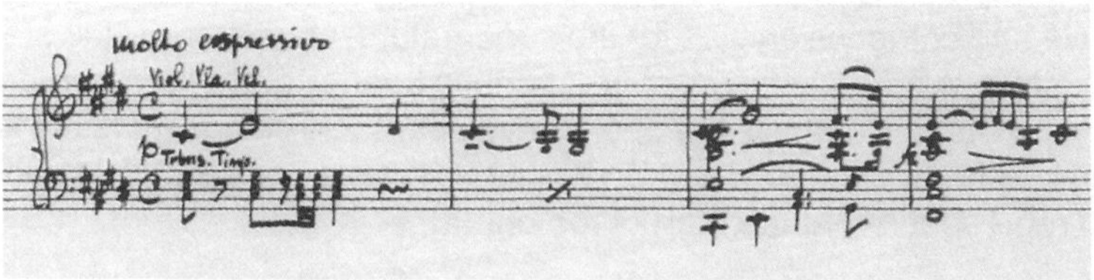

Dvořák also felt a great sympathy for the Watersprite. He is a father type, happy and playful with the creatures in his domain, only becoming anxious and fearful of their contact with human beings. Dvořák characterized him with a most striking little figure.

Dvořák is able to make these few notes change in character so that they are playful on the bassoon, mysterious in the cellos, anxious on the timpani, threatening on the horns.

Jezibaba is a typical Dvořák character, half a witch though towards Rusalka she assumes more of the character of a fairy godmother, for she helps her to become a human being. When in contact with mortals, however, she switches on all her witchery. Finally, the trio of nymphs is used to give musical expression to the enchanted forest. They help to lend relief to the story, and to suggest that another life goes on in the forest as well as the tragic story of Rusalka.

It is easy for the listener to discover where Dvořák's sympathies lay — entirely with the supernatural characters. Even the Prince only receives sympathetic treatment in Acts 1 and 3 where he is in contact with the world of the forest. In the company of human beings, amid the glitter and glamour of the Court in Act 2, he becomes a conventional operatic figure. The Foreign Princess who ensnares the Prince in the second act represents human womanhood with normal sexual powers as against Rusalka's passionless love. Her vocal powers are used as a foil to offset Rusalka's inability to speak in Act 2. Two other delightful characters are the Gamekeeper and the Kitchen Boy, who supply the comic element in the human scenes in rather the same way that the trio of nymphs does in the forest. By bringing these gossips to the enchanted forest in the last act, Dvořák succeeded in lightening the atmosphere with a charming comic episode just before the final tragedy.

The opera ends with the motif of a character who never appears. This motif is heard for the first time in the overture on the horns.

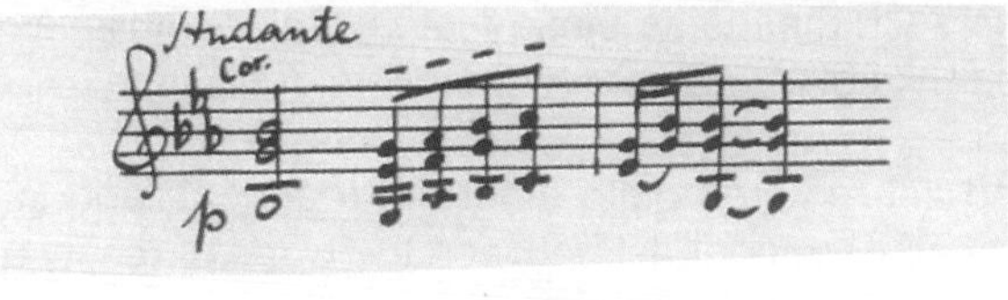

It is sung off-stage by the Hunter as a warning before the Prince meets Rusalka and played at the end of the opera — a most magical sound on muted brass. The Hunter is in reality the conscience of the Prince, and it is as if Dvořák said tenderly in farewell 'You were warned, but you would not heed'.

It is not surprising that with a great symphonic composer like Dvořák the orchestra plays an integral part in the storytelling. At first the long orchestral passages might seem to present a problem to the producer, but when they are analysed from their contrapuntal treatment of the motives and their variations it can be seen that the composer had the unfolding scene clearly in his mind; and far from setting the producer a problem these passages complement both mood and action, and are actually helpful to the development of the drama. It was through his knowledge and experience as a symphonic composer that Dvořák was so successful in capturing both the natural and supernatural atmosphere of the enchanted forest, which is the setting for his fairy tale. His treatment of the orchestra in Acts 2 and 3 is reaching out towards modern impressionism, especially in the economic use of single instruments to obtain orchestral colouring for effects such as dawn, moonlight and rippling water. These techniques, which were new to his work, were very skilfully and successfully developed.

Parallel with this use of the orchestra in a new way there came also a new richness of harmony. An example is his expression of the tragic theme of the lake, based on a progression of three unresolved chords.

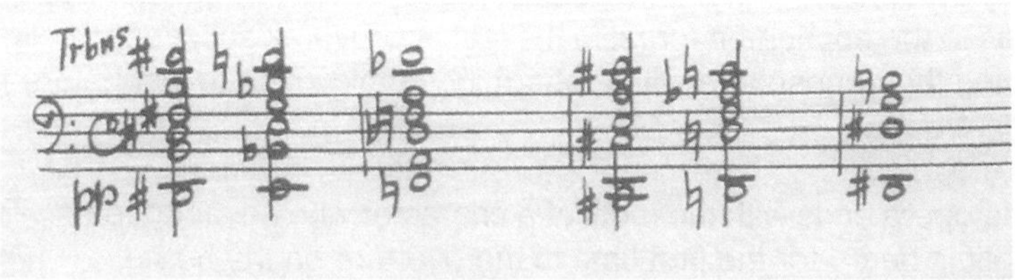

It is through such means as these that Dvořák establishes his place among the ranks of progressive composers of his time.

The second act required quite different treatment, and in it Dvořák solved admirably the contrast between the world of reality and that of the fairy tale. For the other two acts he had to use a new technique, but for the music needed in Act 2 he was already well equipped, and Dvořák the musician could let himself go in great melodic richness and full-blooded orchestration. This excursion into reality is artistically most effective, and just what is needed as a contrast to the spiritual quality of the other two acts.

Having accomplished his opera in the space of five months, Dvořák closed it, as was his custom, with the old Slavonic formula 'Finished, with God's help, on 27th November, 1900'. The National Theatre seized on it eagerly, and the first performance was on March 31, 1901 under the direction of the famous conductor and composer Karel Kovařovic. From the very first performance the work was a great success with the Czech public, and immediately became a repertory opera. It has taken longer to become established internationally. Preparations for a production at Covent Garden were halted by the Second World War, and the forthcoming production at Sadler's Wells will be the first professional stage performance in England.

I was fortunate to be associated with a great production of the opera in Brno in 1934 when Kvapil himself produced it, and in the nineteen years that I have lived in this country it has been one of my dearest dreams to see *Rusalka* on the operatic stage in Britain. [1]

Wendy Toye, who is the producer, and James Bailey, the designer, are working with me in the closest co-operation, as are the gifted cast with Joan Hammond in the title role. It is the hope of us all that this production may incorporate all that is good in the *Rusalka* tradition, and yet bear the stamp of our own times, so that this beautiful opera may be taken to the heart of the public in this country.

....

Diacriticals have been added by the editor

[1] For 1934, read 1938. (ed.)

3

THE CONDUCTOR

by Vilém Tauský

THE CONDUCTOR

by Vilém Tauský

Vilém Tauský contributed this essay to a symposium: 'Tensions in the Performance of Music', edited by Carola Grindea and originally published in 1983. Most of the contributors were Tauský's colleagues from the Guildhall School of Music, London. We are grateful to the publishers, Kahn and Averill, London, for their kind permission to reproduce this valuable text in our present volume.

....

Tension is a quality to be found in many situations in life and it can only be felt by those who are involved in those situations or by those who are witnessing them. Who has not witnessed the tension mount between a mother and her child until the mother slaps him and the child screams? One need only drive alongside a business man hurrying to his appointment and as the traffic lights hold him up, he will look at his watch and beat on the steering wheel with his spare hand to ease the tension. Another example is that of an audience awaiting the appearance of a great artist, when the lights are lowered, the chattering stops and one feels the tension of expectancy. Again, imagine the silence of an audience of several thousand people in a great concert hall, listening intently to the softest pianissimo of the strings. Here is another form of tension. What creates these tensions? In the first case, impatience, in the second frustration, in the third anticipation and lastly, attention.

We think of tension as a kind of invisible resilient force which pulls between a situation and a person, or, in the performance of music, between the performer and the audience. Two factors build the tensions felt by an audience: the composer and the performer.

The composer has crystalised his musical thoughts in writing the work, giving directions as to dynamics, phrasing, and tempi. He builds up tension within the score and it is up to the performer to try to understand the composer's ideas and convey them to the audience, with the same intensity.

If the performer happens to be an orchestral or an operatic conductor his responsibilities are manifold, and so are the problems confronting him, particularly as regards the degree and the different kinds of resulting tensions.

In the first instance, his greatest responsibility is to interpret the work by translating its meaning to the audience in such a way as to convey all its subtleties, even though the composer might not always give clear directions.

Secondly, his instrument is a living body of musicians, each one an individual and this naturally poses problems of communication. The conductor is for the most part a workman whose tools are orchestral players or singers and he must school and control them in such a way that every man knows precisely what to do and when to do it. The conductor is faced with many difficulties in having to cope with a great number of musicians, therefore we will study his work in the two different situations: a) during rehearsals, and b) in performance.

Last, but not least, the conductor must have a sound technique, as the orchestral players, and particularly operatic singers, need a clear beat and exact indications of his intentions.

1: Tensions within the score

There are innumerable examples of various kinds of tensions within the score with which a conductor is confronted.

The beginning of Beethoven's *Fifth Symphony* is a case in point. It is obvious that Beethoven intends to start building tension in the first five bars. No explicit directions are given and musicians have interpreted it sometimes with a slow, doomlike sound, or at other times as a fast, challenging sound. The conductor should feel free to create his own tensions which will largely depend on his reading of the rest of the score.

Two perfect examples of tension in opera arise in the Fourth Act of Puccini's *La Bohème*; one is *musical* and the other *dramatic*. The first occurs at Musetta's entrance. The students have been fooling around with fire-pokers in a mock duel, when the accompanying rumbustious music changes suddenly, with one short fortissimo chord, in a different key. The tension alters to one of tragedy which is poignantly realized by the composer. The other depends upon the conductor and his rapport with the singers. It occurs at the end of the opera when Mimi dies. One bass note holds the tension, glances and words pass between the friends, until, at last, Rudolphe realizes what has happened. Crushing brass chords relieve the former tension, at the same time expressing his overwhelming grief.

This kind of dramatic tension can only be realized through the conductor's skill and perfect timing as well as a close collaboration with the singers.

Here intervenes the question of the role of the conductor and the need for his presence. I am often asked: 'What does the conductor do? Is his presence really necessary? The players never seem to look at him'.

Of course, if the conductor's work were solely to beat out time or to help keep the players together, his job would be of minor importance, though still necessary. But, he has a very different function. He has first to consider the score, decide on the shape and value of the symphony or opera, then form a realization of how the composer has gained his effects, and lastly to help the orchestra interpret them to the audience.

2: Tensions within the orchestra

a) *During Rehearsals*

One of the most important factors in producing a satisfying performance is the work done in rehearsals. Here tension is vital - though of a different nature than in performance - and it consists mainly in holding the interest of the players while the conductor 'strips the picoo down'. The tension in rehearsal cannot and should not be as strong as in performance, and the time spent in 'clearing up' must be fairly allotted. A too tense attitude on the conductor's part may steal some of the energy needed in the performance. As a leader once said: 'You can have it now, or you can have it tonight, but you can't have both'.

Let us look at the functions of the conductor at rehearsals, and then examine what means he takes to carry them out. It is the conductor's responsibility that the orchestra should play the correct notes and, to ensure this, he must first play the work through, using his ears and eyes to check the accuracy of the music. Next, using his artistic intuition, he conveys to the orchestra the ideas he has formed about the shape and balance of the work and the relation between the various sections. He must also consider the balance of wind instruments, as each instrument in this family has a different colour and must be balanced one against the other into one chord. In some particular cases the conductor has to decide on a common breathing to achieve the desired effect. (i.e. the opening chords of the overture to Mendelssohn's *Midsummer Night's Dream*, or the wind chorale at the end of Tchaikovsky's *Romeo and Juliet*).

One of the most effective ways of rehearsing is to take one section at a time and play it through to give the orchestra an idea of the character of the music. The conductor then begins again and interrupts only if technical or interpretative changes are necessary. Finally, it is played in the form in which it fits into the whole work.

Tension is certainly lost and the musicians become bored if from the first note the conductor is incessantly interrupting. I personally do not believe it is necessary to explain the reasons for the effects one is trying to achieve. 'Don't talk about why you do it, just do it,' is my motto. This, the musicians understand and respect perhaps because it allows them to get on with the work.

Freud once said that everything in life could be expressed in terms of 'tumescence' and 'detumescence' - swelling and diminution of swelling. In the perfomance of music we meet with one of the most common uses of tension in expressing the increases and decreases of tone. Yet even some of the best orchestras have to be reminded sometimes that the crescendo and diminuendo must be spaced evenly and gradually, and not played too suddenly. The difficulty is to spread them over a number of bars, otherwise the tension that the composer had in mind is lost and all that one hears is a steady mezzoforte.

An excellent example is the tremendous tension between the Third and Fourth Movement of Beethoven's *Fifth Symphony* or the slowly mounting tension to a great climax, which we find in the symphonies of Bruckner. In the same way, the great crescendi in the overtures and finales of Rossini's operas have to be perfectly spaced to achieve the effect he intended and for which he was known as 'Mr. Crescendo'.

As with crescendi and diminuendi, so accellerandi and ritardandi are a trap for the conductor. An accellerando which is not properly spaced out will certainly ruin the tension towards which it is directed. Similarly a badly calculated ritardando will kill the calming effect which follows a climax, or is the lead to a change of tempo.

Again, in rehearsals, the conductor must clearly establish the execution of accents and fortepianos, as marked by the composer. These should always correspond with the dynamics of the music, and he must carefully distinguish between accents in piano and accents in forte. As to the marking of fortepiano, this presents another difficulty for the orchestra. The conductor will never achieve the tension of a fortepiano if he allows it to be a forte and diminuendo in the same bar.

Though these are considerations of an aesthetic nature, inherent in the interpretation of music, they do present certain problems in rehearsal, depending largely on the skill and tact of the conductor to obtain the right response from the orchestral players.

While still on the subject of rehearsing we must examine the importance of *pauses*, *breaks* and *fermatas*, which are among the most usual ways of creating and relaxing tensions. These are entirely left to the taste and discretion of the conductor. Of course we must differentiate between pauses indicated by the composer, such as one or two silent bars which must be kept in the tempo of the music unless otherwise stated, and those which are marked 'G. P.' or 'Vuota' and can be held at the discretion of the conductor.

This freedom is very important and constitutes the basis of maintaining the tension, particularly in opera. These pauses are used mainly for dramatic effect and they call for a close collaboration between producer, performers and conductor, especially during rehearsals, when decisions have to be made. It is an advantage if the conductor is himself a pianist and is able to work together with the singers at rehearsals from a vocal score. In this way he will be ready to share the technical difficulties and the interpretation it suggests with the singers.

If the cast consists of experienced artists of certain stature, the conductor has to be as flexible as possible and allow them freedom for their own conception of the particular role within the framework of the opera. With less experienced singers, however, he must first impress upon them the need for absolute accuracy, and when this is achieved, he will help them to discover through the music, an interpretation of their own. Thus, they will arrive at a fine performance which should be balanced between musical precision and artistic freedom. A good example is the final scene of Butterfly's death, in *Madam Butterfly* by Puccini, which, although clearly outlined by the composer, gives freedom to the conductor and the singer for a number of interpretations.

As to the controversial subject of *fermatas*, mainly where singers are concerned, the collaboration between the conductor and singers needs tact on the one side and taste on the other. Every singer, naturally, wants to show off his or her voice, and sometimes, especially in Italian opera, the occasion to do so occurs too often to be artistic. In the case of two high notes, fairly close together, if each is given equal rubato value by the singer the tension will be destroyed. The condutor's role is to use his skill and ability to communicate his ideas and convince the singer – if he happens to lack artistic taste – of the need to respect the composer's directions. In fact, this can cause another kind of tension, that of communication.

However, the conductor is not always right when trying to impose the directions given in the score. There are cases in Italian operas when tradition plays a very important part and must be respected. Original scores of famous and established composers, like Verdi or Puccini, were published before the first performance. Later on, from the experience gained from early performances, certain amendments were made which were not always altered in the score. These amendments have now become *tradition* and that is why an operatic conductor should be trained in an Opera House where he can learn the 'unwritten rules'. The final Love Duet in Act 1 of *Madam Butterfly*, or the duets of Alfred and Violetta, in Act 1 and Act 4 of *La Traviata* by Verdi, are very good examples of this oral tradition.

b) *The Performance*

By what means does the conductor hold the tension in performance, that tension which alone can make the music live? First, he must gain the respect of the orchestra or singers through a perfect knowledge of the score, of the thematic material and the orchestration. He must approach the music with sincerity, bearing in mind the composer's intentions and the indication he has given and never supersede them by an interpretation entirely of his own. One sometimes hears young conductors speaking of 'my Berlioz, my Beethoven or my Mozart'. The conductor must think only of how to serve the composer and endeavour to arrive at a stylish interpretation which does justice to the score, promotes the enjoyment of the audience and gradually stamps his own work with integrity. How is the conductor to achieve the tensions of an ideal performance? Inborn musicality, detailed knowledge of the score and sound technique seem to be the first requisites of a conductor.

Musicality is an inborn gift and is not influenced by the personality of the musician. It cannot be added to or subtracted from by human effort. However, sometimes, the personality draws too heavily upon the talent, and the composer suffers from an imbalance of sentiment. It is the role of the conductor to avoid overstressing the emotional value of a work. This fault becomes obvious through exaggerations of tempo in either direction and an over-emphasis of climaxes, thus producing an unbalanced perfomance. Perhaps one should follow Wagner's advice, to 'experience first with the heart and then allow the brain to control the performance'. This emotional experience can only be arrived at through a profound study of the score, the conductor trying to form his own conception of it and hear quite clearly in his own mind how he thinks the composer intended it should sound.

There is a fashion at present [i.e. in 1983. (ed.)] to conduct from memory. The only justification for this would be when the mastery of the score is so complete that its presence is more a hindrance than a help. The audience is there to enjoy the performance rather than to admire the prowess of the conductor. As long as conducting from memory is not undertaken in order to impress the audience, the decision must be entirely a matter of the conductor's choice. What is of primary importance is that he should have the score in his head and not his head in the score.

The building of tension is also achieved by means of rhythm and tempo; two very important factors, because, for the audience they form the basis of music. These factors are very much affected by the temperament of the conductor. He must respect the metronomic marks given by the composer, though very often these are arbitrary, and for some inexplicable reasons, not always correct. In such cases the conductor has to use his own judgement. In my view, the best metronome mark is measured by the feeling in your own heart. No slow tempo must be so slow that the melody is not recognizable; no fast tempo so fast that the melody is no longer recognizable.

The conductor must watch for another weakness which often occurs, especially in romantic music. In a crescendo, orchestras tend to get fast and in a diminuendo, slower. These agogig changes of tempi should be carefully controlled, as, unless they are directed by the composer, they can spoil the overall effect by breaking the music into choppy waves. This happens quite frequently, particularly in some of Tchaikovsky's works, in spite of his most exact directions as to the slightest variations in tempi that he wanted. We only have to look at the opening of the slow movement in his *Fifth Symphony* to realize how scrupulously he has marked the slightest shades of any changes of tempo. In the same way, Mahler, himself a conductor who knew all the pitfalls, marked the changes in great detail, sometimes even adding: 'Don't hurry – wait.' or 'Long pause, short pause'.

In studying the role of the conductor in performance, we must differentiate between the work of an orchestral conductor, who is solely responsible for his performance, and that of an operatic conductor who is less dependent. He has to take many other factors into consideration. This is what Wagner wrote:

> *Just as the right comprehension of the melos of a piece of music suggests the right tempo for it, so the right way of conducting an opera presupposes the true comprehension of the dramatic situation on the part of the conductor. As a matter of fact he must, before all things, have the stage in his eye. This will give him consistently, with due fidelity to the markings of the composer, the criterion as to whether he shall take the tempo faster or slower, how he shall modify it and where he shall expand or contract the volume of orchestral tone. He will not allow himself to draw a melody out at length when the phrasing should be free and animated; he will not beat out a fast tempo, effective as this may be from the merely musical point of view, where the dramatic development goes more slowly; nor will he elaborate orchestral nuances that drown the singers or divert people's attention from the events on the stage.*

After examining the various roles of the conductor during rehearsals and in the performance, we must now study the conductor's technique, without which he would not be able to convey his ideas and intentions to the musicians who have to interpret the score for the audience.

3: Tensions and the conducting technique

Finally, we come to the study of the conducting technique, one of the most important factors in the realization of a fine performance. This is where the conductor may come under severe criticism from both the audience and the musicians he is working with. It is not enough for a conductor to have a thorough knowledge of the score, he must give the orchestral players or singers a feeling of security by a confident conducting technique.

He needs a firm posture and there must be no bending backwards, as if he shrinks from the orchestra, but rather a slightly forward stance, showing that he is in command. The actual beat must be clear, in harmony with the dynamics: small in piano, growing in crescencdo, decreasing for a diminuendo, short and sharp for accents, yet always in the style of the work. No grandiose meaningless gestures, which only irritate the orchestra and distract the attention of the audience.

It is usually a fault with young or inexperience conductors that they use too much of their body. The important tools of the conductor are the arms, hands and wrists, the eyes and the facial expression. The body should only be used to the extent that the position of the orchestra demands. If the conductor uses a stick it should be treated as a prolongation of the arm or wrist. It should be held lightly in the hand, so that a flexible wrist can indicate the beat, while the arm is mainly used to emphasize the dynamics of the music. Under no circumstances must the baton be held stiffly in the hand, because then the wrist is inflexible and the movement becomes clumsy and expressionless. There must be flexibility for the baton even in the palm of the hand.

Breathing is an important factor in conducting. It should be in harmony with the character of the music. Naturally, if the body is overstrained the conductor becomes breathless and it becomes difficult to relax the tension.

The conducting technique should be complemented by the personality of the conductor, which helps to convey his intentions to the orchestra. It is through his personality that he holds, at first, the complete attention of the players or singers. Then, through his eyes, his facial expression, and above all, by encouraging each player or group of players, with an air of expectancy, he will obtain their response.

As to the kind of tensions created through the actual act of conducting, these are similar to those confronting other instrumentalists or singers and these have been studied in detail in the other essays of this book [that is, *Tensions in the Performance of Music.* (ed.)]. There are several factors which have to be taken into consideration when studying the conductor's technique. He has to stand for a long time, both during rehearsal and in performance, facing the orchestral players or the singers, continuously exerting himself to give indications as to tempi and the interpretation of the works. It is very important indeed that there must be release of tension between the exertions. But, what is more important and valuable, is the fact that if the conductor has faithfully carried out the detailed study of the score, analysing the whole shape, its structure and orchestration, and if the work during rehearsals has been done, covering all the aspects discussed in this essay, he will find that in performance, the tensions which are the subject of this study would automatically establish themselves.

What is more, a conductor must work creatively all the time, in rehearsals and in performance. He becomes himself a creator who must add the quality of his vision and imagination to the work, so that forgetful of himself – he recreates together with the orchestra and through them, for the audience, the work as the composer has imagined it.

Glossary (ed.) [1]

Agogic: Type of accent based on duration rather than on volume
Fermata: (It) the prolongation of a note or rest beyond its usual value
G.P.: *Generalpause* (Ger), a rest for the entire orchestra or ensemble
Vuota: (It) Void: a note to be played on an open string or a general pause

[1] Sadie, S., (ed.), *Grove Concise Dictionary of Music,* (London: Macmillan, 1988).

4

VILÉM TAUSKÝ - A PERSONAL MEMOIR

by Fraser Goulding

VILÉM TAUSKÝ - A PERSONAL MEMOIR

by Fraser Goulding

In the Summer Term of 1973, I was appointed répétiteur on the Opera Course at the Guildhall School of Music and Drama, of which Vilém Tauský was the head, and thereby began an association of more than thirty years. From 1973 to 1979, and again in 1982, I acted as Vilém's assistant at Guildhall Opera, playing the piano for rehearsals, and deputising when other work took him away. Thus I gained a unique insight into that musical mind and the way it worked.

We began that summer with Mozart's *The Marriage of Figaro*, and over the years, performed *Così Fan Tutte* and *The Magic Flute*, Britten's *Albert Herring* and *A Midsummer Night's Dream*, R. Strauss' *Ariadne auf Naxos*, Poulenc's *The Dialogues of the Carmelites*, and many other well and not so well known operas and excerpts. Every term brought a different opera, and a different style. Vilém's operatic pedigree is well documented in *Vilem Tausky tells his story*. He began in the traditional way as a répétiteur in Brno, moving up to become assistant conductor then conductor, working with many of the great Czech and German conductors of the time. Once in Britain, he conducted for The Royal Opera, Sadler's Wells and the Carl Rosa Company. The extraordinary interpretative aura Vilém displayed when conducting was a distillation of these and many other influences. As colleague, teacher and mentor his influence, in turn, on countless singers, instrumentalists and conductors is incalculable.

How fortunate we were to learn so many works from a man who had, in turn, prepared them with his own mentors, Zdeněk Chalabala, Erich Kleiber, Clemens Krauss and who had worked with Richard Strauss, Martinů, Britten, Poulenc, and many others on their own operas. For example, at the first rehearsal of *The Dialogues of the Carmelites*, he suddenly said, jabbing a finger at my vocal score, 'Poulenc changed that note'. This happened several times during the rehearsal. The year was 1982, and, he was remembering alterations Poulenc made at Covent Garden in 1953! Preparing operas by Britten, he was able to pass on to us the composer's own interpretation of his work, and how the original cast delivered their roles.

Preparation time at Guildhall Opera was comparatively generous, and for the first few weeks of term, we would work on the music, beginning with each character on his or her own, and gradually building up the ensembles. Vilém would preside over these music calls, making quite clear how he wanted the music to go, by conducting and, where necessary, explaining in more detail. Then, the production rehearsals would begin, and Vilém would be there, watching the stage setting unfold and occasionally commenting if he thought musical groupings or dramatic points could be improved. Later still would come rehearsals with orchestra, where he would galvanise the players and incorporate them into his vision of the music and drama. Finally we arrived at the performances, and he would be in the pit, steady as a rock, looking after his singers and players and at the same time remaining true to his interpretation. All this was done without fuss or unnecessary explanation. He was simply doing the job he loved which he had learnt by example and from experience.

We know that singing and vocal music was a great influence as he was growing up, in particular from his mother, an opera singer, and from his encounters with his 'uncle', Leo Fall. [1]

Certainly, he was a natural opera conductor. He breathed instinctively with the singers, allowing them to expand when they were able, or moving the music on when they were running short of breath, whilst all the time being aware of the overall phrasing and structure of the music. He knew all the tricky moments which needed clear cues and was a consummate rescuer of the occasional wrong entry.

His experience was not confined to opera, although his book contains an appended list of over 100 operas he could conduct at 24 hours notice. To him, music was music, whether it was vocal, orchestral, chamber, solo, light or serious. He conducted an enormous variety of music of all kinds, from the classics to world premières, and made no arbitrary distinctions. He was the first conductor to perform a cycle of Bruckner symphonies (with the BBC Northern Orchestra), and gave the first British performances of several operas by Smetana. In between he might be heard on BBC Radio conducting *Semprini Serenade*, or on television conducting *The Vera Lynn Show*.

---

[1] For his actual relationship to Leo Fall, see fn.[1] on p.47. (ed.)

It was his heartfelt mission to work with students. As well as being Head of Opera at the Guildhall School, he was also Professor of Conducting. Perhaps remembering his own strict teachers he could be very scathing to anyone he felt was not working hard enough and it is probably fair to say that he was even harder on the conducting students than the singers. He believed that conducting was a privilege which had to be earned. To one startled student who announced he would like to study Strauss' *Four Last Songs* and several Mahler symphonies, he said sternly 'Go away and conduct *The Merry Widow* for three years, and THEN you might be able to conduct Strauss and Mahler'. He was not always good at explaining conducting technique. If asked about a specific point, for example, a change of tempo, or awkward pause, he would probably give not very convincing instructions. If one could watch him negotiate such hurdles, it became crystal clear how it could be done.

So what was his conducting style? His beat was rather large, with a comfortable round, rolling motion, smooth rather than jerky except in very rhythmic or jagged passages. He made great use of his left arm, almost sculpting the music with those large fingers and palm. Thus, the phrasing was paramount and it was always clear exactly where, when and how the notes and phrases should be played. He told one conducting student: 'Never mind one, two, three, four; just conduct the music'. He could place perfectly and exactly any chord of any dynamic and intensity. To watch him conduct works by composers as diverse as Mozart, Beethoven, Dvořák, Smetana, Johann Strauss, Offenbach, Britten, Peter Wishart or William Alwyn was sheer pleasure. Players and singers trusted him implicitly to help them do their job. Here was a man who was utterly inside the music, and who knew and felt intuitively just how it should go with those particular performers at that particular time.

In the late seventies, he was conducting a performance of *The Magic Flute* at the Guildhall Theatre in the Barbican. During the scene leading to the Trial by Fire and Water, suddenly the music became slower and much more intense than it had ever been in rehearsal. It was as though he had switched onto a completely different plane. Afterwards he told me that was how Erich Kleiber used to take that passage. At that moment, he knew that the Tamino, Dennis Hooker, was able to sustain the line, and would be able to follow his intentions. He rarely marked anything in a score, and it always amazed me how in hired material he could ignore other conductors' frantic pencil and blue crayon scribbles. Everything was in his head.

He never talked much about his compositions, and I was surprised to learn, after his death, of the number and wide range of works he had written. The variety is another testimony to his simple belief in the power of music; all are written from the heart, in that wonderful rounded manuscript, from a desire to express something in music at a particular time, for example, *Coventry*, a Meditation for String Quartet, and the orchestral suite *From our Village*.

Some singers and players found him domineering and intractable. Certainly, he delighted in scoring points off people, particularly if he thought they were too full of themselves. This was a test, to see who could stand up to the verbal sparring. To a soprano trying to defend herself against what she felt was unjustified criticism, he said 'You know, you will never win', but with a twinkle in his eye.

Some of his sayings have become almost legendary. A few examples may amuse: after a tiring dress rehearsal of an opera: 'Go home and sleep' ... pause ... 'I don't care who with' ... another pause ... 'Then it might be *The Beginning of a Romance*', (the title of the opera). After a spate of split notes in the notoriously difficult *Se vuol ballare*: 'Horns, go home, we don't need you'. To a hapless percussionist in the BBC Symphony Orchestra who was sporting a pair of dark spectacles: 'If you took off your glasses, you might be able to see the music'. Another percussionist, my friend and colleague Stephen Henderson recalls that for recording sessions for *Semprini Serenade* players would often arrive late, as there was no pressure on recording time. Vilém would always start exactly on time by rehearsing the signature tune, regardless of how many were missing. Then as players arrived, saying 'Sorry I'm late, Mr. Tauský', he would reply 'You are sorry. WE are sorry you are late', usually repeated several times for each player.

His public persona therefore could seem severe. In fact he was a kindly man, always concerned for the well being of his family and friends. He had a great sense of humour, and was not at all against change or modernising. When Wilfred Judd set the opening of *The Magic Flute* with the Three Ladies knitting an enormously long serpent, and Papageno with a supermarket trolley, listening to a 'Walkman', Vilém was entranced, and constantly enthused at how well the updating worked. He bought Wilfred a clockwork frog in appreciation.

His last public performance was in 1994, conducting Chelsea Opera Group in Smetana's *The Brandenburgers of Bohemia*. (See overleaf) He had never conducted it before, although he knew the work well, having heard it often in his teens and twenties. Watching him then, sixty years seemed to roll away. He conducted with a ferocious energy and precision I certainly had not seen before. I asked him after the performance where that had come from. He replied simply: 'It is in my blood'.

To me personally, he was an inspiration, and the single most important influence on my musical life. As the weeks, terms and years went by, playing for his rehearsals, or harpsichord continuo in *Figaro* and *Così,* celeste in *The Magic Flute*, working alongside him, and observing all he did, I realised that he was consciously and unconsciously handing on to me the fruits of this vast knowledge and experience. His encouragement and guidance gave me courage to follow my chosen career. From being good colleagues, we became true friends. When rehearsing together, each knew exactly what the other was thinking. He came to hear me conduct whenever he could. His wife Peggy told me that after hearing the overture to *The Pirates of Penzance*, he whispered to her approvingly: 'That was conducted with love'. He was always there to help me with works I was learning; sometimes he would play them for me on the piano, at other times, humming gently and pointing at the score was sufficient. If I felt I had not done as well as I should, he would say: 'Don't be depressed', and give some example from his own experience. On an occasion when I was passed over for a post, he took me to a restaurant, and wrote down on a paper napkin a series of names and events where something similar happened in Prague early in his own career. At another performance, of *Ariadne auf Naxos*, talking about me, I am told he said, proudly: 'Of course he is good. Who do you think taught him?'.

For thirty-two wonderful years, he gave me unstinting guidance and support. In all that time two rather prickly people exchanged never a cross word. I miss him terribly, but he is always there in the background, that commanding, magnetic, comforting presence still influencing my own life in music. His compositions remain, and the priceless knowledge and fruits of his experience which he imparted, will be passed in turn to our successors.

CHELSEA OPERA GROUP

Leader: Diana Cummings
Chorus Master: John Gibbons

THE BRANDENBURGERS IN BOHEMIA

("Braniboři v Čechách")

Opera in three acts
by
Bedřich Smetana
(1824 – 1884)

Libretto by Karel Sabina

First performed at the Provisional Theatre, Prague, on January 5th, 1866

A concert performance in the English translation by Deryck Viney

Conducted by Vilém Tausky

Cast in order of singing:

Oldřich Rokycanský, a knight ....Fan-Chang Kong *(baritone)*
Volfram Olbramovič, Lord Mayor of Prague.........................Mark Beesley *(bass)*
Junoš, a young Prague burgher ....Richard Braebrook *(tenor)*
Ludiše, Volfram's daughter ....Helen Kucharek *(soprano)*
Jan Tausendmark, a young Prague burgher ....Jeffrey Carl *(baritone)*
Vlčenka, Volfram's daughter ....Jacqueline Bremar *(soprano)*
Děčana, Volfram's daughter ....Marion Olsen *(mezzo-soprano)*
Jíra, a runaway serf ....Donald Stephenson *(tenor)*
Old villager ....Jeremy White *(bass)*
Town crier ....Fan-Chang Kong *(baritone)*
Varneman, a Brandenburger captain ....Terry Jenkins *(tenor)*

The action takes place in Prague and the surrounding countryside in the year 1279.

Vilém Tauský's last operatic performance:
'The Brandenburgers in Bohemia'
at the Queen Elizabeth Hall, London, on 13 November 1994

[Collection R. Beith]

5

VILÉM TAUSKÝ - A RECOLLECTION

by Philip Hesketh

VILÉM TAUSKÝ - A RECOLLECTION

by Philip Hesketh

In early 1994, I found myself, in a state of some apprehension, arriving at a large block of flats overlooking Haven Green. I had, some three years previously, taken over as Musical Director of the West London Sinfonia, a fine amateur orchestra based in Ealing and the suggestion had been made that I should make contact with Vilém Tauský, a prominent local resident. As a new young conductor meeting a great master whose name I had known from childhood it was perfectly natural for me to feel a little nervous. However, I had encountered Vilém before and the memories did nothing to still my inner turmoil.

I spent the first years of my professional life as a cellist and my initial studies had been at the Guildhall School of Music where Vilém was Professor of Conducting. He was known as a perfectionist, demanding and frequently irascible and he certainly seemed, to a green young music student, to live up to that reputation. Many were the tales of tension and tempest in the rehearsal studio and those hapless students who, through incompetence or indolence, had received a lashing would lick their wounds ruefully afterwards. Most music students, however, know instinctively when such trials are worth the pain and Vilém commanded enormous respect and devotion amongst us. It is with great regret that I recall my own slightly bizarre and abortive experience of working with the great man. The opera production that had been programmed for that year was *The Coronation of Poppea* by Monteverdi and the full glory and splendour of the nascent Early Music Department was unleashed upon it. This was not, as one can easily imagine, Vilém's natural habitat and his involvement with the project was short-lived, leaving the 'antiphonal continuo units' to hold the thing together. However, as my harpsichord partner in the first of these units was a young pianist and conducting student by the name of Paul Daniel, the performances were in good hands.

All of this was in my mind as I arrived at his apartment but within moments of being admitted he had put me completely at my ease and from then on, at all our subsequent meetings, he was always unstintingly helpful and supportive both to me and to the members of the orchestra.

He was also, of course, extremely challenging. His attitude to excellence in music and conducting was utterly unbending and whilst he was always extraordinarily generous and helpful in correcting faults, he was merciless in pointing them out. Needless to say, on the rare occasions that compliments were truly earned they were given freely and honestly.

It must be said, however, that the nature of amateur music making, with its necessary compromises and accommodations, was often a bit of a mystery to him. An amateur orchestra is run by the players and for the players and consequently, as Musical Director, one is required to make artistic decisions such as programming with one large eye firmly on the musicians' enjoyment of the experience, not only of the performance but also of the hours of preparation and rehearsal. Vilém would have none of this. 'Why?' he would demand in exasperation on hearing of some choice which displeased him. 'Why must you play this?'. 'You should play a Martinů symphony instead' he would declare. 'That is great music'. My explanation that, even though I would love to do this, the players may not agree was met with incomprehension or scorn. 'You are the conductor. The musicians will play what you tell them to play'. Difficult though this made things I am keenly aware that without such prodding and encouragement I would never have introduced my orchestra to such a composer as Josef Suk, whose *Asrael, Pohádka* and *String Serenade* thrilled and delighted musical amateurs who otherwise would probably never have heard them, let alone performed them publicly.

Vilém seemed very happy to be associated once more with an orchestra and he enthusiastically attended rehearsals and performances. 1994/5 was the orchestra's 25th anniversary season and for this he gave us a delightful new piece of his own, the *Serenade for Strings*, which we performed in October 1994. His vast experience in opera was also reflected when we undertook semi-staged performances of Puccini's *La Bohème* and Bartók's *Duke Bluebeard's Castle*. The news that this very well known conductor was actually still active and busy with the orchestra was a great thrill to the players and audiences who had not heard of him since they had listened to *Friday Night is Music Night* many years before.

In 1996 we were delighted when Vilém agreed to become the President of the WLS and marked this singular honour with a performance of Suk's extraordinary and monumental *Asrael Symphony*, which he himself had premièred in this country with the BBC Northern Orchestra in 1954. Vilém's personal experience not only of the music but also of the characters and events behind this intensely autobiographical work was overwhelming and a great privilege for us all.

Another highlight of that year for me came when Vilém agreed to come briefly out of his long retirement and conduct the orchestra in a performance of *Vltava* at Stamford School. Had the years mellowed him? Not a bit! But the musicians will remember that concert all their lives. Vilém remained our President and continued to attend our concerts right up until his death. It is still with a sense of great loss that I realise, at the end of a performance, that he is not sitting in the third row peering myopically at the stage and that there will be no pithy and pertinent post mortem of the orchestra's playing or my conducting before we leave.

Into every life a little rain must fall and, for the conductor, this precipitation often takes the form of the minority of musicians who seem temperamentally unsuited to the activity, namely bored and disillusioned professionals or blasé amateur dilettantes. From time to time a surfeit of such folk can plunge the sunniest disposition into a deep and abiding depression and, on such an occasion a cup of tea and a chat with Vilém was always a great restorative. Music was his whole life; whether studying it, performing it or just talking about it, it was clear that, for him, nothing was more worth doing.

Whilst he was completely at home with the masters of 'serious music' he would also express unqualified admiration for the composers of the great Viennese waltz tradition or post-war BBC light music. In these cynical and discontented days it is wonderfully refreshing to be reminded that Franz Lehár and Leo Fall or Eric Coates and Ronnie Binge all belong to exactly the same world as Mahler and Stravinsky and their music must be approached with just the same open mind, open heart and complete seriousness of purpose. I quickly learned that to express the slightest hint of disdain for the lighter music was, to him, a terrible and tragic mistake and a crime which disbarred one from claiming any true feeling for music.

The wearisome intellectual fastidiousness with which musical sophisticates so pollute the world was incomprehensible to one so honest and big-hearted and in my experience, he simply ignored it.

It was through Vilém that I and several of my colleagues in the orchestra came into contact with the Dvořák Society and here I found a striking reflection of Vilém's attitudes. In an age when politicians and others seeking public approval are told repeatedly and unequivocally that a liking for classical music will brand them as elitist or intellectual (having a mind that works is electoral suicide, apparently) it is important and wonderful to know that such an organisation can not only continue to exist but can thrive.

To my lasting regret I never did programme a Martinů symphony. Indeed, the only piece I have yet conducted by this prolific and wonderful composer is the little known *Intermezzo*, which the WLS played in our commemorative concert on the first anniversary of Vilém's death. This, together with a suite from *Die Dollarprinzessin* by his 'uncle', Leo Fall, would have pleased him mightily, I think. 'Very good, Philip, very good. Leo Fall was a great composer, you know. By the way, you should look after your second violins, they are often flat. And your tempo in *Vltava* was too fast, much too fast. You must learn to think like a Czech. Come for tea and we can talk about it'.

6

THE LIFE AND TIMES OF VILÉM TAUSKÝ

by Richard Beith and Karel Janovický

Tauský at home: 1910-1939 (KJ)

The Military Career of Private Tauský: 1939-1945 (RB)

Tauský in Great Britain: 1945-2004 (KJ)

Tauský's birth town, Přerov (Prerau), circa 1910

[Collection P. Herbert]

TAUSKÝ AT HOME: 1910-1939

by Karel Janovický

The Czechoslovak Music Dictionary of 1965 is silent on Vilém Tauský – why? Before the war in Brno Tauský was one of the city's top musical personalities; he was twice decorated by his own country for his wartime service and after the war he became the most successful champion of Czech music in Britain as well as wider afield.

Tauský's life offers enough material for more than one biography: at different times during his 93 years he was not only a brilliant pianist and répétiteur, composer and conductor, chorusmaster, army sergeant, star of popular light music on the radio, but also a long-serving teacher at the Guildhall School of Music in the City of London, fondly remembered by many singers and musicians who had had the good fortune to attend his opera classes.

Vilém Tauský was born on 20 July 1910 at Přerov in central Moravia. He was the youngest of four children in a family which was half musical: his father, Emil, was a doctor in the service of the state railways, but his mother, Josefina, was an opera singer (she sang, for instance, Susanna in Mozart's *Marriage of Figaro* under Gustav Mahler's baton at the Vienna Court Opera). Vilém's 'uncles' on his mother's side were the operetta composers Leo Fall and Leo Ascher. [1]

He remembered how in their company he used to meet people like Lehár and Oscar Straus, 'listening to their coffee-shop conversation, watching them play cards and being introduced to their publishers'. It was undoubtedly from this fertile soil that his own operettas were to grow. Equally strong, if not stronger, however, were his first impressions of 'serious' music. The director of the local hospital in Přerov and colleague of Vilém's father, Dr Karel Šantrůček, was the husband of Antonín Dvořák's daughter Magda - herself a professional singer.

---

[1] Fall was, in fact, his mother's first cousin, while Ascher was his mother's brother. Two more Falls were musicians also, both younger brothers of Leo: Siegfried became professor of music at the Berlin Conservatoire, and Richard a composer of cabaret chansons and operetta in Vienna. Richard perished in the Auschwitz concentration camp. There were two Fall sisters.

Vilém was always looking forward to hearing the stories of her European concert tours with Edward Grieg. She liked to devote the first half of her programmes to songs by Dvořák, and the second to those of Grieg. Together with Vilém's mother, they often liked to sing duets. From time to time Dvořák's widow, Anna, would visit Přerov.

> *She was a very nice person. She must have noticed how deeply impressed I was by her, and so - to my great joy - she gave me a page from the score of Dvořák's opera 'Jakobín' with corrections in the composer's own hand. My older sister Vally happened to be singing in 'Jakobín' at the time.* [2]

These, then, were the roots of Tauský's career as an opera conductor with a repertoire numbering over 120 works ranging from the classics to 20th century composers (Bartók, Britten and others). [3]

In the wider circle of the Dvořák family he also met Josef Suk, Dvořák's late daughter Otilka's husband. It seems as no accident that Tauský claimed that he first introduced Suk's *Asrael Symphony* to audiences in Britain in two concerts with the BBC Northern Orchestra on 27 and 28 April 1954 in Manchester. [4]

A talent for music, an 'occasional' inclination to study diligently (at the Music School in Olomouc and other places) and opportunities to accompany singers on the piano in the family circle at home would appear to be a particularly fortunate combination of circumstances for any budding musician – should he indeed want to pursue a career in music. And Vilém did want to pursue that option, but he was not the first gifted person in the history of music to be sent by his sensible parents to university to study a 'trade with good prospects'. At the law school Vilém lasted just one semester, soon switching to the Janáček Conservatoire in Brno. He enrolled for composition, submitting his *Cello Sonata* in support of his application.

---

[2] Tauský, M., *Vilém Tauský tells his story*, (London: Stainer and Bell, 1979), p.13.

[3] 115 operas and operettas were listed as conducted by Tauský in *his story*, pp. 159-160, but he continued to add new works, see pp.119-120 of this volume.

[4] *Asrael* had been heard earlier in Great Britain on a Third Programme broadcast conducted by Kubelík on 20 November 1947, but a public performance by Walter Süsskind and the Scottish National Orchestra scheduled for the 1952 Edinburgh International Festival had to be abandoned as the orchestral parts could not be obtained, see *The Scotsman*, 22 August 1952. (ed.)

Since he had finished his secondary school education and taken his 'maturity' examination, he was free at the Conservatoire to devote himself entirely to musical subjects. The atmosphere at the Brno Conservatoire sparkled with the fame of Leoš Janáček's final years, but for Tauský there was little chance to enjoy much more than the sense of the great man's presence and influence, since eleven months into Tauský's first year at the school Janáček was dead. [5]

Four years followed of studies with Janáček's colleagues and pupils: Osvald Chlubna (orchestration), Zdeněk Chalabala (conducting) and Vilém Petrželka (composition). For his graduation, Tauský composed an orchestral *Sinfonietta* which was later to secure him a state prize and a place at the Master School of the Prague Conservatoire. Prague saw a re-crossing of some of the paths that Tauský was to tread for the rest of his life: his professor of composition at the School turned out to be Josef Suk, and it so happened that his fellow students were the pianist Rudolf Firkušný, two years his junior, and the pianist and conductor Walter Süsskind. [6]

When Tauský returned briefly to Czechoslovakia 36 years later in October 1974, a lady ran after him in the street in Přerov, crying, 'This must be Mr Tauský! I am Rudolf Firkušný's sister, Marie'. She wanted to tell Tauský she had got a ticket for his appearance in Olomouc, both to see the opera and to tell him that she had seen Tauský's father the evening before he was taken away by the Germans to be sent to a concentration camp. Dr. Tauský asked her to thank Firkušný for letting the family know that Vilém was alive and that he had successfully found sanctuary in France.

During Tauský's second year of studies in Brno he twice became the recipient of a welcome stroke of luck: the Brno Opera was rehearsing Fibich's *Šárka* when Chalabala's répétiteur was taken ill. Chalabala invited his pupil Tauský to help out at the Opera and, seeing that he was doing well, continued to employ him. Soon Tauský was in on the rehearsals for another opera, Puccini's *Turandot*. At eleven a.m. on the day of the première Chalabala was taken ill. It was decided that Tauský should conduct that night.

---

[5] Leoš Janáček died on 12 August 1928.

[6] Jan Walter Süsskind (1913-1980), music director of the Carl Rosa Opera Company 1943-45 and thus Tauský's immediate predecessor in that post.

It was not an easy assignment: Zinka Kuncová (Turandot) sang in Croat, Jan Kiepura (Calaf) in Italian and the rest of the cast in Czech. But the performance - in Tauský's own words - had gone reasonably well.[7]

Not so long after, the 21-year-old Tauský was standing on the conductor's rostrum in charge of rehearsals for Mussorgsky's opera *Boris Godunov* with the legendary Chaliapin in the main role. At the same time Tauský was using his pianistic talents not only as a répétiteur but also as an orchestral player and soloist in performances of works like Stravinsky's *Firebird* and *Petrushka*, Martinů's *Špalíček* and other scores. The 30s in Brno were a time of a flowering of music and of enthusiasm – a time whose excitement Tauský fully embraced.

On 8 March 1932 the Brno *Beseda* (Friendly Society) put on Carissimi's oratorio *Jeptha* and three Bach cantatas, with Tauský playing the harpsichord. A month or so later the Brno Radio broadcast the play *Marcela* by František Kožík and Svatopluk Ježek, to which Tauský composed a jazz score. And just then Tauský was appointed conductor of the Opera of Moravia's *Zemské divadlo* (Theatre) in Brno. [8]

Amidst all these activities he was only now getting ready for his graduation concert at the Conservatoire, to be held in June: he was to conduct Smetana's tone poem *Šárka*. The critic of the paper *Lidové noviny* thought that:

> *Of all the graduates Vilém Tauský is perhaps the strongest as a conductor thanks to his temperament, ... in his broad, massive and emphatic gestures, his musical strength, as well as the occasional dose of surface effect, there is something reminiscent of Oskar Nedbal.*

The *Brněnská svoboda*, however, begged to differ somewhat, saying that Tauský:

---

[7] The Croatian soprano Zinka Kuncová (1906-1989) later married a Mr Milanov. As Zinka Milanov she became well known in the USA, particularly at the Metropolitan Opera, and elsewhere. (ed.)

[8] The *Zemské divadlo* was built in 1882 and before 1918 was known as the *Stadttheater*. In the immediate post-WWII period it was called *The Janáček Theatre*. It is now known as the *Mahenovo divadlo* or Mahen Theatre.

... puts his every nerve in the service of the musical work, ... little caring for any superficial effect of his spontaneous approach and gestures, since he knows that his busy liveliness is sweeping along both the players and the audience. He points up the dynamics, he lets himself be carried along by the melodies and rhythms, demonstrating that he will make a well-qualified theatre conductor possessed of a full-blooded sense of the dramatic.

The Zemské divadlo, Brno, now the Mahenovo divadlo: Tauský's opera and operetta performances took place here

[Collection R. Beith]

Many of Tauský's own works were being performed: the Brno Radio broadcast his *Wind Quintet*, his *Little Piano Suite*, *Nursery Rhymes* (a cycle of songs with piano accompaniment to words of Slovak folk poetry), and *Songs of Slovácko*. Tauský was appearing in radio 'cabarets' and 'novelty cabarets', sometimes as pianist, at other times as conductor.

Brno was at that time a testing ground for new music and new productions that only got to Prague later on or possibly not at all. 'The difficult music of Roussel's ballet *The Spider's Banquet* was surprisingly well conducted by Tauský; it was the first time he had undertaken such an important task', wrote the *Moravské noviny* on 20 March 1933.

The Brno Radio put on the modernist oratorio *HMS Royal Oak* for narrator, tenor, mixed choir and symphonic jazz orchestra by Ervin Schulhoff, based on a real story from recent history about a mutiny on the Royal Navy's battleship of that name. Tauský's conducting was 'technically safe, paying special attention to the rhythmic aspect', wrote the critic of the *Lidové noviny.* But Tauský was showing also the classical side of his musical talent all this time: in October 1937 he took part in the *Zemské divadlo's* homage to Vítězslav Novák by conducting his ballet *Signorina Gioventù.* According to the *Národní noviny* he displayed 'a lively understanding for the lush polyphony and heady colours of Novák's score'. It had not been an easy task, but according to the critic of the *Moravský přítel lidu* he:

> *tackled his difficult task with great success. The masterly work, scored with virtuoso technique ... was in Tauský's hands clearly articulated and comprehensible.*

At a Dvořák evening a year later Tauský conducted the opera *Tvrdé palice (The Stubborn Peasants).* His feeling for vocal music had been growing during this period: The Moravian Composers' Club put on his *Four Songs* for soprano and piano (with himself playing the accompaniments 'unobtrusively and skillfully', according to the *Brněnská svoboda* on 9 May 1934), the Friends of Art Club his *Písně pěšáka (Songs of an Infantry Man)* in February 1937 and when a book of poems and prose in memoriam of the late President T. G. Masaryk was being compiled, Tauský contributed a male voice chorus *Bože veliký a mocný Bože (God Great and Mighty God)* to verses by one of the book's authors, Otakar Peterka.

Experience gained at Brno Radio and his earlier collaboration with the writer František Kožík allowed Tauský to embark on a large-scale radio project - a Christopher Columbus epic *Cristobal Colón* to a huge symphonic score. The cast included several leading actors of the *Zemské divadlo*, with a 100-strong orchestra conducted by the composer. As the periodical *Obzor* wrote on 19 April 1934, 'the play was so successful that the management of Brno Radio decided to broadcast it again at the end of May'.

Lidové noviny spoke about cogent dialogues, onomatopoeic music, and choral declamation expressing the mood and the crowd's movements around the protagonists of the drama. It all testified to the modernist concept of the work, as well as the élan with which both the creators and the promoters tackled such ambitious projects at the time. In another comment printed eight days after the first broadcast, *Lidové noviny* added:

> *It remains to say something about the music to this radio play, for Vilém Tauský's score performs a role equal to that of the spoken word ... It is true that we are still only at the beginnings of the development of such musico-dramatic forms and cannot lay claim to music that is original and fully convincing artistically ... Tauský's score is not self-sufficient, it and the non-musical elements of the play are interdependent ... but it is tasteful and it serves the radio genre very well, ... effectively helping to mould the totality of the drama.*

Only another short step now lay between Tauský and film music. In June 1938 a film comedy with his music, *Ztratila se 'Bílá paní' (The Picture of the 'White Lady' is Missing)*, appeared in the cinemas: in England within the next five years Tauský was to compose and record music to Jiří Weiss's film *Věrni zůstaneme (Loyal We Shall Remain)* about the Czechoslovak exile army and its fight against Nazism. Tauský dedicated its 90-minute symphonic score to the head of the Czechoslovak government in exile, President Beneš. [9]

Tauský's operetta activities were also bringing in successful results. December 1933 saw the première of Bohumír Polách and Jiří Žalman's *Na růžích ustláno (A Bed of Roses)* with music by Jaromír Weinberger (of *Schwanda the Bagpiper* fame) orchestrated and conducted by Tauský. Though by all accounts a routine-type operetta, nonetheless the work according to the *Brněnská svoboda* newspaper triumphed, thanks to the subtle orchestral garb that Tauský had dressed Weinberger's tunes in, 'but also to the way he lifted the standard of the performance'. [10]

---

[9] The English title eventually given to the film was *Interim Balance.*

[10] In 1937 the operetta was successfully put on at the Vienna *Volksoper.*

Two more collaborative ventures with Weinberger followed: a story of the battle of Austerlitz, *Císař na třešních (The Emperor Picking Cherries)*, and the musical comedy *Apropos co dělá Andula? (By the Way, What's Andula Doing?*). But by May 1935 *Brněnská svoboda* was able to welcome a new and entirely original Tauský work, *Usmívejte se! (Smile!)*, which became the first operetta to be broadcast on Czech Radio. The librettists of this 'modern jazz fairy tale' were the well-tried duo Polách and Žalman. To the *Moravské noviny* critic it came as a:

> *Great surprise, since it has turned out to be a work of real dramatic worth. The music of V. Tauský does dwell in the realm of popular song, but it displays a successful striving for originality and dramatic force.*

In early 1939 Brno saw the premières of two more operettas: Rudolf Friml's *Katuška* ('the impressive and colourful orchestration' by V. Tauský endowed the work with 'an effective dose of youthfulness', according to the *Lidové noviny*) and *Děvčátko v modrém (A Little Girl in Blue)*, originally entitled *Angorská kočička (Angora Cat)*, with Tauský's own original music and a libretto by Václav Poláček.

On 14 March - the very eve of the German invasion of what had remained of Czechoslovakia after the loss of the Sudetenland - Tauský conducted his *Děvčátko v modrém* at České Budějovice.

There was hope at the time that this sparkling operetta with its French setting would be put on in Paris, and so the French capital now became Tauský's immediate destination in what was to be his epic wandering.

Author's note: This is an updated version of the first of two articles, the second being 'Tauský in Exile', which appeared in the Czech music magazine *Harmonie* (June and August 1998), drawing mostly on interviews with Vilém Tauský. The story of the postwar years continues on page 85.

Addendum: Vilém Tauský and the lost composers (ed.)

During his formative years in Brno, the young Vilém Tauský was familiar with several of the Czech composers who were to lose their lives between 1939 and 1945, in internment or in the Holocaust. Karel Janovický has already drawn attention to Tauský conducting Ervin Schulhoff's *HMS Royal Oak* for Brno Radio, see page 52. Schulhoff (1894-1942) was both composer and concert pianist, and well known for playing in four-handed piano duos in Brno, Prague and Ostrava.

The 2009 Schloss Laudon chamber music festival in Austria included a performance of Tauský's *Coventry*, given by the Aron Quartet. It was a considerable surprise to read in the programme booklet that:

> *Tauský accompanied his friend Erwin Schulhoff on propaganda tours of the Soviet Union playing four-handed piano programmes and later worked with Schulhoff on his opera 'Flammen' in Brno.*

The author of this note, Michael Haas, responded to the editor's enquiry by stating that the information came straight from Tauský himself, in an interview in October 2001. [11]

Haas, producer of Decca's respected *Entartete Musik* series of CDs, recorded that Tauský expressed amazement when told that *Flammen* (known to Tauský by its Czech title *Plameny*) had already been recorded. *Plameny* was given its world première at Brno's *Zemské divadlo* on 27 January 1932, with Tauský assisting when he was only 21. Derek Katz has recorded 1933 as the year of Schulhoff's visit to the Soviet Union in which concerts were given in Leningrad and Moscow. Schulhoff's companions on that trip included the composers Alois Hába and Josef Stanislav. Katz also noted that Tauský was not listed in Bek's biography of Schulhoff, although several duo partners were identified. [12]

---

[11] Vilém Tauský was interviewed twice on camera in his last years. Firstly by Michael Haas at Ivor Newton House in October 2001 and secondly by Martin Anderson (standing in for Michael Haas) at the London Jewish Cultural Centre, Golders Green in December 2003. The Society is indebted to Geraldine Auerbach MBE for supplying copies of these two interviews. *Kammermusikfestival Schloss Laudon*, Programme 2009; Michael Haas, personal communication, 2010.

[12] Derek Katz, personal communication, 2010, citing Bek, J., *Erwin Schulhoff - Leben und Werk*, (Hamburg: Von Bockel verlag, 1994)

It is very probable that Tauský's performance of *HMS Royal Oak* was the third since its creation. Schulhoff wrote this work in 1930 and it was premièred by *Frankfurter Rundfunk* on 9 May 1931. A second performance in Breslau at the *Junge Bühne* in 1932 was staged as a ballet, choreographed by Aurel von Millos, and the review from *Lidové noviny* quoted by Karel Janovický was dated 14 February 1933. That review further noted that this 'late night hours' performance was relayed to all stations of Czechoslovak Radio. [13]

Interviewed by Haas, Tauský noted that in Přerov he was a near neighbour of the younger Gideon Klein (1919-1945). Tauský remembered Klein coming back to his home from the library with 'piles and piles of books, all of which he devoured; the town spoke of him as its prodigy genius'. Anderson added that Tauský noted that: 'When he was nine Klein was reading encyclopedias for fun'. Tauský admitted that it was only later that he heard that Klein was a musician and composer. He met one of Klein's sisters in post-war London.[14]

Both interviewers asked if Tauský knew Pavel Haas (1899-1944), the first Czech composer to be sent to Terezín. Yes, he knew Haas and his parents (Zikmund and Olga) who owned shoe shops in Brno. However, he had no recollection of the Brno première of Haas' *Šarlatán* (*The Charlatan*) on 2 April 1938.

It appeared that Tauský didn't know Hans Krása (1899-1944) but had a brief acquaintance with Viktor Ullmann (1898-1944).

---

[13] CD booklet with Channel Classics CCS 25109 including a performance of *HMS Royal Oak* by the Ebony Band; for the Breslau choreographer, see Toepfer, K., *Empire of Ecstasy*, (Berkeley: University of California Press, 1997), p.296. Schulhoff, as a dedicated left-winger, had taken Soviet citizenship, but had not left Bohemia and Moravia when Germany attacked the Soviet Union. Hence Schulhoff was interned because of his new nationality, not for his Jewish faith. He died of tuberculosis in Festung Wülzburg internment camp, near Weissenburg, Bavaria, on 18 August 1942.

[14] A photograph of the Klein family home in Přerov can be found in Slavický, M., *Gideon Klein, A fragment of life and work* (Prague: Helvetica-Tempora, 1996).

Přerov: The Square, circa 1910

[Collection P. Herbert]

Interior view of the salon of the Záloženského House in Přerov, in the late Austrian period; This is the building shown top right above. Tauský would have heard performances here

[Collection P. Herbert]

A typical Free Czechoslovak Forces concert in Great Britain, in which S/Sgt Vilém Tauský featured as accompanist, duo-pianist and choral conductor. Harwich, 10 April 1943

[Collection R. Beith]

THE MILITARY CAREER OF PRIVATE TAUSKÝ: 1939-1945

by Richard Beith

It might have come as a surprise to the young Vilém Tauský if he had learnt on his graduation from the Brno Conservatoire in 1931 that his career as a promising young conductor at the Brno Opera House would be cut short in 1939 by a savage world war. It might have been a bigger surprise to learn that by the year 1945, he would have been transformed first into *soldat* (Private) Tauský, then Corporal Tauský, Staff Sergeant Tauský and finally Second Lieutenant Tauský, the holder of the Czechoslovak Military Cross and the Czechoslovak Order of Merit.

The Tauskýs have described the dramatic events of March and April 1939 when, having conducted his operetta *The Little Girl in Blue*, Vilém Tauský woke up in his hotel room in České Budějovice to find the town square occupied by German tanks and swastika banners hanging from the windows. The Germans had invaded, creating the Protectorate of Bohemia and Moravia. It so happened that the Bmo Opera were lending their costumes for *Jenůfa* to the Paris Opera, so Václav Jiříkovský, the helpful director of the Brno Opera, arranged for Tauský to travel to Paris with the director's son. Vilém Tauský spent a tense month waiting for a French entry visa, facilitated by the Paris-based composer Nikolay Tcherepnin, and for his exit visa from the Protectorate. A 'good Aryan' arranged that the conductor's passport was not stamped '**J**' to denote his Jewish ancestry and Vilém Tauský arrived in Paris on 14 April 1939. [1]

Tauský obtained work as a rehearsal pianist with Colonel de Basil's *Ballets Russes* in Monte Carlo but with the ever increasing chance of a European war he acted on rumours that a Czechoslovak army-in-exile was to be formed in France, gave up his job at the ballet and returned to Paris. Tauský recorded that he signed-up on 22 July 1939 and that whilst waiting for events to unfold, he lived at a villa at Augerville de la Rivière which Mrs Osuská had 'borrowed'. She was the wife of the Czechoslovak Minister in Paris.

[1] Tausky, M., *Vilem Tausky tells his story*, (London: Stainer and Bell, 1979). pp.48-52. Director Jiříkovský was later executed by the occupiers for assisting other people to escape. The pianist Peter Jiříkovský is the Director's great-nephew.

Tauský's fellow residents included Jiří Mucha, son of the painter, and the composer Vítězslava Kaprálová. [2]

Following the British and French declaration of war on Germany, the Czechoslovak volunteers were soon sent to Agde, located on the French Mediterranean coast between Marseille and the Spanish border. Agde was the location of three basic camps which had been built to hold refugees from the Spanish Civil War. Camp number 2 was derelict and was turned over to the Czechoslovaks. Barrack building was the first task, but Tauský recorded that he was soon ordered to form a military band to improve the troops' morale and to propagandise to the French. There was no sheet music and the only piece that could be bought was the piano score for Dvořák's *Humoresque*. By 23 November 1939, the Czechoslovak soldiers at Agde were sufficiently organised to promote a *Grande soirée artistique* for the enjoyment of the local French population. *Le soldat V. Tauský* was recorded as creating and directing the marches *Pour la Patrie* and *Dans le Combat*, see the facsimile programme opposite. [3]

To find sufficient instruments for a marching band was a serious problem, but the composer Bohuslav Martinů, a long-term Paris resident, arranged for the Consulate to buy the instruments of a defunct police band. By January 1940 Tauský, now a Corporal, was in command of a 'full-blooded military band which was capable of performing in public concerts'. On 6 March 1940, the soldiers presented another *Grande soirée*, this time to honour the 90th anniverary of the birth of their late President, T. G. Masaryk. Corporal Tauský started the evening by conducting the *orchestre militaire* in the overture to Smetana's *Hubička (The Kiss)*. [4]

---

[2] Karel Janovický has noted that the Czech expatriate community in Paris included Bohuslav Martinů, Rudolf Firkušný, the artists Jan Zrzavý and Rudolf Kundera, the violinist Jan Šedivka, journalist and poet Ivan Jelínek and others. When war broke out, all the men volunteered to join the exile army. Martinů was turned down on account of his age, but put in charge of culture in Beneš's fledgling exile government.

[3] *his story*, p.55.

[4] *his story*, p.55; Programme: *Grand soirée, a la mémoire du President T G Masaryk, organisée le 6 Mars 1940 á Agde, par des soldats tchécoslovaques pour feter son 90e anniversaire* (Brno, collection Jan Janíček).

P R O G R A M M E

Grande soirée artistique organisée par les soldats de l'armée Tchécoslovaque, le 23 Novembre 1939 pour la population d' Agde.

1. ORCHESTRE: Marche "Pour la Patrie" éxécutée par la musique de l'armée Tchécoslovaque. Créée et dirigée par le soldat V.Tausky.

2. CHOEUR: Choeur solennel"Věno" de B. Smetana, chanté par le choral de l'armée sous la direction du Lieutenant Bohumil Sigmund.

3. ORCHESTRE: Morceaux choisis de grands compositeurs tchéoslovaque "Humoresque" de Antoine Dvořak et "Poème" de Zd, Fibich.

4. SOLO d' ACCORDION: "Rose-Marie", opérette de Friml, jouée par le soldat Hala.

5. CHOEUR: Trois chansons gaies, chantées par le choral del'armée.

6. DANSES: La danse nationale "Česka Beseda" éxécutée par des Officiers de l'armée Tchécoslovaque et leurs Dames et par des invités français qui ont bien voulu nous prêter leur gracieux concours.

7. CHOEUR: Deux marche militaires, chantées par le choral de l'armée.

8. CHOEUR: Un groupe de soldat tchécoslov. de France chantera une marche militaire française "Sambre et Meuse".

9. ORCHESTRE: Une fantaisie de l'Opéra de Rossini"Guillaume Tell".

10. IMITATION: musicale et vocale, accompagnée de l'orchestre, éxécutée par le soldat Emile Glaas.

11. SOLO DE CHANT: "D'Une Prison" du compositeur français Raymond Hahn, chanté par le soldat Alois Lebovič.

12. ORCHESTRE: Ouverture de l'Opéra de Herold "Zampa".

13. ROMANCE FRANCAISE: "a une jolie dame" chanté par le soldat Vladimir Zelený.

14. ORCHESTRE et CHOEUR: Une marche militaire Tchécoslovaque "Dans le Combat" de V.Tausky.

E N T R ' A C T E

15. COMPOSITION SCENIQUE: "Dans la Nouveau Combat" présentée par des soldats Tchécoslovaque. Créée et régie par le Sous-Lieutenant VACLAV GORČICA.

23 November 1939

Edited facsimilie of the programme of the cultural evening given for the population of Agde, location of the Free Czechoslovak Army camp, showing two references to 'soldat V. Tausky'

[Original: Collection J. Janíček]

As the troops were trained, they outgrew the available accommodation at Agde and spread over a larger area of southern France. The Czechoslovak military administration remained in Paris with divisional headquarters in Beziers. When it came, the fall of France was rapid in the extreme. Even then, the French military authorities were slow to make use of the two trained Czechoslovak Regiments. Both the First and Second Infantry Regiments were only ordered to leave for the front on 5 June 1940, two days after the end of the Dunkirk evacuation. Both regiments travelled as far north as the Marne in vain efforts to help stem the French retreat, but by 16 June both regiments were heading back to the Loire and by 23 June, the regiments were 'put at the disposal of the Czechoslovak Army'. That is, the fighting was almost over and the Czechoslovak troops had to fend for themselves and head south back to Agde, or return to their homes in France. [5]

Tauský's recollections confirm that the retreat was far from orderly, although the bulk of the forces did reach Agde. Those wishing to fight on were rescued by a variety of merchant ships provided by the Royal Navy using the harbours at Sète and Port Vendres. Those rescued included Czechoslovak airmen who had been operating with the French Air Force. Several smaller groups, including Tauský's, considered the Atlantic coast of France a good alternative escape route being much nearer to the United Kingdom. Tauský was in a group of thirty-six led by a sergeant. They reached Bordeaux, but turned south coming to rest in the fishing port of Arcachon. There they found a Yugoslav coaler in harbour, the *Trsat Bakar*, scheduled to proceed to Newport in Monmouthshire to load coal. In Tauský's words:

> *With a courage born of desperation, the sergeant and I forced our way on board with our field-ambulance revolvers drawn. In my case the revolver was not even loaded, and I certainly wouldn't have dared to fire it if it had been. But we managed to give the captain the impression that if he did not carry out our orders he would die on the spot.*

---

[5] Souček, J., 'On the French Front' in *On All Fronts, Czechoslovaks in World War II*, (Boulder CO: East European Monographs, 1991), pp.53-61. Many of the Czechs and Slovaks recruited into the Czechoslovak regiments had lived and worked in France for years - they had homes to return to.

After some days at sea they arrived at Newport via Cardiff, to a friendly welcome. From Newport they went by train to rural Cheshire, ending up in a tented camp in the peaceful parkland surrounding Cholmondeley Castle, see illustration on p.82. Four years later, for his part in the escape of this group, Tauský was awarded the Czechoslovak Military Cross. Cholmondeley was to be the home of the Czechoslovak soldiers for three months until they departed for winter quarters in Warwickshire. [6]

By 26 July 1940, when Dr Edvard Beneš, the London based President-in-exile first visited the Czechoslovak Brigade, approximately 3,500 servicemen had reached Cheshire from France. It was at Cholmondeley that they received British uniforms and weapons. At the same time, President Beneš was concerned to generate public awareness of the Czechoslovaks' need to regain their pre-1938 boundaries at the end of the present war. To this end a cultural department was set up by the government-in-exile in London under Dr Viktor Fischl. Patriotic concerts and manifestations were organised to educate the British public as to Czechoslovak aspirations. Vilém Tauský was to play a significant part in this enterprise throughout the war. Even during the Cholmondeley period, concerts were given in Chester (28 July), Liverpool (25 August) and Manchester (8 September 1940). Typically these concerts included performances by the Army Choir, folk dances, musical solos, athletic displays drawing on the Sokol tradition and 'symbolic groupings' such as 'Germany's Aggression'. These concerts were often attended by senior members of the government-in-exile. Dr Ripka (Secretary of State for Foreign Affairs) and General Viest (Deputy Minister of Defence) attended at Chester and President Beneš himself appeared at Liverpool. [7]

---

[6] *his story*, p.57.

[7] 'Czechs Entertain, Concert in a Northern Town', *Liverpool Daily Post*, 29 July 1940, 'Czecho-Slovakian Army Concert', *The Chronicle* (Chester), 3 August 1940; 'Visit of Czech President - Dr Benes at War Fund Concert', *Liverpool Daily Post*, 26 August 1940; 'Czecho-Slovak Folk Songs - A Manchester Concert', *Manchester Guardian*, 9 September 1940. Dr Fischl edited a volume of tributes to Antonín Dvořák on the occasion of the centenary of his birth in 1841: *Antonin Dvorak - His Achievement*, (London: Lindsay Drummond, 1942). Karel Janovický noted that Dr Fischl became a distinguished Israeli diplomat, and later, a well-known author writing in Czech still as Fischl and in Hebrew, under the name Avigdor Dagan. Dr Fischl died in 2006.

Vilém Tauský and the Czechoslovak Army Choir

Although Tauský had conducted the army band prior to the fall of France, it would seem that once in Great Britain, it was his talents as a pianist-accompanist that were initially in demand. The phrase 'Piano accompaniment by Corporal W. Tausky', ('William' rather than 'Vilém'?), regularly appeared in concert programmes of this period. This can be seen in those for the Regent Cinema, Leamington, on 10 November and 8 December 1940, the Memorial Theatre Stratford-upon-Avon on 19 January and the Town Hall, Birmingham on 27 April 1941. The programmes were much as those given during the Cholmondeley period; the Army Band and Choir was conducted by J. Obruča. However, as a member of the choir of the Czechoslovak School at Hinton Hall, Whitchurch, Shropshire, Eva Wilkinson remembered Tauský conducting their choir on the steps of Birmingham Town Hall at the start of the 1941 Christmas holidays. [8]

In early 1942 Tauský was still the piano accompanist for the Czechoslovak Army Choir but he was now 'Sergeant V. Tausky' and was featured in these programmes as one half of a four hand piano duo with Corporal S. Martin. In the De Montfort Hall, Leicester, concert on 18 January 1942, they played *Slavonic Dances* numbers 7 and 8 (Op.46) [B.78] by Dvořák and the Choir included works by Dvořák, Schneider-Trnavský and Smetana. Similar programmes were given in Newcastle upon Tyne on 25 January; in Warrington on 8 February; in South Wales between 13-15 February and in many other locations. At many of these events, the performance of the same two Slavonic Dances was included. Tauský also arranged a selection of 'British tunes' for the Army Band entitled *Rule Britannia* which was regularly featured by the band from mid-1942 onwards.

By 10 April 1943 when a 'Grand Concert' was given in the Harwich Forces Theatre, Tauský was still the accompanist and joint purveyor of *Slavonic Dances* but had been promoted to Staff Sergeant and also conducted the Army Choir.

---

[8] 'By July 1942 Sergeant-Major Obruča had become a Lieutenant and the preview of a concert in Chester noted that '... before the war [he] was for 20 years conductor of the Spa Orchestra in Piestany (Slovakia)', 'Czech Army Band and Choir Next Week', *The Chronicle* (Chester), 11 July 1942; Eva Wilkinson, personal communication, 2006.

ČESKOSLOVENSKÝ ÚSTAV
THE CZECHOSLOVAK INSTITUTE
18, Grosvenor Place, London S.W.I

On TUESDAY, JULY 6th, 1943, *at* 6 p.m.

THE CZECHOSLOVAK ARMY CHOIR

Conductor: Sgt V. TAUSKÝ
Soloists: Capt. J. VÁLEK (Tenor), L/Cpl. L. ROSENBLUM (Bass)
Accompanist: Sgt V. Tauský

PROGRAMME

B. SMETANA : Slavnostní sbor - Festive chorus
B. TOVAČOVSKÝ: Vlasti - To my country

B. SMETANA: Kdo v zlaté struny zahrát zná, -)
He who can pluck the golden strings) Capt. J. VÁLEK
Nekamenujte proroky - Stone not the prophets)

Husitský chorál : Kdož jste boží bojovníci - Hussite Hymn

K. BENDL : Svatý Václave - S. Wenceslas Chorale
J B. FOERSTER : Oráč - The Ploughman

A. DVOŘÁK : Když mne stará matka -)
Songs my mother taught me)
Vodníkova arie z opery "Rusalka" -) L/Cpl. L. ROSENBLUM
Waterman's aria from the opera)
"Rusalka")

B. SMETANA : Jeníkova arie z opery "Prodaná nevěsta" -)
Jeník's aria from the opera) Capt. J. VÁLEK
"The Bartered Bride")

CZECHOSLOVAK FOLK-SONGS (arranged by J. Obruča)
Trenčianské hodiny - The chimes of Trenčín
Teče voda teče - The water is flowing
Bodaj by vás vy mládenci - The devil take you.

Facsimilie of choral concert programme at the Czechoslovak Institute: 6 July 1943

[Original: Collection J. Janíček]

As well as Slovak folk songs such as 'The Bells of Trenčín' and 'And quiet flows the river', the Choir's repertoire in 1943 included Karel Bendl's setting of *Svatý Václave (The St Wenceslas Chorale)*, Dvořák's *Ztracená ovečka* (*The Lost Lamb*), J B Foerster's *Oráč* (*The Ploughman*) and Smetana's *Tři jezdci* (*The Three Riders*). A partial listing of performances, see pages 81-82, indicates that the Army Choir and Army Band were well known throughout Great Britain.

Vilém Tauský as Orchestral Conductor

There seems to be a tradition that military bandsmen served as stretcher bearers and ambulance men in times of war; see the previous reference to 'field-ambulance revolvers'.

Hence when the Czechoslovak Brigade moved to Royal Leamington Spa and area in October 1940, Tauský was billeted at 17 and 19 The Parade, Leamington, the Field Ambulance's base. When Coventry suffered its most devastating air raid on 13/14 November 1940, the Brigade's Field Ambulance was dispatched from nearby Leamington to render assistance. Tauský was greatly moved by this experience and within days had written *Coventry*, a Meditation for String Quartet. Tauský has noted that when the first performance of *Coventry* was given, at the National Gallery in London on 17 March 1941, 'I was very proud when the advertised programme ... read Tausky and Beethoven, feeling that I was in good company'. [9]

From Leamington Spa, Tauský was a regular visitor to London. There, Jaroslav Knapp, secretary of the pre-war Czech Institute, arranged for Tauský to conduct concert performances of operas by Dvořák: *Rusalka* and *Jakobín* and by Smetana: *Dalibor*, *Hubička (The Kiss)*, *Libuše* and *Dvě vdovy* (*The Two Widows*). For the Czechoslovak Red Cross Tauský arranged a book of Czechoslovak Christmas Carols, published by Schott and distributed widely to schools all over Britain. He worked with artists who had found refuge in the country, the pianists Małcużyński and Líza Fuchsová, violinist Maria Lonová (Marie Hlouňová), cellist Karel Horitz (Hořic) and others. Robert Kingsley remembered visiting the London flat of his uncle Bernard Grün, to find his uncle deep in conversation with Tauský and Richard Tauber. [10]

---

[9] *his story*, pp.82-83.

[10] *his story*, p.79; commentary by Karel Janovický; Robert Kingsley, 2005. Grün (b. Moravia, 1901, d. London 1972), contributed music to *Balalaika* (1936).

The Czechoslovak Independent Brigade moved on from Warwickshire in May 1942, firstly to Somerset (May-August), then to the Lowestoft area (August 1942 - May 1943) and Dovercourt and area (May - September 1943). In September 1943 they were reinforced by 1,322 Czechoslovak soldiers from the Middle East and became the Czechoslovak Independent Armoured Brigade stationed around Desborough in Northamptonshire. It is uncertain how many days Tauský spent at such military locations, his musical duties made him into a much travelled figure in war-time Britain. Around this time Tauský conducted the Band of the Coldstream Guards in a concert of Czech music for the Royal Navy, thus breaking a 260 year tradition by following the baton of a foreign conductor. Tauský remembered that 'The occasion, which included hospitality on a destroyer, complete with piping aboard, was quite outstanding'. [11]

Vilém Tauský recalled how through Maria Lonová he was introduced to Felix Aprahamian, the then secretary of the London Philharmonic Orchestra. This meeting resulted in Tauský conducting two concerts at the Orpheum, Golders Green, where the LPO were in residence from February 1942 to April 1943. Because the LPO had a heavy commitment to provincial touring, orchestras other than the LPO also performed at this venue. This was the case on 14 and 28 February 1943 when Tauský conducted the New London Orchestra and the London Symphony Orchestra respectively. On 14 February he conducted a seriously Czech programme: Martinů, *Serenade*, Ostrčil, *Suite* (unspecified), Janáček, *Lachian Dances* and Dvořák, *Piano Concerto*, soloist unknown.

A more popular concert was given on 28 February; after Smetana's overture to *The Bartered Bride*, Moiseiwitsch played the *Second Piano Concerto* of Rachmaninov and the concert closed with Dvořák's Symphony, *From the New World*. Vilém Tauský conducted the London Philharmonic Orchestra on at least ten occasions during WWII. He gave six concerts during the 1942/1943 season, three in 1943/1944 and one in 1944/1945. Dates, locations and programmes are shown on pages 83-84. From 1943 onwards, Tauský seemed to criss-cross Great Britain to conducting commitments. This was not really a surprise; as Pirouet commented, 'in general there was no opportunity to hear the work of overseas musicians (in Great Britain at this time)'.

[11] *his story*, p.82.

Guest conductors were limited to 'a number of refugees from the Nazi domination of Europe, including Vilem Tausky and Dr Heinz Unger'. [12]

Many of these concerts of popular symphonic music were given under the auspices of CEMA, the 'Council for the Encouragement of Music and the Arts', the war-time predecessor of the Arts Council. From the evidence of known concert programmes, it would seem that Vilém Tauský was often asked to conduct from a narrow repertoire of Czech music with the addition of a popular piano concerto. The Overture to *The Bartered Bride*, *Vltava* and *From Bohemia's Woods and Meadows* from *Má vlast* and the Symphony *From the New World* appeared with some regularity. It must be noted though, that Dvořák's Piano Concerto was also heard on a number of occasions, perhaps with a greater frequency than in the opening years of the 21st century.

At least four concerts are known with the Liverpool Philharmonic Orchestra, (not yet 'Royal'). On Sunday 14 March 1943, Staff Sergeant Tauský conducted the first ever complete concert performance in Great Britain of Smetana's patriotic cycle, *Má vlast.* The concert was arranged to coincide with the fourth anniversary of the occupation of Prague. Jan Masaryk attended and spoke after the concert. The local press regarded this as a major musical and political event. Under the heading 'A Czech Concert' it was reported that:

> *The cycle of six symphonic poems of Bedrich Smetana entitled "My Country", which was presented by the Philharmonic Orchestra under Vilem Tausky yesterday was a unique undertaking. The work has not previously been heard in its entirety at a single concert in Great Britain and while to Czech audiences such an event would be a matter of course, we rarely encounter national expression in so concentrated a musical form .... Mr. Tausky handled the orchestra with great vigour, and, of course, with an intimate knowledge of the score.*

---

[12] *his story*, pp.88-81; Pirouet, E., personal communication, 2005; Pirouet, E., *Heard melodies are sweet - A History of the London Philharmonic Orchestra*, (Lewes: The Book Guild, 1998) pp.46-47. The Martinů Serenade was presumably the 1930 four-movement work for strings [H. 199]. The New London Orchestra of 1943 was not related to the current orchestra of the same name. Dr Heinz Unger was born in Berlin in 1895 and came to London in 1933.

The playing had confidence and more than once a sonority and fire that were out of the common. Considering that the bulk of the work was new to players and audience alike, the performance may be accounted highly successful. His Excellency M. Jan Masaryk, the Czecho-Slovak Minister for Foreign Affairs, introduced by the Lord Mayor, said that Smetana's work was part of the Czech heritage, their past and their future was enshrined in it. They were fighting the war to make the world safe for [the works of] Smetana, for Elgar, for Shostakovich, for Szymanowski, and their like. This was an important and historic occasion for them all, to be listening to Smetana in a free city, among a free people. [13]

A second report set the concert firmly in the current context:

The unquenchable national spirit of Czecho-Slovakia found musical expression at a concert promoted by Friends of Czecho-Slovakia (Liverpool), in association with the C.E.M.A., at the Philharmonic Hall, on Sunday afternoon, in commemoration of the fourth anniversary of the Nazi occupation of Prague. It was an occasion to be remembered. M. Jan Masaryk, Czecho-Slovak Minister of Foreign Affairs and Deputy Prime Minister, declared himself deeply touched by the Liverpool Philharmonic's performance of Smetana's remarkable work "Ma Vlast" (My Country) – a cycle of six symphonic poems, in which the composer describes in the language of music his own beloved Bohemia, its natural beauties, its legends, its glories and sorrows, its dauntless faith and resolution. ... The orchestra was conducted by Vilem Tausky, formerly conductor at Brno National Opera House, and now a sergeant in the Czecho-Slovak Army. It was obvious that he was on the happiest terms with the players, and they responded nobly to his confident and discerning direction. [14]

On Sunday afternoon 1 August 1943 he conducted The Municipal Orchestra in the Bournemouth Pavilion in part of a 'Programme of Czechoslovak Music.'

---

[13] 'A Czech Concert', *Daily Post* (Liverpool), 15 March 1943.

[14] 'Smetana's "My Country"', *Liverpool Echo*, 15 March 1943.

The concert opened, as so often, with the Overture to *The Bartered Bride* and continued with the Dvořák *Piano Concerto* played by Líza Fuchsová, but this was directed by the local conductor Montague Birch. The final work was Dvořák's *Symphony in G major*, then known as No. 4. The concert which was warmly reviewed, was held in conjunction with an Exhibition of Czechoslovak Arts and Crafts and a reception hosted by General Rudolf Viest. [15]

The local newspaper report of the LPO concert which took place in Walsall on 18 August 1943 was headed:

UNDER CZECH CONDUCTOR
LONDON PHILHARMONIC'S VISIT TO WALSALL
ELEMENT OF FLAMBOYANCY

The review was the first seen to confirm that: 'As he is serving with the Army of his native country, Mr Tausky appeared on the dais in uniform instead of conventional evening dress'. The review continued:

> *Most of Mr Tausky's pre-war experience was gained in Prague and other Continental cities, and it may be that that accounts for the slight, but nevertheless distinctive variations from the more normal interpretations that he introduced. On the other hand, these may be more the expression of his own personality rather than the result of any "national influence". The most notable of them was an element of what might best be described, perhaps, as flamboyancy in his work.*

With reference to the performance of the Symphony *From The New World*, the reviewer assumed that:

> *... besides rounding off an enjoyable evening for the audience as a whole, it made a special appeal to the contingent of U.S. troops who were present.* [16]

Karel Janovický has noted that the Czech film director Jiří Weiss, who was making his name in London as an independent maker of documentaries, had the idea of capturing on film the different Czechoslovak exile forces' contribution to the war effort.

[15] *The Bournemouth Echo,* 31 July and 2 August 1943.
[16] *Walsall Observer and South Staffordshire Advertiser,* 21 August 1943.

This was not to be propaganda, but an honest historical testimony that could be shown back home in Czechoslovakia after the war. By the autumn of 1943 the shooting was in full swing. The Army gave Tauský a mere three months to write the music – 90 minutes of it – to the full length feature film and to record it with the London Symphony Orchestra. Immediately afterwards he had to return to his unit. He subsequently sent the whole score to President Beneš who thanked him in a letter dated 30 August 1944, see overleaf. What has happened to the score and where it may be kept now are mysteries. But the film, under its English title *Interim Balance*, is kept at the Imperial War Museum, London. Tauský himself only saw it in full for the first time when it was shown at the Czech Embassy in London on the fiftieth anniversary of the end of the war in Europe. [17]

An overtly political event took place in the Stoll Theatre, London, on 28 October 1943 to celebrate the 25th Anniversary of Czechoslovak Independence. Orchestral and choral items were mixed with patriotic speeches. Tauský conducted the Orchestra of Sadler's Wells and his own Army Choir, see page 73. A noteworthy LPO concert in which Vilém Tauský conducted his own *Coventry*, arranged for string orchestra, was given in Coventry on 13 March 1944. It was presented as a 'Lidice Shall Live' concert, in a week which included a visit from President Beneš and performances by the Czech Army Choir and Army Band. Líza Fuchsová contributed solos by Dvořák and Smetana at a women's rally. The composer indicated in his programme notes, below, that *Coventry* could stand for a variety of sufferings, not just the Coventry blitz.

> *On the night of 13th November, 1940, I heard the raid upon Coventry. The ceaseless drone of enemy attack, the howl of falling bombs, and the dull thunder of crumbling buildings - all made their impression on me. But when morning came the lasting impression, the deeper impression, was made in the quietness of desolation. The ultimate importance seemed to be, not in the brutal assault, but in the results upon human life which followed it. It is for this reason that I chose the intimate form of the string quartet in which to speak of the burden of suffering which fell upon the people of Coventry as an outcome of modern warfare.*

[17] Contributed by Karel Janovický.

PRESIDENT
ČESKOSLOVENSKÉ REPUBLIKY

V Londýně dne 30.VIII.1944.

Pane rotmistře,

děkuji Vám za Vaši skladbu,kterou jste mně věnoval. Měl jsem příležitost sledovat Vaši práci pro českou hudbu v Anglii a blahopřeji Vám k úspěchům,jež jste tu dosáhl.

Srdečně Vás pozdravuji.

Rtm.Vilém T a u s k ý ,
c/o. Czechoslovak Forces
in E n g l a n d .

30 August 1944
Letter of thanks and congratulations from President Beneš to Staff Sergeant Tauský. The message in translation:

Dear Staff Sergeant

Thank you for your composition which you have dedicated to me. I have had occasion to follow your work for Czech Music in England and I congratulate you on the successes you have attained here.

I cordially greet you.

25th ANNIVERSARY of Czechoslovak Independence

PROGRAMME

OVERTURE to ... "LIBUŠE" ... by *B. Smetana*
Performed by Sadler's Wells Orchestra
Leader: Walter Price. Conductor: Sergt. Vilém Tauský

ADDRESS by ... H.E. Dr. J. SLÁVIK ....
Minister of the Interior of the Czechoslovak Government

ADDRESS by H.E. P.B.B. NICHOLS, C.M.G., M.C.,
British Ambassador to the Czechoslovak Government

ADDRESS by ... ... V. NOSEK ... ...
Vice-Chairman of the Czechoslovak State Council

HUSSITE CHORAL "WARRIORS OF GOD"
Czechoslovak Army Choir. Choir-Master: Sgt. V. Tauský

ADDRESS by a Czechoslovak Airman, S/Ldr. S.J.

"THE PLOUGHMAN" by *L. B. Foerster*
Sung by the Czechoslovak Army Choir

ADDRESS by a Czechoslovak Woman War-worker

"THREE HORSEMEN" by *B. Smetana*
Sung by the Czechoslovak Army Choir

ARIA of King Vladislav from *Smetana's* opera "DALIBOR"
Soloist: O. Kraus. Sadler's Wells Orchestra
Leader: Walter Price. Conducted by Sgt. V. Tauský

SOKOL MARCH: "INTO NEW LIFE" *Josef Suk*
Sadler's Wells Orchestra
Leader: Walter Price. Conducted by Sgt. V. Tauský

NATIONAL ANTHEMS

28 October 1943
Facsimilie of the Stoll Theatre programme
O. Kraus would be the baritone Otakar Kraus

[Original: Collection G. Melville-Mason]

It is not upon the terror of that night, the ruined city, or the dead and bleeding bodies that I meditate, but on the mental sufferings of the fear-stricken minds, deranged reason and the sorrows of bereavement which arose from them. "Coventry" was performed for the first time by the Menges String Quartet at the National Gallery in London on 17th March 1941. Later ... the sufferings of my own people were symbolised in what happened in the village of Lidice. Further meditation upon the interdependence of human sufferings led me to transcribe "Coventry" for string orchestra and the original dedication "To the memory of an heroic people", still stands as a memorial to these two symbols of the present sufferings of mankind.

It was reported that:

> *The orchestra ... were conducted by a talented and experienced, though still young, Czech conductor, Vilem Tausky. Happily, there is no need to popularise Czech music in England; that was done once and for all, by Dvorak himself.* [18]

On Saturday afternoon, 29 July 1944, Vilém Tauský was in the Town Hall, Leeds, conducting the Northern Philharmonic Orchestra, Leader Edward Maude, in a 'Concert of Czechoslovak Music' under the patronage of HRH The Princess Royal. With proceeds to 'Czech Charities', the programme was:

Smetana: Overture, *The Bartered Bride*
Dvořák *Piano Concerto*, Líza Fuchsová
Suk: *Serenade for Strings*
Smetana: Arias from *The Bartered Bride*, Olga Riedová
Dvořák: Symphony, *From the New World*

Again, this concert was associated with a local 'Czechoslovak Week' which included another exhibition of arts and crafts and a political speech by Dr Maximillian Lobkowicz, the Czechoslovak Ambassador to the United Kingdom.

---

[18] 'Feast of Czech Music by Philharmonic Orchestra', 'Lidice Shall Live Campaign', 'Czech Tribute to Coventry Women', *Coventry Evening Telegraph*, 14, 15, 16 March 1944.

CENTRAL HALL - COVENTRY

Monday, March 13th, 1944, at 6.30 p.m.

"LIDICE SHALL LIVE" CONCERT

REYNOLDS NEWS
(in conjunctioh with Peoples Plays Limited)

presents

THE LONDON PHILHARMONIC ORCHESTRA

(Leader - JEAN POUGNET)

Conductor:

VILEM TAUSKY

Programme and
Notes, price 6d.

13 March 1944
'Lidice Shall Live' concert programme

[Collection: M. Goold]

The Northern Philharmonic Orchestra dated back to 1903 but after the war gave way to the short-lived Yorkshire Symphony Orchestra.[19]

The presence of a rare concerto in the programme was recognised. 'H.H.W.' commented:

> *The programme ... included, in Dvorak's Piano Concerto, a work which the keenest concert-goer is only likely to hear once or twice in a lifetime. Madame Liza Fuchsova ... was thoroughly at home with her native idiom, and in M. Vilem Tausky, she had a conductor to whom the sweeping rhythms of Czechoslovak music came naturally.* [20]

The Czechoslovak Independent Armoured Brigade remained in Northamptonshire until the end of May 1944 when they moved to the Scottish Borders, based at Galashiels. The open spaces were ideal for tank training. At the end of August 1944, following a short period in the Yorkshire Wolds, the Brigade embarked for France as a fighting unit. On 5 October they were posted to Dunkirk to invest the strong German garrison which had been bypassed in the Allies' desire to capture the port of Antwerp. Here they were to remain until VE Day.

Before General Miroslav left England for France, Tauský had been promoted to second lieutenant and awarded the Czechoslovak Order of Merit. Vilém Tauský has noted that he was scheduled to travel with the Brigade to France but developed a pneumonic infection necessitating hospitalisation. Two months later he was attached to the remnant of the Czechoslovak Army HQ at 134 Piccadilly, W1. Tauský occupied himself with office work when he wasn't involved in making music. [21]

On Monday 30 October, 1944, when most of his fellow soldiers were probing the German forces in Dunkirk, Vilém Tauský conducted another 'Independence Day Celebrations' event at the Central Hall, Westminster. The 'Independence Day' was the foundation of the Czechoslovak Republic in 1918 and the concert was given 'Under the auspices of the Czechoslovak State Council'. Lieutenant Tauský con-

---

[19] Grundy, D., *The Glorious Experiment, The History of the Yorkshire Symphony Orchestra 1947-1955*, (Shrewsbury: Abbotsbury Books, 1987), p.79.

[20] *The Yorkshire Post*, 22, 24 and 29 July 1944.

[21] *his story*, p.84. In having his soldiers given a 'lower-risk' task, it could be argued that President Beneš wanted to preserve his 'western' brigade for the future.

ducted the London Philharmonic Orchestra, leader Jean Pougnet, the concert opening with the two National Anthems and an address by Jaroslav Stránský, Minister of Justice in the government-in-exile. The musical programme has been listed with the other LPO concerts.

By the early winter of 1944 Tauský was again conducting the Liverpool Philharmonic Orchestra, leader David Wise, in the North West of England. Both concerts, on Monday 4 December at the Centenary Hall, Stockport, and on Tuesday 5 December at the Champness Hall, Rochdale, were described as 'ENSA Symphony Concerts for War Workers', organised for the Ministry of Labour and National Service. ENSA was the 'Entertainments National Service Association' which covered a wide range of duties including entertaining the forces. The programme was identical on each night:

> Smetana: Overture, *The Bartered Bride*
> Smetana: *Vltava* and *From Bohemia's Woods and Meadows*
> Dvořák: *Slavonic Dances* Nos. 3 in A flat, 9 in B major
> Dvořák: Symphony, *From the New World*

At Rochdale, the reviewer was not partial to all-Czech programmes:

> *At the ENSA concert for war workers given by the Liverpool Philharmonic Orchestra in the Champness Hall on Tuesday evening, the programme consisted entirely of Czech music ... Apart from Dvorak the only Czech composers who are at all well known are Smetana and Suk, and of their work there is little of supreme importance ... It was, none the less, an evening of considerable enjoyment.* [22]

In Stockport, however, they regarded the concert as an unalloyed joy

> *The programme of Czechoslovak music for the war workers' concert ... on Monday was a happy choice. Nor could there have been a more amiable conductor than Lieut. Vilem Tausky, of the Czech Army, and the Liverpool Philharmonic Orchestra reflected his mood. It was a concert noteworthy because of its gaiety, and was rapturously acclaimed by the 1700 war workers present.* [23]

---

[22] 'Music in Rochdale', *Rochdale Observer*, 9 December 1944.

[23] 'War-Workers' Concert', *Stockport Express*, 7 December 1944.

The Stockport review appeared to refer to Tauský's recent presence in France, in Autumn 1944, but that has not been confirmed. A visit with the Czechoslovak Army Choir or Army Band would have been quite logical once he was fully restored to health.

By VE Day Vilém Tauský was still based at the Czechoslovak Army HQ in Piccadilly wondering what the future would bring. During the summer of 1945 he met H. B. Phillips of the Carl Rosa Opera Company who offered him the musical directorship of that company. It took some time for Tauský to be demobilized and to become a naturalized British citizen, but his military career was over.

Tauský and the BBC in wartime

Peter Herbert has noted that reference to 'W.Tausky' first appeared in BBC files on 14 April 1942. Greg Terian has extracted the following data from Tauský's file in the BBC Written Archives Centre regarding his collaboration with the BBC between 1943 and 1945:

28 October 1943: Tauský conducted 37 members of the London Symphony Orchestra in Studio 1, Maida Vale, on Czechoslovak Independence Day. This was a Czech Transmission of the European Service and the music was written, arranged and conducted by Tauský. The Czechoslovak Army Choir and eight members of the Fleet Street Choir also took part.

12 December 1943: Tauský conducted singers, the BBC Theatre Chorus and Orchestra at the Bedford studio in a programme of Smetana's operatic music. This was transmitted on the BBC Home Service.

14 April 1944: Tauský conducted the BBC Scottish Orchestra in a programme of European music, recorded in the Glasgow studio. The music played and the date of transmission are not known.

27 July 1944: Tauský and the BBC Theatre Orchestra gave a 'Czech Programme' for the Latin American Service which was recorded in the Bedford studio. This was broadcast on 31 July and consisted of: Smetana, Overture *The Secret* and the symphonic poem *Richard III*; Dvořák: Overture *Othello* and Janáček: *Lachian Dances* 1 and 2.

17 July 1945: Tauský and the BBC Theatre Orchestra recorded another 'Czech Programme' for the Latin American Service at the Bedford studio. Music played and date of transmission were not recorded.

Terian has also recorded a comment made by Geraldine Mucha who worked for the BBC Czech Service during the war. She recalled Tauský arriving at the studios for an orchestral engagement wearing battledress. She noted that with little time available for rehearsal, all present were astonished by the quality of performance achieved. [24]

The musical legacy

The legacy of Vilém Tauský's military career can be discussed in at least three areas: his stimulation of Bohuslav Martinů in the winter of 1939/1940, his own compositions and his decision to remain in Great Britain and make a new career here.

From 1937 Vilém Tauský had collaborated with Martinů during that composer's visits to Czechoslovakia. In 1939, Martinů, residing in Paris, was considered too old for military service but was active in supporting the Free Czechoslovak soldiers; his help in acquiring instruments for their new band has already been noted. It was for Corporal Tauský's band that Martinů wrote his heartfelt *Polní mše (Field Mass)*, a substantial work for solo baritone, male voice choir and instrumental ensemble. If the instrumentation looks slightly odd, that is only because those were the instruments available to Tauský at that time.

The composition was started on 4 November 1939 and finished the next month. As a result of changing fortunes, the work was never given a public performance in France; this had to wait for Kubelík's Prague première in 1946. It was claimed that Martinů wrote a *Vojenský pochod* (*Military March*) dedicated to 'The Czechoslovak Division in France', but Tauský told Terian that the March never existed. [25]

Reference to the list of Tauský's compositions elsewhere in this volume shows that he did not entirely give up composing during wartime. Of the works listed, the moving quartet movement *Coventry* is the most remembered.

---

[24] Terian, G., personal communication, 2009.

[25] Terian, G., 'Lost Martinů', *Newsletter*, Dvořák Society of Great Britain, No.80, July 2007.

Coventry is currently in the repertoire of the Martinů Quartet and they have performed it on a number of occasions, in Coventry itself in November 2000 on the 60th anniversary of the destruction of that city, and at the Leamington Festivals in 2001 and 2004. *Coventry* is also available in a modern recording and, in the string orchestra version, has been played in the Czech Republic in recent years.

In conversation with the author at Leamington Spa in May 2001, Vilém Tauský confirmed that it was Jan Masaryk who advised him in 1945 not to go back to liberated Czechoslovakia. Other contributors to this volume will discuss his post-war activities, but Vilém Tauský's decision to stay and make his career here in the United Kingdom was to be of inestimable value to musical life in the British Isles for several decades after the end of the second world war.

....

Acknowledgments, with particular reference to the history of the Czechoslovak Brigade in Great Britain, 1940-1944.

Warm thanks to the helpful staff of the Aberdeen Library; Barnet Local Studies & Archives Centre; Bournmouth Library; Bristol Record Office; Chester City Archive; Clacton-on-Sea Library; Colchester Library; Coventry Central Library; The Mitchell Library, Glasgow; Leeds Central Library; The Central Reference Library, Liverpool; The Manchester City Library; Reading Library; Rochdale Metropolitan Borough Council Leisure and Recreation Service; Stockport Local Heritage Library; Walsall Local History Centre; The Leamington Library, Warwickshire County Council Libraries and Heritage and the Watford Central Reference Library.

A partial listing of concerts given by members of the Czechoslovak Brigade:

1940

28 July	Gaumont Palace Cinema, Chester
25 August	Royal Court Theatre, Liverpool
8 September	Odeon Theatre, Manchester
13 October	Wulfrun Hall, Wolverhampton
10 November	Regent Cinema, Leamington Spa
8 December	Regent Cinema, Leamington Spa

1941

19 January	Shakespeare Memorial Theatre, Stratford-upon-Avon
27 April	Town Hall, Birmingham
6 June	British Thomson-Houston Works, Rugby
25 June	Temple Speech Room, Rugby
10 October	The Lyric, Glasgow
31 October	YMCA Canteen, Kineton, Warwickshire
9 November	Civic Hall, Wolverhampton
16 November	Danilo Cinema, Redditch
26 November	Boulton Paul Aircraft Limited, Wolverhampton
27 November	Canteen, I.C.I. Kynoch Works

1942

18 January	De Montfort Hall, Leicester
25 January	The Stoll Picture Theatre, Newcastle upon Tyne
8 February	Odeon Cinema, Warrington
13 February	Rolls Hall, Monmouth
14 February	Great Central Hall, Newport
15 February	Park Hall, Cardiff
26 February	Walton Hall, Warwickshire
28 February	Temple Speech Room, Rugby
5 March	Regal Cinema, Grays, Essex
14 July	Town Hall, Chester
15 July	Philharmonic Hall, Liverpool
16 July	Colonnade, Princes Park, Southport

1943

1 January	Royal Albert Hall, London [Grand Pageant of the Empire and her Allies]
10 April	Forces Theatre, Harwich
2 May	Regal Cinema, Walton-on-Naze
28 May	Royal Grammar School, Colchester
6 June	Town Hall, Clacton-on-Sea
13 June	The Playhouse, Saxmunden
30 June	Church Hall, Dovercourt, Essex [Scenes from Smetana's opera *Hubička, The Kiss*]
4 July	Winchester Cathedral [Commemorative service]
6 July	Czechoslovak Institute, London
12 August	Royal Albert Hall, London, BBC 'Polish-Czechoslovak Promenade Concert'
22 August	The Town Hall, Reading

1944

9 July	Picture House, Selkirk

Vilém Tauský's first home in Great Britain, July-October 1940: a tent in the grounds of Cholmondeley Castle, Cheshire, the first home of the Czechoslovak Brigade Top right: President Beneš

[Collection R. Beith]

Concerts given by Vilém Tauský with the London Philharmonic Orchestra, 1943-1944.

3 August 1943 Colston Hall, Bristol, at 6.30pm

Smetana: *From Bohemia's Woods and Fields*
Mozart: *Piano Concerto No.24* in c, Solomon
Dvořák: *Symphony No.2 [7]* in d

10 August 1943 Town Hall, Watford, at 6.45pm

Smetana: Overture *The Bartered Bride*
Dvořák: *Symphony No.5 [9], from the New World*
Grieg: *Piano Concerto*, Cyril Smith
Ravel: *Bolero*

17 August 1943 Town Hall, Birmingham, at 6.30pm

Smetana: *From Bohemia's Woods and Fields*
Suk: *Meditation on an old Bohemian chorale*
Grieg: *Piano Concerto*, Cyril Smith
Dvořák: *Symphony No.2 [7]* in d

18 August 1943 Town Hall, Walsall, at 6.30pm

Smetana: *From Bohemia's Woods and Fields*
Rachmaninoff: *Piano Concerto No.2* in c, Eric Harrison
Dvořák: *Symphony No.5 [9], from the New World*

19 August 1943 Albert Hall, Nottingham, at 6.30pm

Smetana: *From Bohemia's Woods and Fields*
Rachmaninoff: *Piano Concerto No.2* in c, Eric Harrison
Dvořák: *Symphony No.2 [7]* in d

20 August 1943 De Montfort Hall, Leicester, at 6.30pm

Smetana: *From Bohemia's Woods and Fields*
Suk: *Meditation on an old Bohemian chorale*
Grieg: *Piano Concerto*, Cyril Smith
Dvořák: *Symphony No.5 [9], from the New World*

7 November 1943 Adelphi Theatre, London, afternoon concert

Smetana: *From Bohemia's Woods and Fields*
Suk: *Meditation on an old Bohemian chorale*
Beethoven: *Piano Concerto No.4*, Susan Slivko
Dvořák: *Slavonic Dances*, Op.46

27 December 1943 Colston Hall, Bristol, at 6.00pm

Purcell: *Trumpet Voluntary*
Handel/Savage: *Concerto for Orchestra*
Rutland Boughton: *The Immortal Hour, 'Fairy Song', 'Song of Creation'*
Rachmaninoff: *Rhapsody on a Theme of Paganini*, Eric Harrison
Dvořák: *Four Slavonic Dances*
Puccini: *Tosca, 'E Luceven le Stelle', 'Recondita Armonia'*, Francis Russell
Weinberger: *Schwanda the Bagpiper, 'Polka and Fugue'*

13 March 1944 Central Hall, Coventry, at 6.30pm

Smetana: *From Bohemia's Woods and Fields*
Tauský: *Coventry, Meditation for Strings*
Dvořák: *Slavonic Dances*, Op.46 Nos 1, 3, 7 and 8
Dvořák: *Symphony No.5 [9], from the New World*

30 October 1944 Central Hall, Westminster

Smetana: *From Bohemia's Woods and Fields*
Suk: *Meditation on an old Bohemian chorale*
Dvořák: *Piano Concerto* in g Op.33, Lísa Fuchsová
Suk: *Fantasia for Violin and Orchestra*, Op.24, Maria Lonová
Smetana: *Má vlast*: *Tábor* and *Blaník*

Tauský in Great Britain: 1945-2004

by Karel Janovický

With the war in Europe at an end, Tauský was offered the post of music director of the Carl Rosa Opera Company which, with its 60 years' tradition, was the country's only opera company during the war and the most active one for a time afterwards. Tauský directed it until 1949. During his first year with the Carl Rosa he still conducted in uniform, since only in December 1946 was he officialy demobilised. Two years later he gained British citizenship. In the meantime he married Margaret Mallett (*née* Powell), a mother of two he had met during the war. Thus he gained a family and, in Peggy, a collaborator who became the co-author of his biography.

Looking back at it today, it may seem that the Carl Rosa repertoire was little more than run-of-the-mill. Yet in a world ravaged by war it was often and for many a revelation. Certainly thanks to Tauský the Carl Rosa Opera Company introduced works which Britain had never seen before and which under his baton became a marked success: Smetana's *Hubička (The Kiss)*, for instance, played for a whole year. Tauský experimented with giving a few of the performances of *The Kiss* in the original Czech, thus anticipating the trend by four decades. Only when the Royal Opera Covent Garden came on the post-war scene did the slow and at times patchy process of once again singing all opera in the original begin. The Slav languages were left till last, Czech taking its turn only after successful productions of Mussorgsky's *Boris Godunov* and *Khovanshchina* in Russian.

It was the existence of the Royal Opera, together with London's second opera stage at the Sadler's Wells Theatre, plus a drop in the younger post-war audience's interest in opera, that led to Tauský's tenure at the Carl Rosa being curtailed. He found himself free but still able to promote Czech music. During the following years he introduced to the British public Dvořák's *Jakobín*, Fibich's *Šárka*, Martinů's *Veselohra na mostě (Comedy on the Bridge)* and two more Smetana works totally unknown in this country, *Dvě vdovy (The Two Widows*) and *Braniboři v Čechách (The Brandenburgers in Bohemia)*. He conducted the *Brandenburgers* with the Chelsea Opera Group in November 1994 (see page 38) when *The Times*' critic wrote that 'in the postwar years few did more to champion Czech music than Tauský' and that at 84 he 'brought vigour to the score and especially to the many patriotic choruses'. [1]

During his years as a freelance conductor his engagements ranged from opera and symphonic music to what he described as 'quality light music'. At the Royal Opera, for instance, he conducted *Tosca*, for six years he conducted the Dublin Grand Opera, he gave guest appearances with the Hallé Orchestra in Manchester and he assisted at the birth of the BBC's 'light' orchestras in Belfast and Manchester, needed when music on the radio was reorganised into 'light' and 'serious' genre channels. His popularity went up and up: one particular evening he was heard on the light channel in a recording from Manchester and live from Covent Garden in Strauss's *Salome* on the serious channel - a greater genre contrast is hard to contemplate. In April 1954, with the BBC Northern Orchestra, he gave the first performance in Britain of Suk's *Asrael Symphony* and in the same year marked the 50th anniversary of Dvořák's death with a complete cycle of Dvořák's symphonies. Again, with the same orchestra he played Fibich's *Second* and *Third Symphonies* and Novák's symphonic poem *O věčné touze (Eternal Longing*) and his *Serenade* Op.36, while the BBC during this time broadcast his performances of Janáček's operas *Osud* and *Jenůfa* (the latter in Czech), well before they came to be performed on the stage in Britain.

In 1955 Tauský conducted all six of the Martinů symphonies to mark the composer's 65th birthday. The project was split between two orchestras, the London Philharmonic and the BBC Symphony Orchestra - and the BBC broadcast them all. Some of the performances were the first in Britain, and, as the Martinů scholar, Jaroslav Mihule, has written, this was the first time that the complete cycle was performed anywhere in the world. [2]

There was only another short step that was keeping the popular star of the concert platform from the microphone. In October 1956 Tauský took over the reins not only of the BBC Concert Orchestra - the prestigious 'light' orchestra in London - but also of presenting its concerts at the microphone, most often live.

---

[1] Higgins, J., *The Times*, 15 November 1994.

[2] Mihule, J., *Martinů* (Prague: Karolinum, 2002), p.492.

This engagement lasted eleven years and once again was marked by Tauský's introducing to the British public such composers as Oskar Nedbal and Vítězslav Novák – in Novák's case his *Slovácko Suite*. Tauský was invited to Copenhagen, Vienna, Oslo, Hamburg and other places to conduct and also to perform his own work. The harmonica virtuoso Tommy Reilly performed Tauský's *Concertino for Harmonica and Orchestra*, recorded later by Reilly with the Academy of St-Martin-in-the-Fields conducted by Sir Neville Marriner. Three more works from this period are Tauský's orchestral suite *From our Village*, the *Oboe Concerto* and the *Scherzo for Orchestra*. [3]

The experience he gained during the years with his military band stood him in good stead as he now composed brass and military band music, the most popular of it being the march *Call to Action*. Two more marches, *Men of Tomorrow* and *Czechs are Marching*, have made their mark. The Warsaw Pact invasion of Czechoslovakia in 1968 inspired Tauský to write a *Concert Overture for Brass*, using the tunes of two Czech folk songs. [4]

The top rung on the ladder of popularity for a musician of Tauský's ilk in England is undoubtedly a Proms appearance at the Royal Albert Hall in London. Tauský first conducted a Prom concert in 1955 when Sir John Barbirolli was taken ill and Tauský stepped in to conduct the Hallé Orchestra. Once he had taken over the BBC Concert Orchestra he made a number of Proms appearances with it, the programmes testifying to the high quality he strove for under the label of 'light music'. Included in his 1958 Prom, for instance, were Bruch's *Violin Concerto* and the Letter Scene from Tchaikovsky's *Eugene Onegin*.

---

[3] The Oboe Concerto is a 'freely adapted' work by the 18th century Czech composer Vaňhal. The score is dated 25 July 1956. It was premièred by Evelyn Rothwell (Lady Barbirolli). Tauský also 'arranged' a Vaňhal *Divertimento* for string orchestra. Both these works were published by the Oxford University Press.

[4] Tauský was a guest conductor and examiner at the Royal Military School of Music, Kneller Hall, conducted and adjudicated at the National Brass Band Championships at the Royal Albert Hall in London and was an adjudicator for the BBC's weekly Challenging Brass competition. He was later appointed to the BBC Music Advisory Council and conducted a charity performance of the Choir of 1,000 Cornish Voices with a brass band at the Royal Albert Hall.

Sadler's Wells Trust Ltd

Director Norman Tucker

Administrative Director Stephen Arlen

presents

Sadler's Wells Opera

Musical Director Alexander Gibson

in

Rusalka

An Opera in Three Acts by Antonin Dvorak

Libretto by S. J. Kvapil

English Version by Christopher Hassall

Conductor Vilem Tausky

Producer and Choreographer Wendy Toye

Designer James Bailey

Technical Assistant to James Bailey William Hurndell

Saturday 28 February 1959

Rusalka was first performed on 31 March 1901 in Prague

Third performance at Sadler's Wells

Programme for the third performance of Dvořák's 'Rusalka' at Sadler's Wells Theatre, with Joan Hammond in the title role, on 28 February 1959

[Collection: R. Beith]

When Tauský and the BBC Concert Orchestra appeared at the 1965 Edinburgh International Festival, their two concerts included a Haydn symphony, Prokofiev's *Violin Concerto*, Malcolm Williamson's *Symphonic Variations* (a world première) and scenes from Gershwin's opera *Porgy and Bess*.

The BBC contract - though demanding - allowed him nonetheless to make guest appearances in opera. In 1959 at Sadler's Wells he gave the first professional performance in this country of Dvořák's *Rusalka*. It seemed odd at the time that this lovely work by the ever popular Dvořák should have had to wait so long to be seen and heard, and it was typical of Tauský to take it under his wing. Tauský took part in the teaching of young voices at the English National Opera School from its inception in the early 50s and he also took part in the founding of the Welsh National Opera. The *South Wales Echo* wrote after his appearance with the Welsh National Opera in London in 1954:

> *... much credit must be given to Vilem Tausky who, in four seasons, has widened the approach of the company ... The Bartered Bride must now be ranked as one of the finest in the repertoire. Vilem Tausky ... has put the stamp of authority on this production ... In Cavaleria Rusticana he brings to the score a sense of urgency and passion, and builds up a masterly tension in every big climax.* [5]

When his BBC Concert Orchestra contract came to an end, Tauský in 1968 joined the staff of the Guildhall School of Music, rising later to the position of director of its opera department. In the meantime he also took on the advanced conducting course. (I remember visiting his class at the School as a BBC reporter for an interview; while waiting for him to finish I was struck by the high standard of the voices among the opera students and by the joy with which they fine-honed their performance under his guidance.)

The list of operas which Tauský put on with his students at the School between 1965 and 1980 runs to some 70 titles, including Janáček's *Počátek románu (The Beginning of a Romance)*, new works like Britten's *Midsummer Night's Dream*, as well as early works like Monteverdi's *L'Incoronazione di Poppea*.

---

[5] Tausky, M., *Vilem Tausky tells his story*, (London: Stainer and Bell, 1979), pp.114-115.

Tauský with a young Prince of Wales

[Photo: courtesy B. Rayson]

However, more followed later. In recognition of his work at the School Tauský was made a Freeman of the City of London in 1979. Six years later, having reached 75, Tauský officially retired but continued teaching at the Guildhall School of Music until 1991. [6]

There are some 200 titles in the BBC Gramophone Library catalogue under the name Vilém Tauský. Many of them are studio recordings of arias and operetta excerpts, but there are also live recordings of Proms concerts from Tauský's time with the BBC Concert Orchestra, as well as scenes from operas by Verdi, Gounod, Tchaikovsky, Puccini and others. Important among them are recordings of Joan Hammond accompanied by various British orchestras under Tauský's direction, since it was the Hammond - Tauský tandem which first brought to the public's attention Rusalka's 'Song to the moon', thus making it very popular (it became a 'Housewives' Choice' on the BBC) and paving the way for the historic Sadler's Wells production of the opera in 1959. This production was marred on the first night, which my wife and I attended, by a thick London peasouper that gradually seeped into the auditorium as the performance progressed.

[6] He was also made a Fellow of the Guildhall School of Music and was a Liveryman of the Worshipful Company of Musicians.

Tauský at his piano, which used to belong to the composer Eric Coates. London, 21 October 1997

[Photo: K. Janovický]

In 1981 Her Majesty the Queen appointed Tauský CBE for his services to music. In Czechoslovakia Tauský visited only twice and only briefly at that: the Czech concert agent Alexander Percy-Holeček spent over a year persuading the authorities to permit Tauský to come to his native Moravia in October 1974 on the occasion of the 90th anniversary of the Czech Theatre in Brno.

During his visit he conducted Smetana's *Tajemství (The Secret)* in Brno, *Fidelio* in Ostrava and *Madam Butterfly* in Olomouc. A year later Percy-Holeček arranged a visit to Slovakia where Tauský conducted the Košice State Philharmonic in its home town and also at Michalovce and Humenné.

'These two visits,' Tauský wrote, 'have done much to heal the wounds of the war'. (Eight members of his family had died in the concentration camps.) 'I have been greeted by many old friends as if I had never been away'. [7]

Official recognition, however, had to wait till well after the fall of the communist regime.

---

[7] *his story*, p.156.

In October 1999 he visited Prague where at the Bohuslav Martinů Institute he received the Martinů Medal.

Tauský receiving the Martinů Medal from Ivan Štraus, Chairman of the Martinů Foundation, Prague

[Photo: Z. Chrapek, courtesy G. Melville-Mason]

A year later he was given the Jan Masaryk *Gratias Agit* Award for his services to Czech music, presented in London by the then Czech Ambassador Pavel Seifter. In 2001 he visited Prague again and received the Gold Medal of the Music Academy.

Shortly before his death on 16 March 2004 he was awarded the Janáček Medal. Thanks to the efforts of the devoted companion of Tauský's later years, Brenda Rayson, his ashes were buried at the cemetery in Brno on 20 July 2005 - the 95th anniversary of his birth - and the Janáček Medal which, due to declining health he had been unable to receive in person, was after a fitting ceremony at the Janáček Museum handed over to her.

A homecoming at last for Tauský - a fine musician greatly admired in his adoptive country as a conductor, composer and teacher, untiring in his championship of Czech music.

Author's Note: This is an updated version of the second of two articles in the Czech music magazine *Harmonie* (June and August 1998), drawing mostly on interviews with Vilém Tauský. I am grateful to Brenda Rayson for additional information.

At a Supraphon/Dvořák Society presentation evening at the Czech Embassy London

[Photo: courtesy G. Melville-Mason]

P r o g r a m :

ANTONÍN DVOŘÁK:	**Serenáda E dur pro smyčcový orchestr** Moderato Tempo di Valse Scherzo. Vivace Larghetto Finale. Allegro vivace
VILÉM TAUSKÝ:	**COVENTRY – meditace pro smyčcový orchestr**
	Přestávka
ANTONÍN DVOŘÁK:	**Dva valčíky**
KAREL JANOVICKÝ:	**Preludium a dvojitá fuga pro smyčcový orchestr**
MARK KOPYTMAN:	**Ornaments pro klavír a smyčcový orchestr** - světová premiéra

Tauský's 'Coventry', in the string orchestra version, performed by the Orchestra Atlantis conducted by Vítězslav Podrazil at Plzeň in the Czech Republic, on 24 May 2007

7

THREE LETTERS TO VILÉM

by Graham Melville-Mason

THREE LETTERS to VILÉM

by Graham Melville-Mason

In May 1994 Vilém Tauský joined many other distinguished British musicians in donating valuable items of musical interest to the Musicians' Benevolent Fund for auction to raise money for the Fund. His donation included three autograph letters which he had received in the 1950s from old friends from his Czech life – one from the composer Osvald Chlubna (1893-1971) and two from Bohuslav Martinů (1890-1959). Before parting with them, he gave me copies and said that I may find them of 'musicological use' sometime in the future. In this tribute volume to Vilém, it seems appropriate to include translations of these letters and I am grateful to Karel Janovický for help in deciphering Martinů's handwriting and in translation from the Czech originals.

Osvald Chlubna was a composition pupil of Janáček at his Brno Organ School from 1914-15 and later in his master class from 1923-24. Like many Czech composers of the period, he was dual qualified having studied also at the technical and commercial colleges in Brno, so earning his living as a bank clerk until 1953 while teaching counterpoint and instrumentation at the Organ School and later instrumentation and harmony at the Conservatory part-time from 1918 to 1935. From 1953 until 1959 he became a full-time teacher at the Conservatory while also teaching music theory at the Janáček Academy (JAMU) from 1956 to 1958. Throughout this time he continued to compose works in almost every genre. Chlubna taught Vilém Tauský instrumentation and Vilém referred to him as 'a favourite disciple of Janáček' and as 'perhaps the musician closest to Janáček'. Jan Trojan, in his *New Grove* article, called Chlubna 'an outstanding orchestrator' and noted that he was responsible in 1918 for orchestrating the last act of Janáček's *Šárka*. Vilém, in his biography, tells of his involvement in the completion of Janáček's last opera, *Z mrtvého domu (From the House of the Dead*) for production in 1930, along with Chlubna, the conductor Břetislav Bakala (1897-1958) and producer Otakar Zítek (1892-1955), Chlubna being responsible for completing the unfinished final bars and the more optimistic alternative ending to the opera. He was also the first to reconstruct Janáček's *Dunaj* symphony.

in Brno on 9 April 1957
Bratří Čapků 8
Brno

Dear friend,

you will perhaps wonder that I am writing to you. But the director of the music archive of the Czech Music Fund was in London recently, and so I had asked him for your address, so that I could write to you and send my regards. That you, too, still remember me I once heard at the Radio and many acquaintances came to tell me about it. I thank you for it. However, I would also like to remind you that in 1958 there will be great Janáček celebrations in Prague, as well as in Brno, and that Brno is supposed to have an international conference about Janáček's work, during which there will be performances of all the Janáček operas. You could come and hear them in their true presentation by Frant. Jílek, now Chief of the Brno Opera. Perhaps you still remember him.

As for myself, I am still busy writing. I now have seven stage works, of which one ballet: High Jinks on Wires [*Hrátky na drátkách*], treated musically by way of Czech dances. But, regretfully, not placed yet.

Once again, I greet you and wish you success,
Yours,
Osvald Chlubna

(František Jílek (1913-1993) was a fellow student of Vilém's and they began their conducting careers together, first as répétiteurs, in the Brno Opera under Zdeněk Chalabala (1899-1962) – also a Janáček pupil - who had been conductor there since 1926.)

Vilém first made the acquaintance of Martinů during his Brno years, in 1932 when he was the pianist for the first performance of the ballet *Špalíček* (H.214) and later in Paris with the Czechoslovak Army before the German occupation of France, when Martinů wrote his *Polní mše (Field Mass)* for Vilém and his Czechoslovak musicians.

Thereafter Vilém was to champion Martinů's music throughout his long conducting career. He had the distinction of being the first conductor ever to perform the complete cycle of Martinů's symphonies, which he did for the BBC to mark the occasion of the 65th birthday of the composer in 1955, although he had no idea that he was the first until the Martinů scholar Jaroslav Mihule pointed it out to him over a lunch in London in August 1990. Vilém also presented a programme on the composer for the BBC television series *Monitor* and invited Martinů to take part. Unfortunately this was not possible and these two letters from Martinů relate to the occasion, the first being shown on the programme.

March 7 – 55

Dear friend:

Your kind letter has brought back many memories, memories of Brno and of our plans, as well as of Paris and of everything turning out in the opposite way to how we had imagined it. I do not know anything about any project at the BBC, nor about what you have just written to me about and what has made me happy. As to the few words to your lecture, I would not like to get used to that and create 'precedents' and I would also not like to write any reflections on art and artists and on myself, but so as not to turn you down I am sending you a little article which you may like to use as an introduction to the project of performing all my symphonies.

Here goes: [in English] In the beginning of things England was for me only a colour in the geographic map. France was red, England was yellow. Later on I learnt that Handel came there, Berlioz came and Dvořák came. And they liked him and his music. I thought: 'England, England, very far from my little village on the border of Moravia! They like Dvořák over there, maybe, one day they will like my music too!' Youngster's dreams. There was not yet a radio at this time and I didn't have the scores, except in my head. And the years went on, the world changed in an unexpected way. Half of my dreams became true, my music shall be performed in England. If they like it over there the second half of my dream shall become true also. This of course, I do not know, I am only hoping it shall. The scores, I have many of them now, might be of some of them will evoke the old memories of Dvořák in a new version. It could seem that this music has not so much in common with him but it does.

[in Czech] If you want to use the article at all, add some form of ?? [illegible] and as to my new works, mention La Locandiera [*Mirandolina* (H346)], an opera on C. Goldoni's text, and the cantata *The Epic of Gilgamesh*, also my latest Symphony No.6 entitled *Fantaisies symphoniques* which has now been played in Boston and New York, and do not forget *Julietta*.

Cordially,

Yours,

B. Martinů

July 11.55

Dear friend:

Excuse this belated letter, I had a lot of work to do, since I did not want to carry unfinished manuscripts to the States. To my great regret I have to confess to you that we were unable to get a single note of all those BBC concerts, even though we got angry over the transistor and quarrelled by our Radio and even at our friends' house. It is almost impossible to get the BBC here, I do not know why. B + Hawkes have written to me that you gave a beautiful performance of the 5th. Symphony. I would have liked to get the Fantaisies which I have not heard yet, write to me how they strike you. In America it has created a sensation and I would like to know why. I would generally like to know how the orchestra reacted to my Symphony and how the Festival went – successfully or not successfully. Could you drop me a few lines.

We are in Nice till the end of this month, then the address will be B.M. c/o Ch. Quennehen, 62 rue Pierre Charron, Paris 8.

Thank you very much for all those performances and I cordially greet you both,

Yours,

B. Martinů

8

THE REPERTOIRE OF VILÉM TAUSKÝ

by Graham Melville-Mason

Hull Philharmonic Society

Programme—Second Concert

Thursday, 12th April, 1956

Guest Conductor: **VILEM TAUSKY**

GOD SAVE THE QUEEN

PART 1

1	**Overture—The Thieving Magpie**	*Rossini*
2	**Symphony No. 1** .... Commissioned by the Society	*Joubert*
3	**Piano Concerto** .... Soloist—**ISO ELINSON**	*Grieg*

Interval (15 *minutes*)

Coffee served in Reception Room

PART 2

4	**Symphony No. 6**	*Tchaikowsky*

Programme of the Hull Philharmonic Society concert in the City Hall, Hull, 12 April 1956, conducted by Vilém Tauský

[Collection R. Beith]

THE REPERTOIRE OF VILÉM TAUSKÝ

by Graham Melville-Mason

Sir Thomas Beecham, late in his life, commented that nobody ever gave him credit for all his hard work, remembering only the apparent ease with which he rehearsed, performed and lived, yet behind the façade lay a powerhouse of preparative activity, concern and generosity. Towards the end of his life Vilém Tauský said, with a touch of sadness in his voice, that nobody remembered the wide repertoire that he had conducted throughout his long life but only associated him with *Friday Night is Music Night.* How truly unfair to both men.

From his first attempt to conduct Smetana's *Prodaná nevěsta (The Bartered Bride)* as a teenage schoolboy and his baptism with the first movement of Beethoven's *Symphony No.6 in F (Pastoral)* in the conducting class of Zdeněk Chalabala at the Brno Conservatoire, where he also came under the supervision of Leoš Janáček from his first year there in 1927 until the composer's death a year later, Tauský must have conducted a range of works running into four figures until he finally laid down his baton in London on 13 November 1994, aged 84, with a performance of Smetana's opera *Braniboři v Čechách (The Brandenburgers in Bohemia).* After all these years of a constantly active life in music based mainly in Brno, Prague, France and Great Britain, it would be a well nigh impossible task to trace all the works that Tauský conducted, from classical Bohemian pieces, through the world of opera and operetta, comprehensive cover of the music of Smetana, Dvořák, Janáček and Martinů through to twentieth century works by British composers of his post-war adopted country. For that wide service to British music, he deservedly received the CBE in 1981.

To get at least some idea of the enormous extent of his repertoire as a conductor, it is possible here just to draw on the more readily available sources – his own accounts in conversation with him, his biography up to 1979, the BBC Sound Archives at Caversham, various programme booklets, newspaper reviews and – perhaps most valuable and indicative of all – his 'little black book' in which he recorded the works he conducted with the BBC Northern Orchestra (now the BBC Philharmonic Orchestra) between 1952 and 1956. Vilém said that he regretted not continuing these entries after he came to his London posts from Manchester, although all his BBC engagements with programme details were recorded in the Music Index of the Music Contracts Department at Broadcasting House. [1]

As a second year Conservatoire student, Tauský's talents and potential were recognized. Following some good work in class on Fibich's *Šárka*, Chalabala invited him to stand in for the indisposed répétiteur at production rehearsals at the opera house and not long after, the dirtector of the opera, Václav Jiřikovský offered him a position as répétiteur. Naturally, following this appointment with the opera at Brno, it was inevitable that his first important gaining of conducting experience came from the world of opera – the best training in the tradition of most of the finest European conductors from the nineteenth and twentieth centuries. His first chance to be in charge in the pit came after a year when he replaced an ill Chalabala in Puccini's *Turandot* and in 1932 he was given full responsibility for a production of Roussel's ballet *Le Festin d'araignée (The Spider's Banquet)*. At this time also he was given charge of both Mussorgsky's *Boris Godunov* and Gounod's *Faust* as Chalabala was again ill.

These first ten years in the Brno opera house saw him widen his theatre repertoire by conducting Tchaikovsky's *Eugene Onegin*, Rimsky-Korsakov's *Tsarskaya nevesta (The Tsar's Bride)* and *Snegurochka (The Snow Maiden)*, as well as *Boris Godunov* from the Rusian repertoire. In addition he conducted several Czech operas and the popular works of Puccini and Verdi, the last including *Il Trovatore* and *Rigoletto*. By the end of this period, in 1937, his ballet conducting brought him into contact more with contemporary works, such as Prokofiev's *Romeo and Juliet*, Stravinsky's *Apollon Musagète*, Nikolay Tcherepnin's *Vaňka* and his fellow countryman Vítězslav Novák's *Signorina Gioventù*. Perhaps his finest hour in Brno came in 1938, just before the Nazi occupation forced his exile, when he conducted the new production of Dvořák's *Rusalka*, produced by Jaroslav Kvapil, who had written the libretto for the composer. Later that year he conducted the première of his own operetta, *The Girl in Blue* in České Budějovice but the German presence there brought the decision that it was time to leave. His escape to Paris, renewed contact with Martinů, who wrote his *Polní mše (Field Mass)* at the end of 1939 for

[1] For his biography see: Tauský, M., *Vilem Tausky tells his story*, (London: Stainer and Bell, 1979). For two sample pages from the 'Little Black Book', those listing works by Dvořák, see pp.124-125.

Vilém's assorted military musicians, then escape to England via Wales has been recounted elsewhere in this volume, see pages 59-62.

Once in Britain, his superior officers sought to continue to use their talented musician who had begun morale boosting performances while at the Czech camp at Agde in the south of France. During this period he conducted a motley band of instrumentalists. A concert programme from Agde on 23 November 1939, see page 61, shows him conducting Dvořák's *Humoresque* and the Fibich *Poème*, together with Rossini: *William Tell Fantasy*, Herold: Overture: *Zampa* and two marches of his own. Gradually his choir began to make good propaganda for the Czechoslovak forces in Britain by travelling to give concerts in various parts of the country. (As a boy, I remember hearing them, little knowing that the cheerful, rotund conductor would one day become a good friend!). While at the Czechoslovak army's first British base at Cholmondeley Park in Cheshire he organized concerts of Czech music, light and serious, vocal and instrumental, then beginning to take them to nearby towns such as Chester and Whitchurch where there were colonies of Czech civilians, as well as to local schools where there were Czech refugee children.

Soon these activities became wider known and he was joined occasionally by some distinguished artists from London, such as the Polish-Argentinian pianist Witold Małcużyński, and the Czechs, pianist Líza Fuchsová and violinist Marie Hlouňová. News of Vilém's presence and talents seem to have spread quite quickly and before long he was being asked to conduct elsewhere, the war having removed a number of younger men to the front. As early as his first London visit only a month after arriving, he met up with Jiří Mucha, now a war correspondent and last seen in Paris, as well as the baritone Otakar Kraus whom he had known since his time at the Brno Opera and with whom he was to work in more than a hundred performances with the Carl Rosa Opera Company after the war. Having arrived in Cheshire in July 1940, the Czech army was moved to a more permanent base in and around Leamington Spa in the October of that year, thus bringing Vilém closer to London and more musical activity which would increase the demand on his services and the opportunity to widen his repertoire, not only Czech and international but also British. For his Czech Army concerts he wrote a number of Czech folk and national song arrangements for the choir and band, including *The Czechs Are Marching*, *Waltzing Through Czechoslovakia* and *Under Czech Skies*, works which would continue to appear occasionally in his programmes for years to come. For Christmas 1941 he arranged and published eight Czech carols, the proceeds going to the Czech Red Cross. In addition to some Smetana and Dvořák, already he had begun from time to time to slip in the occasional work by Janáček and Martinů and was gratified to find appreciative listeners among British audiences.

At this time also, in conjunction with the Czech Institute there, he was sent to London to conduct concert performances of a number of Czech operas, including Smetana's *Hubička (The Kiss)*, *Dalibor*, *Libuše* and *Dvě vdovy (The Two Widows)*. Later on, he brought Dvořák's *Rusalka* and *Jakobín* to British audiences for the first time. Chamber concerts were also organised and he conducted his Czech Army Choir. The real opportunity to broaden his repertoire and conducting career came also on one of these London visits when he met Felix Aprahamian, at that time Sir Thomas Beecham's secretary to the London Philharmonic Orchestra, through Marie Hlouňová. (Like Felix, she lived in Muswell Hill and took shelter in his house during air raids.) To Vilém's pleasant surprise, Felix immediately invited him to conduct under the auspices of the the London Philharmonic Orchestra. As a result he conducted the London Symphony Orchestra at Golders Green on 28 February 1942.

The first concert announcement in Great Britain to mention Vilém Tauský by name?
[From the 'Hendon and Finchley Times', 26 February 1943, Courtesy Barnet Local Studies & Archives Centre]

COUNTY BOROUGH OF READING

PROMENADE CONCERT

IN THE TOWN HALL
SUNDAY, 22nd AUGUST, 1943, at 7 p.m.

THE

CZECHOSLOVAK ARMY CHOIR

Pianist: LIZA FUCHSOVA

PROGRAMME

1 (a) WARRIORS OF GOD — *XVth Century Choral*
(b) KING WENCESLAS - CHORAL — *K Bendl*

2 TWO EVENING SONGS — *B.Smetana*
(a) WHO KNOWS TO STRIKE THE GOLDEN STRINGS
(b) DO NOT STONE THE PROPHETS

Tenor Solo: CAPT. VALEK

3 PIANOFORTE SOLOS
TWILIGHT WAY - WALTZ IN A MINOR — *A.Dvorak*
TWO CZECH DANCES (a) OATS (b) DUPAK — *B.Smetana*

INTERVAL

4 (a) THE LOST LAMB — *A.Dvorak*
(b) THE PLOUGHMAN — *G.B.Foerster*
(c) THREE HORSEMEN — *B.Smetana*

5 PIANOFORTE SOLOS
OPUS 12, No 3 — *J.Suk*
SLOVAK VILLAGE BAND — *V.Novak*
FANTASY ON CZECH FOLK SONG — *B.Smetana*

6 (a) THE LOVER — *P.Krizkovsky*
(b) THREE CZECHOSLOVAK FOLK SONGS — *J.Obruca*
THE BELLS OF TRENCANY
QUIET FLOWS THE RIVER
THE DEVIL WITH YOU, LADS

Edited facsimilie of concert programme at the Town Hall, Reading, 22 August 1943

[The original autographed by Líza Fuchsová, Captain Válek and Vilém Tauský: Collection J. Janíček, Brno]

FRIENDS OF CZECHOSLOVAKIA
in association with C.E.M.A
PHILHARMONIC HALL
SUNDAY, MARCH 14, 1943
at 2.30 p.m.
in the presence of

His Excellency M. JAN MASARYK

(Czechoslovak Minister of Foreign Affairs and
Deputy Prime Minister)
B.SMETANA'S
"MA VLAST" — "MY COUNTRY"
First complete concert production in
Great Britain

LIVERPOOL PHILHARMONIC

ORCHESTRA

Conductor: S/SGT. VILEM TAUSKY
(Formerly conductor of the Brno National
Opera House)
All profits will be devoted to the Czechoslovak
Red Cross Fund for victims of the Gestapo.
PRICES 7/6 5/- 3/6 2/6
Booking Offices: Philharmonic Hall, Rushworth & Dreaper, Ltd, Byrom's, Houghton St.

Facsimilie of concert announcement from the 'Daily Post' (Liverpool), 12 March 1943

Little did he know then that Golders Green would be very familar territory in his later years with the BBC Concert Orchestra in its home at the Golders Green Hippodrome. Previously on 14 February he had conducted the New London Orchestra in Martinů: *Serenade*, Janáček: *Lachian Dances*, Ostrčil: *Suite in c minor* and Dvořák: *Piano Concerto in g minor*. These events immediately opened other doors, including being invited by Walter Legge to conduct concerts for the wartime ENSA and CEMA organisations, where he worked with many well established and already famous soloists. In 1943 we find him conducting the Liverpool Philharmonic Orchestra on 14 March giving the complete Smetana *Má vlast (My country)* cycle of symphonic poems for the first time in Britain. (Sir Henry Wood's 1909 Proms performance of all six symphonic poems took place on separate nights). On 1 August he shared an all Czech programme with the Bournemouth Municipal Orchestra in which he conducted Dvořák: *Symphony No.8 in G (Op.88) [B.163]*. On 10 August he was with the London Philharmonic Orchestra for a concert in Watford Town Hall, playing Smetana, Dvořák, Grieg and ending with Ravel's *Bolero*. An account of this concert given in his biography shows that he had Dennis Brain as his principal horn, who had previously played for him in a solo capacity. [2]

Before that, on 28 October 1943, he took part in a major event to mark the 25th anniversary of Czechoslovak Independence. At this emotional diplomatic and political event he led the musical contribution, conducting the Sadler's Wells Orchestra and the Czech Army Choir. The programme opened appropriately with Smetana: Overture: *Libuše* and closed with Suk: *Sokol March: Towards a New Life*. His work with British orchestras expanded in 1944; on 13 March in the Central Hall, Coventry, he conducted the London Philharmonic Orchestra in the string orchestra version of his own *Coventry* and on 27 July he conducted the BBC Theatre Orchestra in Smetana: Overture: *Tajemství (The Secret)* and Symphonic Poem: *Richard III*, Dvořák: Overture: *Othello* and Janáček: *Lachian Dances Nos.1 and 2*. On 29 July he conducted the Northern Philharmonic Orchestra in Leeds Town Hall in another all Czech programme: Smetana: Overture: *The Bartered Bride*, Dvořák: *Piano Concerto in g minor* (soloist Líza Fuchsová), Suk: *Serenade for Strings*, Arias from *The Bartered Bride* (soloist Olga Riedová) and Dvořák: *Symphony No.9*. In December he was with the Liverpool Philharmonic Orchestra in Rochdale and Stockport.

---

[2] A complete list of all the concerts which Tauský conducted with the London Philhamonic Orchestra in 1943-1944 can be found on pp.83-84. (ed.)

These programmes were again Czech: Smetana and Dvořák. With the end of the war approaching in 1945, during which time he had given over two hundred concerts for war workers alone, demands on Vilém's services remained considerable even though the Czechoslovak Brigade had moved to the continent at the end of August 1944. With his decision to remain in England, on the advice of Jan Masaryk, his musical career immediately took off, thanks to the excellent reputation he had gained with British musicians and orchestras for the high standard of his performances and his genial personality. While he had not conducted any full scale opera during the war years, his Brno operatic background was known and in the summer of 1945 he received an invitation to become musical director of the reforming Carl Rosa Opera Company

His first opera with the company was Puccini: *Tosca* at Wimbledon on 20 November 1945, with a cast that included Joan Hammond and his friend and compatriot Otakar Kraus. He was to remain as musical director until 1949 and the many operas he conducted there also included Bizet: *Carmen*, Gounod: *Faust*, Leoncavallo: *Pagliacci*, Mascagni: *Cavalleria Rusticana*, Offenbach: *The Tales of Hoffmann*, Puccini: *Madam Butterfly* and *La Bohème*, Verdi: *La Traviata, Il Trovatore* and *Rigoletto*, Wagner: *The Flying Dutchman*. One of the last productions he conducted before leaving the Carl Rosa company was very dear to his heart and this was bringing to the British stage for the first time Smetana's *Hubička* in October 1948, which was a great success and attracted considerable press interest and acclaim.

This period coincided with an invitation to conduct the Grand Opera Society of Dublin, while orchestral invitations continued. On 15 February 1948 he had returned to the Liverpool Philharmonic Orchestra with Smetana: *Má vlast* and in 1949 Radio Éireann in Dublin invited him to conduct a Dvořák programme of the Overture: *Šelma sedlák* (*The Peasant a Rogue*) and *Symphony No.7 in d minor (Op.70) [B.141]*. BBC engagements were also increasing and the *Radio Times* shows also that his own compositions were appearing in programmes of other conductors. Radio Éireann continued to invite him and on 4 May 1951 he conducted a programme of Smetana: *Vyšehrad*, Martinů: *Violin Concerto No.2 [H.293]* (soloist Jaroslav Vaněček) and Suk: *Pohádka (Fairy tale) (Op.16)*.

14 November 1951 saw Vilém Tauský making his Royal Opera House,

Covent Garden début, taking over the direction of Tchaikovsky's *Pikovaya dama (The Queen of Spades)* from Erich Kleiber, returning on 31 October 1952 to conduct Puccini: *Tosca.* In that season also he conducted *Salome* by Richard Strauss. His relationship to the stage was reflected in a programme with the London Symphony Orchestra at the Royal Albert Hall on 30 March 1952 in which he conducted ballet suites from Tchaikovsky: *Swan Lake* (Op.20) and *The Sleeping Beauty* (Op.66), Chopin: *Les Sylphides* and the programmatic Rimsky-Korsakov: *Sheherazade* (Op.35). 1952 also saw him begin a three year relationship with what might be considered an adjunct of Welsh National Opera, when he conducted a week of opera at Briton Ferry with a distinguished cast each year, including Bizet: *Carmen*, Verdi: *Il Trovatore* and *Rigoletto.*

With his appointment to the BBC Variety Orchestra in Manchester in 1950 his light music repertoire expanded and during this period he was invited to conduct the BBC Northern Orchestra (now the BBC Philharmonic) and so started another long and fruitful association with further opportunities to widen his symphonic repertoire, including Bruckner: *Symphony No.1 in c minor* and *Symphony No.2* in the same key. His first concert with that orchestra was in November 1951, consisting of Dvořák: Overture: *Othello*, the first performnace of Tauský: *Fantasia da Burlesca for violin and orchestra* (Frederick Grinke) and Schumann: *Symphony No.4 in d minor.* An important landmark was his conducting the complete cycle of Dvořák's nine symphonies in 1954 to mark the fiftieth anniversary of the composer's death. His performance of *Symphony No.1* on 30 May 1953 was the first in Britain since the work had been recovered. From the early 1950s Vilém's diary was ever full. In 1951 he was also appointed musical director of Welsh National Opera where he remained until his appointment as Chief Conductor of the BBC Concert Orchestra in 1956. Among his operas there were Gounod: *Faust*, Leoncavallo: *Pagliacci*, Mascagni: *Cavalleria Rusticana*, Puccini: *La Bohème* and *Tosca*, Šmetana: *The Bartered Bride*, Strauss, J.: *Die Fledermaus*, Verdi: *La Traviata, Rigoletto*, and *Sicilian Vespers*. During this period also began the long association with Sadler's Wells when, in July 1953 he was invited to conduct the Christmas production of Humperdinck: *Hansel and Gretel*, soon to be followed by Bizet: *The Pearl Fishers.*

Vilém Tauský's busy life continued to alternate between concert hall, BBC studios and the opera house. He returned to the Royal Opera

House in 1953 conducting Tchaikovsky: *The Queen of Spades* in January and Verdi: *Il Trovatore* in November and December – even spending Boxing Day conducting *Hansel and Gretel* at Sadler's Wells in the afternoon and *Il Trovatore* at the Royal Opera House in the evening! His extraordinary capacity for work continued through the 1950s, with the start of his association with Britten's English Opera Group in 1954, conducting Lennox Berkeley: *The Dinner Engagement* coupled with Arne: *Love in a Village* and performances of Walton: *Façade* including one at the York Festival. In the same year he conducted Berkeley's *Nelson* at Sadler's Wells. In January 1954 he was also back at the Royal Opera House conducting Puccini: *Turandot*. In the same year also he conducted the Puccini: *Il Trittico (Il Tabarro, Suor Angelica* and *Gianni Schicchi*) at Sadler's Wells. Although it was December 1956 before Janáček's *Jenůfa* reached the British stage with Rafael Kubelík at Covent Garden, Kubelík had given a BBC broadcast of the work in May 1951 and Vilém gave a further studio broadcast on the BBC Third Programme on 25 November 1954. Both he and Kubelík had Gré Brouwenstijn as Jenůfa for the broadcasts.

1955 was marked by a most significant event in the concert calendar when the BBC invited Vilém to conduct the complete cycle of Martinů's six symphonies to mark the composer's sixty-fifth birthday. Vilém had known Martinů since 1932 when he took part in a performance of the composer's *Špalíček* and had prepared the première of his opera *Hry o Marii (The Plays of Mary)* in Brno in 1935. For many years he believed this to have been the first time the whole cycle of symphonies had been given in Great Britain until the Martinů scholar Jaroslav Mihule informed him that indeed it was the first time the complete cycle had been given anywhere in the world. Among other important British premières of Czech works conducted by him in his Manchester period were Suk: *Symphony No.1 in E* on 26 January 1952 and Suk: *Symphony No.2 in c minor (Asrael)* on 27 April 1954, Suk: *Pohádka* on 18 April 1953 and Novák: *O večne touze (Eternal Longing)* on 20 March 1956.

His repertoire was also widening in the field of British music, for which he was soon to be as well known as for Czech music and for which he was later to be honoured. On 1 January 1955 he conducted Geoffrey Bush: Overture: *Yorick* and received a letter of thanks from the composer, see overleaf.

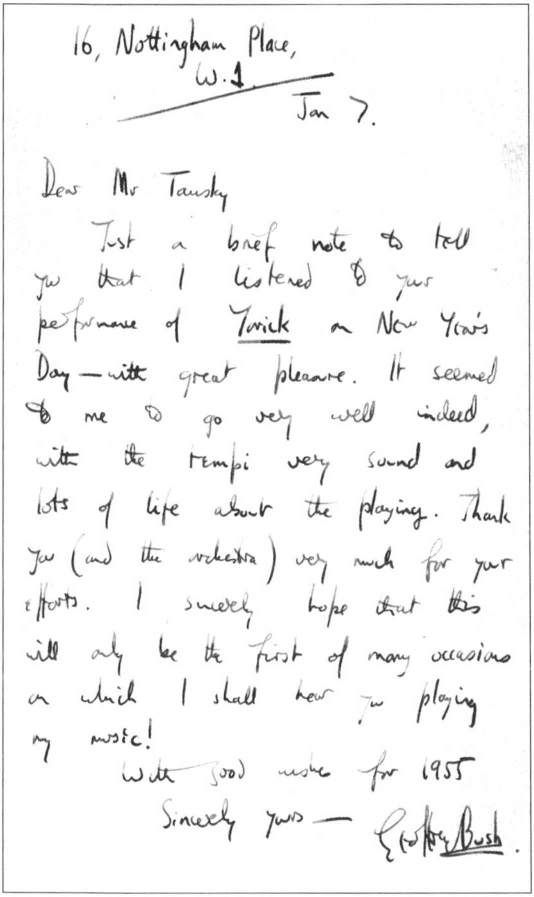

16, Nottingham Place,
W.1

Jan 7.

Dear Mr Tausky

Just a brief note to tell you that I listened to your performance of Yorick on New Year's Day — with great pleasure. It seemed to me to go very well indeed, with the tempi very sound and lots of life about the playing. Thank you (and the orchestra) very much for your efforts. I sincerely hope that this will only be the first of many occasions on which I shall hear you playing my music!

With good wishes for 1955

Sincerely yours — Geoffrey Bush.

He did not forget the operettas of his 'uncle', Leo Fall and in March 1955 he conducted a broadcast of Fall: *Madame Pompadour*. Also in 1955 he arrived at the Royal Albert Hall to conduct the Viennese Evening at the Proms, taking over from an indisposed John Barbirolli.

This year also saw the start of his great success with students of opera, when Gordon Thorne of the Royal Manchester College of Music asked him to conduct a broadcast performance of Ciléa: *Adriana Lecouvreur* with the BBC Northern Orchestra in December. The Maurice was John Mitchinson. In October 1956 Vilém was appointed chief conductor of the BBC Concert Orchestra, a position he was to hold for ten very successful and popular years. That repertoire was enormous, ranging from Strauss and Sullivan to Stravinsky and included commissions from British composers such as Malcolm Arnold, Eric Coates, Iain Hamilton, Gordon Jacob, Elizabeth Lutyens, Phyllis Tate and Malcolm Williamson. In this period he was occasionally asked to include works of his own, notably his Harmonica Concertino and the Suite: *From Our Village*. Malcolm Williamson's *Our Man in Havana* also featured and he even conducted Gilbert and Sullivan in Denmark, giving both *Trial by Jury* and *H.M.S.Pinafore* there. *Friday Night is Music Night* was established before Vilém took over the orchestra, a series of popular concerts with well-known soloists playing, as he put it, everything from Mozart to *My Fair Lady*! In 1957 he was invited to conduct the St.Cecilia's Day concert for the Musician's Benevolent Fund with the Concert Orchestra, when he included Coates: *The Three Elizabeths* which he often played thereafter. In 1958 Vilém and the orchestra were invited to play at the BBC Proms in their own right, in a programme which included Bruch: *Violin Concerto No.1*, Litolff: *Concerto Symphonique No.4* and extracts from Tchaikovsky: *Eugene Onegin*. He continued to conduct elsewhere from time to time, as we know from his programme with the Hull Philharmonic Society at Kingston upon Hull on 12 April 1956, see page 104. The John Joubert *Symphony* had been commissioned by that Society.

Although Vilém Tauský was not the first to conduct staged Janáček in Great Britain, he did conduct the first concert performance here of *Příhody Lišky Bystroušky (The Cunning Little Vixen)* with the BBC Northern Orchestra in Manchester in 1958. In 1959 operas that he conducted included Giordano: *Andrea Chénier* and Strauss: *Die Fledermaus*. However, the most significant operatic event was his giving the British première of Dvořák: *Rusalka*, which is recounted in detail elsewhere in this volume. A by-product of this was an invitation back to the BBC Northern Orchestra to conduct the music for *Humoreske: A Radio Portrait of Antonín Dvořák* transmitted on 5 July 1959. By the end of the 1950s his reputation among his fellow professionals and orchestral players was well established and much appreciated, as the confidential reports in the BBC testify and press criticism endorses.

The review after a concert in the Colston Hall Bristol in 1961, which is quoted in his biography is typical. On this occasion he had played Vaughan Williams: Overture: *The Wasps*, Gershwin: *Rhapsody in Blue* and Arnold: *Scottish Dances*. In 1964 he came again to the attention of Gordon Thorne, then principal of the Guildhall School of Music, who had attended a performance of Auber's *Fra Diavolo*, resulting in Vilém being asked to conduct the Nicolai: *Merry Wives of Windsor* with the Guildhall opera students and a year later Wolf-Ferrari: *School for Fathers*. In 1966, on retiring from the BBC, he was asked to become senior tutor of opera at the Guildhall and subsequently its Director of Opera, a post he held until 1992. In addition in 1973 he was asked to take over the advanced conductors' course. At Sadler's Wells his appearances ranged from Lehár: *The Land of Smiles* to Williamson's *The Violins of St.Jacques*, the latter staged in 1966 and dedicated by the composer to Vilém and his wife Peggy. [3]

An invitation to the 1965 Edinburgh International Festival saw him conduct three performances of Britten: *Albert Herring* in the King's Theatre and then on 9 and 11 September he conducted the BBC Concert Orchestra in the Usher Hall. The first programme consisted of Haydn: *Symphony No.48 in C*, the world première of Williamson: *Symphonic Variations*, Prokofiev: *Violin Concerto No.1 in D (Op.19)* with Wanda Wilkomirska and Tchaikovsky: *Capriccio Italien*. The second programme opened with Smetana: Overture: *The Bartered Bride*, followed by Haydn: *Trumpet Concerto in E flat*, Haydn: *Aria des Schutzgeistes*, Svendsen: *Carnival in Paris*, Hamilton: *Concerto for jazz trumpet* and Gershwin: *Porgy and Bess*. As soloists he had Mattiwilda Dobbs (soprano), Inia Te Wiata (bass), David Mason and George Swift (trumpets).

Another outlet for his ever widening repertoire was linked with the Oxfordshire village of Towersey, where he and Peggy bought a cottage in 1960 and involved themselves in local life whenever they were there. This eventually led to inviting distinguished soloists to join their local performances, such as Owen Brannigan as Noah when Vilém put on Britten: *Noye's Fludde* in July 1966. Performances of British music continued to feature in his programmes and he was involved with the commissioning and production of works by young British composers for the Guildhall opera students, including operas by Geoffrey Bush, Peter Wishart, Carey Blyton and Patric Standford. Invitations continued to arrive to conduct most of the major British symphony orchestras and he was invited to both conduct and adjudicate at the annual National Brass Band competitions in the Royal Albert Hall, eventually writing his

---

[3] *his story*, p.130.

Concert Overture as the test piece for one year. In 1969, in the same venue, he started to conduct annual Viennese concerts for Victor Hochhauser.

After his period as a BBC staff conductor with the Northern and then Concert orchestras, the BBC continued to invite him to broadcast, often talking on Czech composers and giving complete studio performances of Smetana: *Dalibor* and *Hubička*, as well as Weinberger: *Švanada dudák* (*Schwanda the Bagpiper*). Janáček had also featured with *Jenůfa* and the first British performance of *Osud*, *(Fate)*, albeit not staged. *Osud* was recorded before an invited audience in the Camden Theatre, London on 16 October 1971 and broadcast on Radio 3 on 22 January 1972. Just as with giving the first professional staged performance of Dvořák: *Rusalka* at Sadler's Wells in 1959 (he had conducted a studio broadcast in 1957), he also gave the first British performance of Smetana: *Hubička* with the Carl Rosa Opera Company in October 1948 at the King's Theatre, Hammersmith, thereafter taking it on tour including to the Hippodrome, Coventry and the King's Theatre, Southsea. During a short return to Czechoslovakia in October 1974 he conducted Smetana: *Tajemství,* in Brno, Beethoven: *Fidelio* in Ostrava and Puccini: *Madam Butterfly* in Olomouc. In 1975 he was invited to the Slovak Spring Festival and conducted some contemporary British music in Košice including works by Malcolm Williamson and Gerard Schurmann. He did not return again until 1999. While remaining active at the Guildhall School of Music in opera productions up to 1992, his concert appearances became less with advancing years. Much to his satisfaction, he bowed out on 13 November 1994 still widening his repertoire and completing his conducting of all Smetana operas with *Braniboři v Čechách* (*The Brandenburgers in Bohemia)*, at eighty-four as active and alert as ever.

The Appendices which follow list:

1 Operas and Operettas conducted by Vilém Tauský

2 Works performed during the Manchester years: 1952 to 1956

Appendix 1

Operas and Operettas conducted by Vilém Tauský

Albert, E.d'	*Tiefland*
Arne	*Love in a Village*
Auber	*Fra Diavolo*
Beethoven	*Fidelio*
Berkeley, L.	*The Dinner Engagement, Nelson*
Bizet	*Carmen, Djamileh, Doctor Miracle, The Pearl Fishers*
Blacher	*The Flood, Romeo and Juliet*
Blyton	*The Girl from Nogami*
Boughton	*The Immortal Hour*
Britten	*Albert Herring, A Midsummer Night's Dream, The Rape of Lucretia*
Bush, G.	*Lord Arthur Saville's Crime*
Chabrier	*Une Education Manquée*
Chailley	*Trial by Tea*
Cimarosa	*Il Maestro di Capella*
Donizetti	*Don Pasquale, The Night Bell, Rita*
Dvořák	*Jakobín, Šelma sedlák, Rusalka*
Fall	*Madame Pompadour*
Fibich	*Šárka*
Flotow	*Martha*
Giordano	*Andrea Chénier*
Gluck	*L'ivrogne corrigé*
Gounod	*Faust, The Mock Doctor, Romeo and Juliet*
Haydn	*La Canterina*
Hindemith	*The Long Christmas Dinner*
Humperdinck	*Hansel and Gretel*
Kálmán	*Countess Maritza*
Lehár	*The Land of Smiles, The Merry Widow*
Leoncavallo	*Pagliacci*
Martinů	*Comedy on the Bridge, Hry O Marii*
Mascagni	*L'Amico Fritz, Cavalleria Rusticana*
Massenet	*Le Jongleur de Notre Dame, Le Portrait de Manon, Werther*
Menotti	*The Medium, The Telephone*
Milhaud	*Le pauvre matelot*
Moniuzsko	*Halka*

Mozart	*Bastien and Bastienne, Così fan Tutte, Don Giovanni, The Magic Flute, Il Seraglio*
Musgrave	*The Abbot of Drimock*
Mussorgsky	*Boris Godunov*
Nicolai	*The Merry Wives of Windsor*
Offenbach	*Daphnis and Chloë, Husband on the Mat, The Tales of Hoffman*
Puccini	*La Bohème, Gianni Schicchi, Madama Butterfly Manon Lescaut, Suor Angelica, Il Tabarro, Tosca, Turnadot*
Rossini	*The Barber of Seville, Il Cambiale di Matrimonio, La Scala di Seta*
Saint-Saëns	*Samson and Delilah*
Smetana	*Prodaná nevěsta, Braniboři v Čechách, Dalibor, Hubička, Tajemství, Dvě Vdovy, Libuše, Čertova stěna*
Smyth	*The Boatswain's Mate*
Stravinsky	*Mavra*
Strauss, J. II	*Die Fledermaus, The Gypsy Baron, Vienna Blood*
Strauss, R.	*Ariadne auf Naxos, Der Rosenkavalier, Salome*
Sullivan	*The Mikado, HMS Pinafore, Trial by Jury*
Suppé	*Das Pensionat*
Tchaikovsky	*Eugene Onegin, The Queen of Spades*
Thomas	*Mignon*
Verdi	*Aida, Don Carlos, Falstaff, La Forza del Destino, The Masked Ball, Nabucco, Rigoletto, Sicilian Vespers, La Traviata, Il Trovatore*
Weinberger	*The Outcasts from Pokerflat, Schwanda the Bagpiper*
Williamson	*The Violins of St.Jacques*
Wishart	*The Clandestine Marriage*
Wagner	*The Flying Dutchman, Tannhäuser*
Wolf-Ferrari	*The Inquisitive Women, School for Fathers*

In addition, Vilém Tauský also conducted a number of other operas during his tenure as Director of the Opera Department of the Guildhall School of Music from 1966 to 1992. The Archives of the Guildhall School of Music, including this period, are held in the London Metropolitan Archives, 40, Northampton Road, London EC1R 0HB, Tel:020 7332 3820, e-mail: ask.lma@cityoflondon.gov.uk and should contain this information.

Appendix 2

Works Performed During the Manchester Years – 1952 to 1956

Bach, J.S.	*Toccata in F (arr. Elgar)* (x2)
	Air on a G string (x1)
Baines, F.	*Symphonic Study No.3* (x1)
Balakirev	Tone Poem: *Russia* (x2)
Bartók	*Violin Concerto* (x1)
	Rhapsody No.1 (x1)
	Suite (arr. Serly) (x1)
Beethoven	*Overture: Coriolanus* (x4)
	Overture: Egmont (x4)
	Overture: Fidelio (x2)
	Overture: Leonora No.1 (x6)
	Overture: Leonora No.2 (x3)
	Overture: Prometheus (x5)
	Symphony No.1 in C (x4)
	Symphony No.2 in D (x3)
	Symphony No.4 in Bb (x1)
	Symphony No.5 in c (x2)
	Symphony No.6 in F (x2)
	Symphony No.7 in A (x1)
	Piano Concerto No.1 in C (x2)
	Piano Concerto No.2 in Bb (x1)
	Piano Concerto No.3 in c (x1)
	Piano Concerto No.4 in G (x3)
	Violin Concerto in D (x2)
Benjamin	*Prelude to Holiday* (x5)
Berkeley, L.	*Symphony* (x1)
	Nelson: Intermezzo (x1)
Berlioz	*Overture: Beatrice and Benedict* (x4)
	Overture: King Lear (x1)
	Overture: Le Corsaire (x2)
	Overture: Le Carnaval romain (x3)
	Reverie and Caprice (x1)
	Romeo and Juliet: Dance of the Sylphs (x2)
Bizet	*Overture: Patrie* (x2)
	Carmen Suite No.4 (x6)
	L'Arlésienne Suite No.2: Minuet and *Farandole* (x1)
	Bohemian Scenes (x4)
Bliss	*Suite: Checkmate* (x1)

	Incidental Music: Things to Come (x3)
	The Enchantress (x2)
Bloch	*Violin Concerto* (x2)
	Symphonic Poem: Winter-Spring (x1)
Boccherini	*Symphony in A* (x4)
Borodin	*Overture: Prince Igor* (x2)
	Symphony No.2 in b (x5)
	Prince Igor: Polovtsian Dances (x2)
	Nocturne (arr. Sargent) (x3)
Bowen	*Symphony No.3* (x3)
Brahms	*Academic Festival Overture* (x2)
	Symphony No.1 in c (x2)
	Symphony No.4 in e (x2)
	Piano Concerto No.2 in Bb (x2)
	Variations on a theme of Haydn (x4)
	Serenade No.1 in D (x3)
Brenta	*Piano Concerto* (x1)
Bruch	*Symphony No.3 in E* (x2)
	*Kol Nidrei (*x1)
	Romance in a (x1)
Bruckner	*Overture in g* (x1)
	Symphony No.1 in c (x4)
	Symphony No.2 in c (x2)
Bush	*Overture: Yorick* (x4)
Chabrier	*Suite Pastorale* (x1)
Cherubini	*Overture: Anacreon* (x2)
	Overture: The Water Carrier (x1)
Chopin	*Piano Concerto No.2 in f* (x2)
	Suite: Les Sylphides (x2)
Cimarosa	*Overture: The Impressario* (x1)
	Oboe Concerto (x1)
Coates	*Cinderella* (x2)
	London Suite (x1)
	Overture: Merrymakers (x3)
	Saxo Rhapsody (x1)
	Suite: Springtime (x1 TV)
Copland	*El Salon Mexico* (x1)
	Quiet City (x1)
Cornelius	*Overture: The Barber of Bagdad* (x6)
Debussy	*Clair de lune* (x2)
	Danse (orchestrated Ravel) (x1)

	Danse Sacrée et Profane (x1)
	Fantasy for piano and orchestra (x1)
	Marche ecossaise (x1)
	Nocturnes: Fêtes (x2)
	Nocturnes: Nuages (x1)
	Petite Suite (x 6)
	Prélude à l'après midi d'un faune (x2)
	Sarabande (orchestrated Ravel) (x4)
	Suite Bergamasque (x1)
Delibes	*Suite: Sylvia* (x1)
Delius	*On Hearing the First Cuckoo in Spring* (x1)
	Song Before Sunrise (x3)
	The Walk to the Paradise Gardens (x2)
Demuth	*Ballade for viola and orchestra* (x1)
	Suite Champêtre (x1)
Dohnanyi	*Variations on a Nursery Theme* (x1)
Dukas	*The Sorcerer's Apprentice* (x1)
Dvořák	*Symphony No.1 in c [B.9]* (x1)
	Symphony No.4 in d (Op.13) [B.41] (x5)
	Symphony No.5 in F (Op.76) [B.54] (x2)
	Symphony No.7 in d (Op.70) [B.141] (x2)
	Symphony No.8 in G (Op.88) [B.163] (x5)
	Symphony No.9 in e (Op.95) [B.178] (x1)
	Overture: Carnival (x2)
	Overture: Othello (x6)
	Overture: Šelma sedlák (Op.37) [B.67] (x5)
	Piano Concerto in g (Op.33) [B.63] (x2)
	Violin Concerto in a (Op.53) [B.108] (x1)
	Romance for violin and orchestra (Op.11) [B.39] (x1)
	Symphonic Poem: Holoubek (Op.110) [B.198] (x2)
	Symphonic Poem: Píseň bohatýrská (Op.111) [B.199] (x4)
	Symphonic Poem: Vodník (Op.107) [B.195] (x3)
	Symphonic Variations (Op.78) [B.70] (x1)
	Scherzo capriccioso (Op.66) [B.131] (x6)
	Czech Suite in D (Op.39) [B.93] (x3)
	Legend No.1 in d (Op.59 No.1) [B.117] (x2)
	Legend No.6 in c sharp (Op.59 No.6) [B.117] (x2)
	Nocturne in B (Op.40) [B.47] (x5)
	Slavonic Dance No.4 in F (Op.46 No.4) [B.78] (x1)

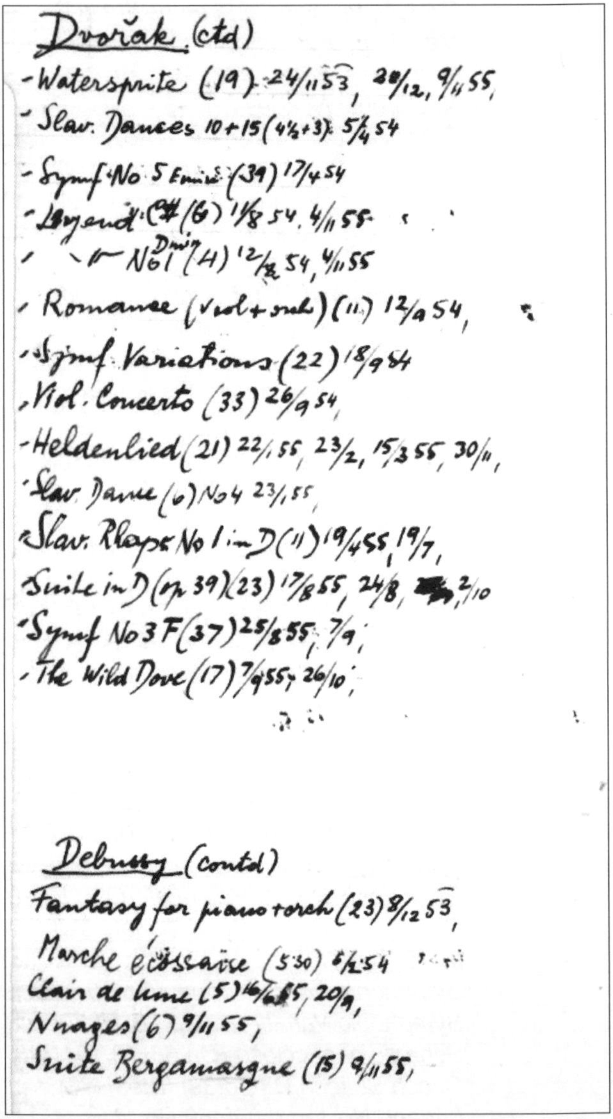

Dvořak (ctd)
- Waterspite (19) 24/11 53, 20/12, 9/11 55,
- Slav. Dances 10+15 (4½+3) 5/4 54
- Symf No 5 E min (39) 17/4 54
- Legend C# (6) 1/8 54. 4/11 55
- " " No 1 D min (4) 12/8 54, 4/11 55
- Romance (viol + orch) (11) 12/9 54,
- Symf. Variations (22) 18/9 54
- Viol. Concerto (33) 26/9 54,
- Heldenlied (21) 22/1 55, 23/2, 15/3 55, 30/11,
- Slav. Dance (6) No 4 23/1 55,
- Slav. Rhaps No 1 in D (11) 19/4 55, 19/7,
- Suite in D (op 39) (23) 17/8 55, 24/8, 2/10
- Symf No 3 F (37) 25/8 55, 7/9,
- The Wild Dove (17) 7/9 55, 26/10,

Debussy (contd)
Fantasy for piano + orch (23) 8/12 53,
Marche écossaise (5'30) 6/2 54
Clair de lune (5) 16/6 55, 20/9,
Nuages (6) 9/11 55,
Suite Bergamasque (15) 9/11 55,

Two pages from Tauský's 'Little Black Book', showing the meticulous records which were the source of this Appendix

[Courtesy B. Rayson]

Dvořak (ctd opposite)

- Symf. No 4 in G (37) 22/1 52, 18/7 53, 19/7, 22/7, 16/10,
- Othello (14) 27/1 52, 28/1, 4/10, 5/10 22/1 54, 21/7 55,
- Nocturne (strings) (7) 17/6 52, 9/7 53, 13/11 53, 6/7 54, 21/1 55,
- Scherzo Capriccioso (12) 21/10 52, 24/10, 13/11 53, 30/6 55, 4/11 55, 11/12,
- Symf d min (posth) (36) 21/1 53, 6/2 53, 7/3, 26/7 54 [50 12/10 55]
- Peasant Rogue (9) 5/2 53, 6/3, 26/9 54, 21/12, 26/1 55,
- Slavonic Rhapsody No 2 (g) (18) 25/4 53, 31/5, 18/8 54, 8/5 55 13/4 56
- Symf (C minor Zlonice) 30/5 53
- Carneval (10) 12/8 53, 4/11 55,
- Symf No 2 (d min.) (38) 28/8 53, 29/8
- Piano Concerto (36) 6/10 53, 7/3 54

Delius

Walk to the Paradise Garden (8) 29/1 52, 23/4 54,

Song before Sunrise (5) 17/6 52, 3/11 53, 6/4 56,

On hearing the 1st Cuckoo in Spring (7) 13/1 56,

Debussy

Petite Suite (14) 31/1 52, 9/7 53, 26/3 54, 14/5, 25/1 55, 13/4 56,

L'après midi (10) 20/4 53, 5/4 55,

Danse sacrée et profane (11) 30/5 53,

Fêtes (6) 9/6 53, 9/11 55,

Dance (orch. Ravel) (6) 27/8 53, 28/8

Sarabande (orch. Ravel) (5) 27/8 53, 28/8, 7/3 54, 22/6 55,

	Slavonic Dance No.10 in e (Op.72 No.10) [B.145] (x1)
	Slavonic Dance No.15 in C (Op.72 No.15) [B.145] (x1)
	Slavonic Rhapsody No.1 in D (Op.45 No.1) [B.86] (x2)
	Slavonic Rhapsody No.2 in g (Op.45 No.2) [B.86] (x5)
Elgar	*Violoncello Concerto* (x1)
	Pomp and Circumstance March No.4 (x1)
	Salut d'amour (x1)
	Sea Pictures (x1)
	Serenade for Strings (x3)
	Wand of Youth Suite No.2 (x5)
Falla	*Dances from the Three Cornered Hat* (x1)
	Nights in the Gardens of Spain (x1)
Ferguson	*Overture for an Occasion* (x3)
Fibich	*Symphony No.2 in Eb* (x2)
Field	*Martini Fantasia* (arr. Bush) (x1)
Franck	*Les Éolides* (x4)
	Symphonic Variations (x2)
Fricker	*Concertante for cor anglais and strings* (x1)
Gerhard	*Piano Concerto* (x1)
German	*Henry VIII Dances* (x3)
	Theme and Six Diversions (x3)
Gershwin	*An American in Paris* (x1)
Gibbs	*Fancy Dress Suite: Dusk* (x1)
Glinka	*Overture: Russlan and Ludmilla* (x5)
	Kamarinskaya (x3)
Gluck	*Overture: Alceste* (x1)
	Overture: Iphigenia in Aulis (x1)
	Sinfonia in G (x1)
	Air de Ballets No.1 (arr. Gevaert) (x2)
	Ballet Suite (arr. Mottl) (x2)
	Dance of the Blessed Spirits (arr. Mottl) (3)
Goetz	*The Taming of the Shrew* (x2)
Goldmark	*Overture: Springtime* (x7)
	Sakuntala (x2)
Gounod	*Ballet Music: Faust* (x3)
	Ballet Music: Romeo and Juliet (x3)
Grétry	*Zemire et Azor: Pantomime and Passepied* (x1)

Grieg	*Piano Concerto* (x3)
	Lyric Suite (x2)
	Sigurd Jorsalfar (x2)
	Two Elegiac Melodies (x2)
	Two Norwegian Melodies (x2)
Haim	*Pastorale* (x2)
Handel	*Piano Concerto* (arr. Lambert) (x1)
	Concerto for Orchestra (arr. Savage) (x1)
	Music for the Royal Fireworks (arr. Harty) (x2)
Harty	*Comedy Overture* (x1)
	With the Wild Geese (x3)
Haydn	*Symphony No.6 in D (Le Matin)* (x1)
	Symphony No.7 in C (Le Midi) (x2)
	Symphony No.8 in G (Le Soir) (x1)
	Symphony No.22 in Eb (The Philosopher) (x3)
	Symphony No.44 in e (Trauersinfonie) (x1)
	Symphony No.48 in C (Maria Theresa) (x1)
	Symphony No.49 in f (La Passione) (x2)
	Symphony No.67 in F (x3)
	Symphony No.83 in g (La poule) (x6)
	Symphony No.92 in G (Oxford) (x1)
	Symphony No.93 in D (x1)
	Symphony No.96 in D (Miracle) (x2)
	Symphony No.98 in Bb (x2)
	Symphony No.100 in G (Military) (x2)
	Symphony No.104 in D (London) (x2)
	Trumpet Concerto in Eb (x2)
Holst	*Concerto for two violins and orchestra* (x1)
	Beni Mora (x2)
	A Moorside Suite (x1)
Honegger	*Symphony No.4* (x1)
	Pastorale d'été (x1)
Humperdinck	*Overture: Hansel and Gretel* (x5)
	Hansel and Gretel: Dream Pantomime (x3)
	Suite: Sleeping Beauty (x3)
d'Indy	*Symphony on a Mountaineer's Song* (x1)
	La forêt enchantée (x1)
	Tableaux de voyage (x2)
Ippolitov-Ivanov	*Caucasian Sketches* (x3)
Ireland	*A London Overture* (x5)
	Overture: Satyricon (x4)

	Legend for piano and orchestra (x1)
Jacob	*Passacaglia on a Well-known Tune* (x2)
Jacobsen	*Theme and Variations* (x1)
Janáček	*Lachian Dances* (x5)
	Suite for strings (x1)
	Overture: Z mrtvého domu
Jirák	*Symphony No.5* (x1)
Johnstone	*The Oak and the Ash* (x3)
Jones, K.	*Miramichi Ballad* (x2)
Khachaturian	*Piano Concerto* (x1)
King	*Fantasy for piano and orchestra* (x1)
Kreutzer	*Overture: Das Nachtlager in Granada* (x3)
Lalo	*Symphony in g* (x1)
	Symphonie Espagnole (x1)
	Violoncello Concerto (x1)
	Divertissement (x3)
Lambert	*Suite: Horoscope* (x4)
Le Galliemme	*Overture in Eb* (x2)
Lehár	*Waltz: Gold and Silver* (x2)
Liszt	*Piano Concerto No.1 in Eb* (x4)
	Symphonic Poem: Les Preludes (x5)
	Symphonic Poem: Orpheus (x1)
	Hungarian Fantasy (x1)
	Hungarian Rhapsody No.1 in F (x1)
	Hungarian Rhapsody No.4 in d (x7)
Lyadov	*Musical Snuff Box* (x2)
Lyapunov	*Piano Concerto in eb* (1)
Mahler	*Symphony No.5: Adagietto* (x4)
	Kindertotenlieder (x1)
Malipiero	*Symphony No.7* (x1)
	Vivaldiana (x2)
Martin	*Ballade for saxophone and orchestra* (x1)
Martinů	*Symphony No.4* (x1)
	Symphony No.5 (x2)
	Symphony No.6 (x1)
	Serenade for small orchestra (x1)
Massenet	*Ballet Music: Le Cid* (x2)
	Alsatian Scenes (x1)
Matthews, E.	*Queen of Ithaca* (x1)
Méhul	*Symphony No.1 in g* (x1)
	Overture: The Two Blind Men of Toledo (x5)

Mendelssohn	*Symphony No.1 in c (Op.11)* (x3)
	Symphony No.3 in a (Op.56) (Scottish) (x2)
	Symphony No.5 in D (Op.107) (Reformation) (x3)
	Overture: *The Hebrides* (x3)
	Overture: A Midsummer Night's Dream (x4)
	Overture: A Calm Sea and a Prosperous Voyage (x3)
	Overture: The Fair Melusine (x1)
	Piano Concerto No.1 in g (Op.25) (x2)
	Violin Concerto in e (Op.64) (x3)
	Midsummer Night's Dream: Nocturne and Scherzo (x2)
Messager	*Ballet Music: The Two Pigeons* (x4)
Miaskovsky	*Symphony No.7* (x1)
Milhaud	*Suite Provençal* (x3)
Moeran	*Wythorne's Shadow* (x1)
Mozart	*Symphony No.19 in Eb (KV 132)* (x2)
	Symphony No.29 in A (KV 201) (x3)
	Symphony No.30 in D (KV 202) (x3)
	Symphony No.32 in G (KV 318) (x1)
	Symphony No.34 in C (KV 338) (x5)
	Symphony No.35 in D (KV 385) (Haffner) (x4)
	Symphony No.36 in C (KV 425) (Linz) (x1)
	Symphony No.39 in Eb (KV 543) (x1)
	Symphony No.40 in g (KV 550) (x1)
	Overture: Così Fan Tutte (KV 588) (x3)
	Overture: Don Giovanni (KV 527) (x1)
	Overture: Lucio Silla (KV 135) (x1)
	Overture: The Magic Flute (KV 620) (x1)
	Overture: The Marriage of Figaro (KV 492) (x1)
	Ballet Music: Les Petits Riens (x1)
	Piano Concerto No.12 in A (KV 414) (x1)
	Piano Concerto No.15 in Bb (KV 450) (x1)
	Piano Concerto No.17 in G (KV 453) (x1)
	Piano Concerto No.26 in D (KV 537) (x1)
	Concerto for two pianos in Eb (KV 365) (x1)
	Violin Concerto No.1 in Bb (KV 207) (x1)
	Violin Concerto No.4 in D (KV 218) (x1)
	Oboe Concerto in C (KV 314) (x3)
	Horn Concerto No.2 in D (KV 417) (x1)
	Cassation No.1 in G (KV 63) (x2)

	Cassation No.2 in Bb (KV 99) (x1)
	Divertimento No.2 in D (KV 131) (x1)
	Divertimento in Bb (KV 137) (x1)
	Divertimento in F (KV 138) (x4)
	Serenade No.7 in D (KV 250) (Haffner) (x2)
	Serenade No.13 in G (KV 525) (Eine kleine Nacht musik) (x2)
	German Dances (KV 605) (x4)
	A Musical Joke (KV 522) (x2)
Mussorgsky	*Khovantchina: Prelude and Persian Dance* (x5)
	Night on the Bare Mountain (x2)
	Gopak (x2)
	Scherzo in Bb (x2)
Nielsen	*Symphony No.2 (The Four Temperaments)* (x3)
	Overture: Masquerade (x1)
	The Dream of Gunnar (x2)
	Dance of the Cockerels (x3)
Novák	*Serenade in D (Op.36)* (x2)
	Symphonic Poem: Eternal Longing (Op.33) (x1)
Offenbach	*Overture: La Belle Hélène* (x3)
	Tales of Hoffmann: Barcarolle (x1)
Pfitzner	*Overture: The Christmas Elf* (x1)
Phillips	*Sinfonietta* (x3)
	A Surrey Suite (x1)
Piston	*Violin Concerto* (x1)
Pitfield	*Theme and Variations* (x1)
	Sketchbook of Women (x2)
Pizzetti	*Symphonic Preludes: Oedipus Rex* (x2)
Poulenc	*Concerto for two pianos* (x1)
Prokofiev	*Symphony No.1 (Classical)* (x4)
	Suite: The Love for Three Oranges (x3)
Puccini	*Manon Lescaut: Intermezzo* (x3)
Purcell	*Suite: Comus* (arr. Lambert)
Rachmaninov	*Piano Concerto No.1 in f sharp (Op.1)* (x1)
	Piano Concerto No.3 in d (Op.30) (x1)
	Piano Concerto No.4 in g (Op.40) (x1)
	Rhapsody on a Theme of Paganini (Op.43) (x1)
Rameau	*Le Bosquet* (arr. Penny) (x1)
Ravel	*Piano Concerto in G* (x1)
	Pavane for Dead Infanta (x4)
	Le Tombeau de Couperin (x1)

	Suite: Mother Goose (x2)
Rawsthorne	*Overture: Street Corner* (x2)
	Concertante pastorale (x3)
Reger	*Four Böcklin Pictures* (x3)
	Ballet Suite in D (Op.130) (x2)
Reizenstein	*Cyrano de Bergerac* (x2)
Respighi	*Suite: The Birds* (x5)
	Rossiniana (x3)
Rezniček	*Overture: Donna Diana* (x3)
	Ballet Music: Donna Diana (x1)
Rheinberger	*Organ Concerto No.2 in G* (x1)
Rimsky-Korsakov	*Piano Concerto in c sharp (Op.30)* (x1)
	Overture: May Night (x1)
	Overture: Russian Easter Festival (x1)
	Capriccio Espagnol (x5)
	Suite: Le Coq d'Or (x2)
Rossini	*Overture: The Barber of Seville* (x3)
	Overture: The Italian Girl in Algiers (x1)
	Overture: Silken Ladder (x3)
	Overture: The Thieving Magpie (x2)
	Overture: William Tell (x1)
	Ballet Music: William Tell (x1)
Roussel	*The Spider's Banquet* (x2)
Saint-Saëns	*Piano Concerto No.2 in g (Op.22)* (x1)
	Africa (Op.89) (x2)
	Violoncello Concerto No.1 in a (Op.33) (x3)
	Introduction and Rondo Capriccioso (Op.28) (x2)
	Le Rouet d'Omphale (x6)
	Dance Macabre (x4)
	Ballet Suite: Henry VIII (x1)
	Suite Algérienne (x2)
	Wedding Cake Caprice (x1)
Schreker	*Ein Tauzspeil* (x3)
Schubert	*Symphony No.2 in Bb* (x2)
	Symphony No.4 in c (x1)
	Symphony No.5 in Bb (x1)
	Symphony No.8 in b (Unfinished) (x1)
	Overture in the Italian Style in C (x7)
	Overture in e (x2)
	Overture: Fierrabras (x3)
	Overture: Rosamunde (x5)

	Ballet Music: Rosamunde (x2)
	Atzenbrugg Dances (x2)
Schumann	*Symphony No.1 in Bb (Spring)* (x3)
	Symphony No.2 in C (x2)
	Symphony No.3 in Eb (x1)
	Symphony No.4 in d (x3)
	Overture, Scherzo and Finale (x3)
	Overture: Julius Caesar (x2)
	Overture: Manfred (x3)
Scriabin	*Symphony No.2 in c* (x2)
Seiber	*Besardo Suite No.1* (x1)
Shostakovich	*Symphony No.1 in f* (x1)
	Symphony No.5 in d (x1)
Sibelius	*Symphony No.1 in e* (x2)
	Violin Concerto in d (x1)
	The Swan of Tuonela (x3)
	Pohjola's Daughter (x1)
	Suite: Karelia (x2)
	Romance in C (x4)
	Valse Triste (x1)
Sinigaglia	*Overture: Le Baruffe Chiozzote* (x1)
	Piedmontese Dance No.2 (x2)
Smetana	*Symphonic Poem: Vltava* (x5)
	Symphonic Poem: Šárka (x6)
	Symphonic Poem: From Bohemia's Wood and Groves (x3)
	Symphonic Poem: Blaník (x1)
	Overture: The Bartered Bride (x1)
	Overture: The Secret (x1)
	Bartered Bride: Dances (x4)
Spontini	*Overture: La Vestale* (x1)
Stanford	*Irish Rhapsody No.5 in g* (x3)
	Songs of the Sea (x1)
Stanley	*The Power of Music* (x2)
Strauss, Eduard	*Mit Dampf* (x1)
Strauss, Johann II	*Overture: Die Fledermaus* (x3)
	Waltz: Acceleration (x3)
	Waltz: Artist's Life (x3)
	Waltz: A Thousand and One Nights (x4)
	Waltz: Roses from the South (x2)
	Waltz: Voices of Spring (x1)

	Waltz: Where the Lemon Trees Blossom (x1)
Strauss, Josef	*Music of the Spheres* (x2)
Strauss, R.	*Horn Concerto No.2 in Eb* (x1)
	Symphonic Poem: Don Juan (3)
	Overture and Dance: Ariadne auf Naxos (x2)
	Burleske for piano and orchestra (x2)
	Suite: Der Rosenkavalier (x2)
	Der Rosenkavalier: Waltz (x1)
	Feuersnot: Love Scene (x1)
	Salome: Dance of the Seven Veils (x1)
Stravinsky	*Suite: Petrushka* (x2)
Suk	*Symphony No.1 in E* (x2)
	Symphony No.2 (Asrael) (x2)
	Fantasia in g for violin and orchestra (x1)
	Suite: A Fairy Tale (x5)
	Meditation on an Old Czech Chorale (x1)
Suppé	*Overture: Morning, Noon and Night in Vienna* (x2)
Svendsen	*Norwegian Rhapsody No.1* (x2)
Takacs	*Suite of Old Hungary* (x2)
Tauský	*Symfonietta* (x1)
	Rhapsody on Smetana (x3)
	The Little White Cat (x1)
Tchaikovsky	*Symphony No.4 in f* (x1)
	Overture: Romeo and Juliet (x2)
	Piano Concerto No.1 in bb (Op.23) (x2)
	Piano Concerto No.2 in G (Op.44) (x1)
	Suite: Nutcracker (x1)
	Suite: Swan Lake (x2)
	Suite: Sleeping Beauty (x2)
	Suite: Caprices d'Oxane (x6)
	Eugene Onegin: Polonaise (x4)
	Eugene Onegin: Waltz (x2)
	Marche Slave (x1)
	Andante Cantabile (String Quartet No.1 arr. string orchestra) (x1)
Tippett	*Fantasia on a Theme of Handel (*x1)
Toye	*Waltz: The Haunted Ballroom* (x2)
Turina	*Symphonic Rhapsody* (x1)
Vaňhal	*Divertimento* (arr. Tauský) (x3)
Van Wyk	*Saudade for violin and orchestra* (x1)
Verdi	*Overture: Louisa Miller* (x1)

	Overture: Sicilian Vespers (x1)
	Ballet Music: Sicilian Vespers (x1)
	Four Sacred Pieces (x1)
Vinter	*Hunter's Moon* (x1)
Wagner	*Overture: The Flying Dutchman* (x4)
	Overture: Rienzi (x1)
	A Faust Overture (x3)
	The Ride of the Valkyries (x2)
	Siegfried's Journey to the Rhine (x1)
	Forest Murmurs (x1)
Waldteufel	*Waltz: La Barcarolle* (x1)
	Skater's Waltz (x1)
Walton	*Viola Concerto* (x1)
	Spitfire Prelude and Fugue (x5)
Weber	*Symphony No.1 in C* (x7)
	Overture: Euryanthe (x4)
	Overture: Der Freischütz (x1)
	Overture: Oberon (x1)
	Overture: Preciosa (x1)
	Clarinet Concerto No.2 in Eb (x2)
Weinberger	*Overture: Knightly Tournament* (x1)
	Schwanda the Bagpiper: Polka and Fugue (x2)
Whettam	*Concerto scherzoso for harmonica and orchestra* (x1)
Williams, V.	*Overture: The Wasps* (x4)
	Suite: The Wasps (x2)
	Oboe Concerto (x1)
	Job (x1)
	An Oxford Elegy (x1)
	Folksong Suite (x2)
Wilson, S.	*anon* (x1)
Wolf-Ferrari	*Overture: Susana's Secret* (x1)
	Concertino for oboe and orchestra (x1)
Wood, H.	*London Cameos* (x1)
Wood, R.W.	*Piano Concerto* (x1)
Wright, K.	*Tobacco Suite* (x2)

During this period Vilém Tauský also conducted on televison and with the BBC Symphony and other BBC house orchestras, as well as with London and regional symphony orchestras.

9

VILÉM TAUSKÝ AND THE HISTORY OF *RUSALKA* IN THE BRITISH ISLES BETWEEN 1945 AND 1969

'It could have no better advocate'

by Peter Herbert

THE CZECHOSLOVAK INSTITUTE
18, GROSVENOR PLACE
S.W.1.

Wednesday, 28th February, 1945, at 6 p.m.

ANTONÍN DVOŘÁK :

Scenes from the Opera

RUSALKA

CAST:

Prince	ROBERT LAWRENCE
Princess....	OLGA RIEDOVÁ
Rusalka....	BLANKA SKALICKÁ
Witch	SARAH TOMASCHOFF
Water-sprite	JULIUS GUTMANN
First Nymph	MARA MENŠÍKOVÁ
Second Nymph....	HEDA BERNEROVÁ
Third Nymph....	MAY CAMPBELL
Huntsman	HYNEK FRIED

CONDUCTOR :
VILÉM TAUSKÝ (at the piano)

ADMISSION FREE . . . ALL VISITORS WELCOME

Facsimilie of poster/programme for Vilém Tauský's 1945 'Scenes from Rusalka'

[Original: Collection J. Janíček]

VILÉM TAUSKÝ AND THE HISTORY OF *RUSALKA* IN THE BRITISH ISLES BETWEEN 1945 AND 1969

'It could have no better advocate'

by Peter Herbert [1]

Prior to the arrival in the United Kingdom of the then Corporal Tauský, it appears that no one had ever performed more than the occasional aria from Dvořák's most famous opera; even that cannot be certain. There had been plans for a visiting production at Covent Garden in the summer of 1939, but that never came to fruition; see the addendum on page 210. The first substantial concert entirely devoted to *Rusalka* was performed in London on 28 February 1945, with Second Lieutenant Vilém Tauský conducting from the piano. No conductor has ever done more to promote the work in this country: his was the hand that guided no less than four productions (of varying scale) of the opera between 1945 and 1968. To Tauský the work was the very lifeblood of Czech music but to the British public it had been virtually unknown. That it should now be such a prominent part of the international operatic repertoire is astonishing in view of the manner in which it had languished. It would be importunate to suggest that today's international renown is the responsibility of that one man. However, without the pioneering work of Vilém Tauský in the United Kingdom, *Rusalka*'s rise to such importance would certainly have been both slower and harder.

The perception and reception of Dvořák's operas in the UK has been patchy at best and dismissive at worst. It has rested with a small body of enthusiasts to maintain any profile for this music and without the

---

[1] The genesis of this essay lies in the acquisition by the author of a programme for the first night performance of Vilém Tauský's production of *Rusalka* at Sadler's Wells in 1959. With the programme was a substantial collection of cuttings from newspapers and journals. Unfortunately the original collector failed to record either the name or date of any of them. Research at the British Library's newspaper collection at Colindale and in other resources has enabled the identification of most of these and led to the discovery of several more. Permission to use these items was sought from all identified publishers. The author most gratefully acknowledges the kind permission granted to reproduce all bar one of these. Apologies are given to any source used that can be identified at a later date. For the quoted sub-title, see p.205. (ed.)

vital participation of the BBC and conductors such as Vilém Tauský and Rafael Kubelík, such a fine work as *Rusalka* might have sunk forever beneath the waves. It was left to the English National Opera and David Pountney's pioneering — if controversial — production in 1983 finally to raise general awareness that *Rusalka* was an opera whose time had come. Both nationally and internationally it has since proved a draw fully worthy of its place amongst the great operatic standards. *Rusalka* had been slow to travel from the beginning. Whilst never fading from popularity at home after its 1901 première, the opera's journey outside its Czech homeland had been painfully slow. Gustav Mahler had planned a production but it stalled over his desire to cut out the Kitchen Boy and Gamekeeper. *Rusalka*'s first foreign outing was indeed in Austria in 1910 but did not reach America until 1993 at the Metropolitan Opera.

This survey aims primarily to examine the various British performances of *Rusalka* under the baton of Vilém Tauský. In particular it looks at the critical reaction to the 1959 Sadler's Wells production. The context of that production is important and other performances of *Rusalka* will also be described at least briefly.

1. The perception of *Rusalka* in the United Kingdom in the mid 20th century

A telling statement appears in Rosa Newmarch's foreword to her translation of *Antonín Dvořák* by Karel Hoffmeister. Rosa Newmarch could be permitted what amounts to a royal 'we' because she had tirelessly campaigned for performances of Czech operas, especially those of Janáček and Dvořák. The ignorance of which she speaks here, though, was certainly that of the British public as a whole. [2]

> *But for the amplification of the material dealing with Dvořák's operas, of which we are unhappily ignorant, and the omission of one or two references to polemical questions — of which we can happily afford to remain ignorant — the book departs very slightly from the original.*

Hoffmeister was undoubtedly a Dvořák enthusiast but he bowed to the prevailing impression of the libretti that he chose to set to music.

[2] London: John Lane, the Bodley Head Ltd., 1928.

Productions, too, had often failed to present Dvořák's operas well. Whilst Hoffmeister called *Dimitrij* 'that masterly work' and enthused about *Jakobín*, he reserved his greatest enthusiasm for *Čert a Káča* (The Devil and Kate) and *Rusalka*.

> *... (for) the second of this pair of fairy-tale operas the text was written by Josef [sic] Kvapil. That is as good as saying that it is a poem in pleasing musical verse, full of tender, shimmering and shadowy moods, the work of an artist who was also a fine connoisseur of the stage and its requirements. Perhaps, therefore, as regards stage business 'Rusalka' is open to criticism; but its priceless play of emotions and refined versification satisfied the master that he would never find anything better suited to his purpose. Here were no elements alien to his nature.* [3]

'In every respect *Rusalka* is a fine opera,' said Hoffmeister.

That Dvořák operas were virtually unknown outside the Czech lands is demonstrated by H. C. Colles in his chapter *The Operas* in Viktor Fischl's highly perceptive symposium. Colles draws heavily on Hoffmeister and talks of *Rusalka* following a single performance in Prague on a day that had included a visit to Nelahozeves. Of the above quotation, Colles suggests that 'the foreigner must take the native critic's word for this'. At this time he had rather faint praise for the opera by saying that:

> *...a poetic influence was at work on the composer akin to that found in the best of the earlier choral works for the concert room, but not conspicuous in his earlier operas.* [4]

The miasma surrounding the operas of Dvořák in the English language was hardly dissipated by Alec Robertson, whose *Master Musicians* book is now in dire need of replacement by one in greater sympathy with Czech opera in general. Indeed, Robertson's lack of any first

---

[3] *Čert a Káča* was the very first Dvořák opera to be performed in the United Kingdom. It was staged by the Oxford Opera Club in 1932 using a translation by Miss A. Raleigh, conducted by Reginald Jacques and Trevor Harvey. The producer was Hans Strohbach. The erroneous 'Josef Kvapil' in the quotation is correctly given as 'Jaroslav Kvapil' in Hoffmeister's original text.

[4] Colles, H. C., *The Operas,* in Viktor Fischl (ed), *Antonín Dvořák: His Achievement,* (London: Lindsay Drummond Ltd., 1942).

hand knowledge of Dvořák's life or works rather perpetuated the composer's own, genuinely humble, reference to himself as 'a simple Czech Musikant'. To Robertson is owed the suggestion that the Vodník, Rusalka's father, is 'a sort of benevolent Alberich', an idea reiterated by numerous critics in later years. Robertson wanted cuts in the second act and this was taken up enthusiastically in the future by the BBC in the 1950s and 60s (and, shamefully, as recently as 2008 in a stage production in Minnesota).

> *There is no reason why — with some judicious cuts in the second act — it should not repeat its success over here. There is just one thing that make it seem overlong, and that is the squareness of the rhythms. The vocal parts are almost invariably in two-and four-bar phrases.* [5]

Thus in the space of two and a bit pages, Robertson dismissed *Rusalka* and his verdicts on the remainder of the operas did nothing to enhance Dvořák's reputation as an opera composer in the English-speaking world. Another book on Dvořák likely to be known by a post-war British audience was *Antonín Dvořák* by Otakar Šourek, but only 3,300 copies were printed. Šourek's enthusiasm for *Rusalka* and indeed, most of the other operas, was enormous but Alec Robertson's book now held sway. Americans had the advantage of Šourek's earlier book, *Dvořák – Life and Works* translated from Paul Stefan's German by Yandray Wilson Vance and published in 1941. That book was the basis for two fictionalised accounts of the composer's life but none of these were likely to be known to the post-war British public; the fictionalised books in any case being of very little material value. [6, 7]

Wartime audiences in London and elsewhere in Great Britain had the benefit of a number of Dvořák centenary concerts in 1941. One event was of especial interest: on Monday 15 September there was a concert devoted to Dvořák's operas. Extracts from *Armida, Dimitrij* and *Jakobín* were sung to piano accompaniment. The concert opened with four numbers from *Rusalka*, beginning with the 'Song to the moon'.

---

[5] Robertson, A., *Dvořák*, (*The Master Musicians*), (London: J. M. Dent and Sons Ltd., 1945).

[6] Šourek, O., *Antonín Dvořák* (Prague: Orbis, 1952).

[7] Purdy, C. L., *Antonín Dvořák, Composer from Bohemia*, (New York: Julian Messner, Inc. 1950); Straaten. J. van, *Slavonic Rhapsody. The Life of Antonín Dvořák*. (New York: Allen, Towne and Heath, Inc., 1948).

The programme produced for the London events was unusually lavish for those days. The full text of all the numbers was given in Czech and English, together with descriptions of the drama as it unfolded.

If Dvořák's operas were an unknown quantity in the middle of the 20th century, this reflected the attitude that had reigned at one time about Dvořák's music as a whole. In a series of perceptive articles for *The Musical Times* in 1941 as part of the celebrations for the Dvořák Centenary that year, H. C. Colles pointed out most ably how it had been the public that led the Germano-centric critics in Dvořák's lifetime. It had been the admirable work by the London musical societies that had brought Dvořák to these shores and this led to an entirely fresh questioning as to why there was at that time of the 19th century an absence of any sort of truly British idiom in British music. To the critics, Dvořák had been a quirky individualist from a German nation: it was the public that perceived the value in his work first. [8]

The initial critical approach to Dvořák's music in the last quarter of the 19th century is closely paralleled by that pertaining to his operas fifty to seventy-five years later. A most exceptional few apart, the belief amongst critics was that the operas of Dvořák were late coming to British shores because they were inferior to the accepted canon of works. The attitude of most of them was to be at best patronising and at worst roundly condemnatory. The public, though, was to listen to and be enchanted by the music rather than the untrustworthy words of largely ignorant men. H. C. Colles was one of very few critics to have taken the trouble actually to go to Prague to see Czech opera. Indeed he attended the great festival of Dvořák's operas at the National Theatre in May 1929. [9]

---

[8] Colles, H. C., *The Musical Times*, 82 April, May and June 1941. Talking about critical reviews of Dvořák's *Stabat Mater*, Colles said: 'They are a series of rather characterless commendations varied only by the suggestion … that if Dvořák had received the benefit of a Public School education he might have paid more regard to the 'quantities' of the Latin verse. ... What the public realized at once was that here was a work pulsing with a sincere and personal emotion, an emotion which could never degenerate into sentimentality because of its utter sincerity'.

[9] Henry Cope Colles (1879-1943) was the music critic for *The Times* from 1911. He lectured at the Royal College of Music and edited the third and fourth editions of *Grove's Dictionary* as well as writing several books on music.

I escaped from a crowded London season ('The Ring' at Covent Garden and the rest of it) in order to find out what no one else who stays in London can know: what Dvořák means to his own people. ... Dvořák means something quite definite to us English folk, ... but his operas have no part in that meaning. [10]

The cited article clearly demonstrates the difference in attitude to music by the Czech nation as a whole when compared with the British. The Czech belief in opera was as the foundation of musical life rather than the eclectic British attitude to opera as a thus far unattained pinnacle; a history that...

... had induced a tone of mind averse to summary judgements, tolerant of minor defects even when they appeared in the work of a master ... a wholesome attitude of acceptance first and criticism afterwards.

Colles was fully aware that a wholesale change of attitude to Dvořák's operas and, indeed, to opera as a whole, would be necessary for acceptance of a wider body of work in the British Isles. He recognised that he had shared a common belief in the centrality of the then core repertory but he had also taken the trouble to investigate matters of which he had been ignorant. Apart from him and a very few others, the mass of critics would remain largely inured to change for more than another twenty-five years.

The range of different types of performance for an 'unknown' opera is remarkable. They are dominated, unsurprisingly, by performances under Czech conductors. Critical reaction (in so far as any has been discovered) to most of these performances was mixed at best and dismissive at worst. There was a general belief that *Rusalka* represented the best of a very mediocre Dvořákian opera oeuvre. During this same period, the public was also first made aware of the operas of Leoš Janáček and it could well be argued that an attitude more sympathetic to Dvořák has come about largely on the coat tails of the huge impact made by the music of his fellow countryman.

---

[10] Colles, H. C., 'Antonín Dvořák. 1. Opera at home', *The Musical Times,* 82 (1178) April 1941, pp.130-133.

The support of the BBC must surely have been critical in establishing the music of the opera amongst the listening public. No critical response has been located about either the first or last of the broadcasts listed overleaf; overwhelmingly, the critical response was negative to most aspects of the work. Study of the criticisms of the Sadler's Wells production in particular demonstrate the prevalence of received wisdom dominating the critics' opinions; thoughtful and constructive criticism was relatively rare and of far greater value.

Up to at least 1959, music criticism tended to damn *Rusalka* with faint praise, complaining about its dramatic weakness whilst admitting the beauty of the music. Thus Vilém Tauský's productions would meet with such criticisms. Afterwards and, certainly after 1964, the work began to be viewed in a new light. This is in spite of the huge popularity from the early 1950s of parts of the opera, particularly the aria 'O silver moon' with Tauský conducting the Philharmonia Orchestra and which was a substantial seller for HMV following its recording in 1952 and which has appeared in numerous compilations to this day.

The stunning success of the Czech National Theatre productions of Czech operas at the Edinburgh International Festival of 1964 included a production of *Rusalka* but the principle triumph redounded to the glory of Janáček. Tauský's new production of *Rusalka* for the BBC in 1968 appears to have received no critical attention. The depths of Rusalka's lake were unplumbed for a further fifteen years until David Pountney's production for English National Opera forced even the critics finally to realise the potential of the work as well as its glorious music.

There can be little doubt that between 1948 and 1969, Vilém Tauský and the BBC did more to maintain the presence and awareness of *Rusalka* than any opera company. Sadler's Wells, whose 1959 production was the first professional staged performance in the United Kingdom, gained wide coverage in national newspapers and magazines at a time when the composer's own image and popularity were in decline following nearly a century of frequent performances of his works. The opera's current popularity throughout the world has finally brought Dvořák's opera to that level of international acclaim that it has always had in its own national environment and cannot be without consequence for his other works.

Rusalka in Performance and Broadcast

Date	Type of performance	Conductor	Rusalka
28/02/1945	Concert	Vilém Tauský	Blanka Skalická
21/05/1948	BBC 3rd Programme (Recordings)	Alois Klíma	Milada Musilová
06/04/1949	BBC Home Service (Live concert)	Stanford Robinson	Gré Brouwenstijn
08/04/1949	BBC 3rd Programme (Live concert)	Stanford Robinson	Gré Brouwenstijn
09/05/1950 11/05/1950 12/05/1950	John Lewis Partnership (stage performance)	Geoffrey Corbett	Mary Maxwell
19/05/1954	BBC Home Service (Live concert)	Rafael Kubelík	Gré Brouwenstijn
25/04/1957	BBC Home Service (Recorded concert)	Vilém Tauský	Joan Hammond
18/02/1959 20/02/1959 24/02/1959 28/02/1959 11/03/1959 19/03/1959	Sadler's Wells [11] (Stage performances)	Vilém Tauský	Joan Hammond
19/03/1959	BBC 3rd Programme (Live broadcast)	Vilém Tauský	Joan Hammond
20/10/1963	BBC 3rd Programme (Recorded stage performance)	Rafael Kubelík	Jadwiga Wysoszanska
19/08/1964 21/08/1964 25/08/1964 29/08/1964 31/08/1964	Edinburgh International Festival (Stage performances)	Jan Hus Tichý	Milada Šubrtová & Libuše Domaninská
20/10/1968 06/11/1969	BBC Radio 3 (Recorded concert)	Vilém Tauský	Joan Carlyle

[11] The performance scheduled for 20 February was cancelled because of ill health of several members of the cast.

2. Concert, Czechoslovak Institute, 28 February 1945 [12]

Vilém Tauský's endlessly fascinating biography contains anecdotes on every page and, while the author may have drawn attention to that which he thought important himself, he unfortunately neglected an audience that relishes the detail that he excluded. One such account appears on page 79 of the book. [13]

> *In London, Jaroslav Knapp, secretary of the pre-war Czech Institute at 6 Grosvenor Square, was doing much to provide a wide audience of both British and Czech people with concerts, lectures and exhibitions of Czech art. I was sent to London to prepare and conduct concert versions of Czech operas. Among these were 'The Kiss', 'Dalibor', 'Libuše' and 'The Two Widows' by Smetana. This last, an enchanting comedy, has still not been given a professional stage performance in Britain. 'Rusalka' and 'Jacobin' by Dvořák were also heard for the first time in Britain.* [14]
>
> *In these operas I had to work with very uneven casts. Some of the singers were professionals of high standing, and others had good voices but little operatic experience.*

---

[12] In the following sections, the cast and characters are given as they appear in the programme or *Radio Times* but Czech diacritical marks have been added or corrected. No attempt has been made to add diacriticals or to correct spellings in the various newspaper or journal articles quoted.

[13] Tauský, M., *Vilém Tauský tells his story*, (London: Stainer and Bell, 1979), p.79.

[14] The Czechoslovak Institute was created by the British Government under the auspices of the British Council. It was opened at the end of January 1941 by the British Foreign Secretary, the Viscount Halifax, at 18 Grosvenor Place, London. The Czechoslovak Embassy was situated nearby at 8 Grosvenor Place, with the Office of the Czechoslovak President being at number 9. The Institute was intended to act as a centre for Czechoslovak life in London. It provided a library, meeting rooms and offices. All sorts of talks, discussions and exhibitions were held at the premises. In the autumn of 1945 the Institute was obliged to move to 6 Upper Belgrave Street where it remained until closed by the British Government in 1950: 'Since the Communist coup in Czechoslovakia in 1948, the Czechoslovak Institute in London has been inactive', said Mr. Ernest Davies, Secretary of State for Foreign Affairs, in the House of Commons.

One British lady, married to a Czech, was rather lacking in imagination, and felt quite at sea among these professionals when she was given the part of the witch in 'Rusalka'. She did her rather stolid best, but Peggy [Tauský's wife (ed.)] told me afterwards that I hadn't improved matters by bellowing at her in desperation, 'I don't vant Mrs. Tomašov of St. Albans. I vant a vitch!' [15]

Tauský's account sheds fascinating light on the hive of activities that must have been the Czechoslovak Institute during the War. The above list of Smetana and Dvořák operatic performances probably represents some of the very earliest performances in the United Kingdom, albeit only in concerts to the accompaniment of piano. Dvořák's *Jakobín*, for example, had hitherto been thought not to have received any sort of performance until 1947. Information about all these performances would cast a valuable light on the history of Czech music in London during the course of the War.

Tauský knew and loved *Rusalka* very much and reminisced about it always with the greatest affection. In his biography he speaks of his first production with the voice of one who believed Dvořák to be one of the greatest of all composers. His account is worthy of full quotation because it demonstrates Tauský's depth of insight of the work. When it came to future productions, he knew exactly what he required because he had great experience of a superb production and, what is more, of working closely with the actual librettist of *Rusalka* as producer.

In the Brno Opera House I think my career reached its zenith in 1938 when I was entrusted with a new and outstanding production of Dvořák's 'Rusalka'. [16]

---

[15] It is interesting that those responsible for the programme advertising the event rendered the name of the unfortunate lady performing the part of Jezibaba as 'Tomaschoff' which could be Bulgarian or even a Russian transliteration. It is puzzling that other names are given in Czech spelling. There has been a suggestion that *Rusalka*, Blanka Skalická, had appeared with the Prague National Theatre. The Julius Gutmann playing the part of the Watersprite could have been Julius Gutman, the singing teacher who counted Adele Leigh and Peter Pears amongst his pupils. No other participants have been identified thus far.
[16] *his story*, pp.46-47.

It is a fairy tale full of fantasy and imagination. The producer was Jaroslav Kvapil, who had written the libretto for Dvořák, and he made wonderful use of our very modern stage resources to create the mysterious atmosphere of the magical forest. During the rehearsals Kvapil told us many stories of the great man, mostly concerning his poetic simplicity. The one which always remains with me concerns the time when Kvapil, as a very inexperienced young man, first took his libretto to read to Dvořák. 'Rusalka' is the familiar story of a water nymph who longs to be human to gain the love of a prince, and the story ends in tragedy for them both. Dvořák listened silently, absorbed as a child. At the end of the reading he asked, 'What happens next?' and Kvapil, who had not finished the third act, told him in his own words the rest of the story. Anxiously he awaited the great man's verdict, but there was utter silence until Dvořák murmured to himself, 'Poor prince, poor prince!' and Kvapil saw that his eyes were full of tears.

In the context of Tauský's book, it is implied that *Rusalka* was given in the early years of the War. However, a photocopy of a programme (or poster) has come to light which gives full details; see page 136.

3. BBC Third Programme 21 May 1948 [17]

The first BBC broadcast of *Rusalka* was from a recording provided by Czechoslovak Radio. The cast and credits were as follows:[18]

Rusalka	Milada Musilová
The Watersprite	Karel Kalaš
The Witch	Marta Krásová
A hunter	Jan Soumar
The Prince	Beno Blachut
A cook	Miloslava Fidlerová

[17] This recording should not be confused with the later 1952 recording, available on CDs from Supraphon (SU3811-2 602), with Ludmila Červinková, Beno Blachut, Eduard Haken, Marta Krásová, Marie Podvalová, Maria Tauberová, Miloslava Fidlerová and Věra Krilová, conducted by Jaroslav Krombholc.

[18] *Radio Times* 14 May 1948. Czech diacritical marks were not used in the original publication, which also misspelled Pinkaš as 'Pinkan'.

Wood Nymphs	Miluše Dvořáková Ludmila Hansalíková Štěpánka Štěpánová

Chorus of the Czechoslovak Broadcasting Corporation
Chorus Master — Jiří Pinkaš

Orchestra of the Czechoslovak Broadcasting Corporation
Conductor — Alois Klíma

The broadcast was on the 21 May 1948 at 7:40 in the evening. It was accompanied by no other information in the *Radio Times*. As far as can be ascertained, nothing from this recording has ever been released on record or CD. It is to be hoped that the Beno Blachut Society may be able to discover and release this most interesting performance. Blachut's 'Prince' is said to be 'unforgettable'.[19]

4. BBC Home Service 6 April 1949 and BBC Third Programme 8 April 1949

Less than a year separated the BBC's first broadcast of *Rusalka* and its second one, on Wednesday 6 April at 8 o'clock in the evening on the Home Service, followed by a second complete live broadcast on Friday 8 April on the Third Programme. The performances were originally to be in English with a translation by Karel Brušák but in the event a translation was commissioned from Christopher Hassall. Brušák would undoubtedly have provided a more idiomatic and sympathetic text, but Hassall's was to see extensive service in the coming years. The accompanying drawing on page 16 of *Radio Times* of 1 April 1949 depicted a very smitten terrestrial Rusalka ogling the Prince as he divests himself of his clothing. [20, 21]

---

[19] Bohuslav Vítek, sleeve-notes to Vltava CD, CR 0137-2-631 *Beno Blachut. Slavné operní árie 1947-1956.*

[20] Christopher Vernon Hassall (1912–1963) was an English actor, dramatist, librettist, lyricist and poet, who found his greatest fame in a musical partnership with Ivor Novello after working together in the same touring company. He was also a biographer of Rupert Brooke and Edward Marsh.

[21] Karel V. Antonín Brušák, (1913-2004), was a poet, teacher, author and broadcaster. Escaping from Paris before the Nazis took the city, then via Gibraltar to Britain, he worked for the BBC for several years and had a long career at Cambridge.

The first choice for the role of Rusalka would have been an interesting one: the services were sought of Elizabeth Schwarzkopf. Similar problems arose with the vital part of the Watersprite, with Trevor Anthony being the first choice. The role of Jezibaba passed from Edith Coates, through Noreen Berry to Zilla Tregenna. Ignorance of the opera had the first proposals including a 'Merman' and three 'elves'. Both broadcasts were relayed from live performances in the Camden Theatre and with the same cast for each performance. The cast was as follows:

Rusalka, a water-nymph	Gré Brouwenstijn
The Watersprite	Norman Lumsden
The Witch	Zilla Tregenna
A huntsman	Newton Goodson
Prince	James Johnston
Foreign Princess	Rosina Raisbeck
The gamekeeper	Murray Davies
The kitchen boy	Anna Pollak
Three Sylphs	Nora Moore Bettine Young Doris Abrahams
BBC Theatre Chorus	
Chorus Master	John Clements

BBC Theatre Orchestra
Conductor Stanford Robinson

The radio audience was treated to a commentary written by Mark Lubbock and narrated by the actor, Andrew Cruikshank, then reaching the peak of his stage career. Act 1 was broadcast at 8.00 p.m. with Acts 2 and 3 lasting from 9.30 to 11.00 p.m. The half hour interval took the form of the 9 o'clock news and a Budget talk by Sir Stafford Cripps. [22]

Radio Times featured a 700-word introductory article by Harold Rutland in his regular *Music Diary* entitled *The Water-Nymph who Loved a Mortal.* The article tells the story of the opera very well and, clearly familiar with the work already, Rutland was astonished at its neglect in Britain. The BBC's Archives at Caversham do not have any record of the audience reaction to these broadcasts.

> *Even allowing for the hazards and the cost of operatic production, there can be no doubt that we in this country are far less enterprising in opera than in other spheres of music. It is inconceivable (...) that the 'New World Symphony' should have taken anything like forty-eight years to reach us. Yet that is what has happened to 'Rusalka', Dvořák's most successful opera. It won immediate popularity in Prague in 1901 as a delightful presentation of the familiar story of the water-nymph who falls in love with a mortal. But although plans were made for the opera to be produced at Covent Garden shortly before the war, and a recording of it, made in Prague, was recently heard in the Third Programme, the performances to be broadcast on Wednesday (Home) and on Friday (Third) will in fact be the first to be given here.* [23, 24]

---

[22] Andrew Cruikshank, 25.12.1907–29.04.1988, a Scottish actor who became best known for his part as Dr. Cameron in the long-running BBC TV series, *Dr. Finlay's Casebook* between 1962 and 1971. His unmistakable, warm voice would have perfectly suited the narration.

[23] *Radio Times* 1 April 1949.

[24] Harold Rutland (1900-1977) pianist, composer and writer. His articles on music for *Radio Times* ran for many years with a consistent high standard of erudition and readability. He wrote for many journals, including *The Musical Times,* which he edited for some years. He was also a Manager of the RPO.

5. John Lewis Partnership Music Society, 9, 11 and 12 May 1950 [25]

The story of the origins and performance of the first ever live staged performance in Britain of *Rusalka* is of great interest and for this reason the production is covered in detail. [26]

The *Gazette* of the John Lewis Partnership reported the forthcoming performances of *Rusalka* on 29 April 1950 as follows:

> *'In opera', wrote Mr. Eric Blom, in The Observer of the 16th April, 'our amateurs are often ahead of the professionals when it comes to exploration', and gave as an example our Opera Group's coming production at Peter Jones, on the 9th, 11th and 12th of May, of Dvorak's 'Rusalka'. This will be the first stage performance of this opera in England. There was to have been one in 1939, but it was 'frustrated by the machinations of Mars'.*

The *Gazette* of the John Lewis Partnership of May 1950 reported:

> *The Partnership's Opera Group, not content with the originality of its mere existence (how very few "opera societies" ever dream of really doing opera!) are this year, in fact next week, on Tuesday, Thursday and Friday, the 9th, 11th and 12th, producing an opera that has never been seen, though parts of it have been heard, in this country before — Dvorak's 'Rusalka'. It is being produced by Mr. Sumner Austin and [he has] very kindly written us an article on it which appears on page 164.*

---

[25] The John Lewis Partnership's Music Society has never lacked an adventurous spirit. It was founded in 1925 as a choir and expanded into a Music Society in the 1930s and at that time John Spedan Lewis gave tremendous support to Glyndebourne by purchasing 200 seats a year. The Society's first opera performance was of Mozart's *Magic Flute* in 1947. The enterprise of the John Lewis Music Society has continued to the present day with frequent performances of pieces old, new and specially commissioned. In 1963 the Society chalked up another British first performance for Dvořák when they presented B.67, *Šelma sedlák (The Peasant a Rogue,* also known as *The Cunning Peasant* or *The Scheming Farmer*).

[26] Quotations from The Gazette of the John Lewis Partnership are by the kind permission of the Archive of the John Lewis Partnership.

It is a difficulty of exploration that there are no roads and no signposts. And if you explore an opera that has only had one orchestral performance broadcast and no stage production in this country, you may find some difficulty in providing yourself with the words and music. The B.B.C. have very kindly helped our Opera Group by lending their vocal scores. Orchestral parts, however, have had to be obtained from Prague, and that has not proved so easy. First attempts produced no reply at all, favourable or unfavourable, but eventually persistent efforts proved successful and a deal was done with Dvorak's executors. At long last the day came when the orchestral parts arrived in London.

'For the first time on any English stage'. This is an opportunity that no lover of opera can afford to miss. There are three performances — on Tuesday, Thursday and Friday at 7 p.m. at Peter Jones. Membership of the Music Society (which costs you 5/- a year — 2/6d. if you are a Junior) entitles you to two seats. Admission is by invitation only, and the Social Secretary's Office is busy making final seating arrangements but will give any help and information to those who want it.

Utilising the BBC's vocal scores meant that Christopher Hassall's translation was used. Costumes were borrowed from Sadler's Wells. Mosco Carner's verdict on some of the costumes, 'the Watersprite looked as if he had walked on to the stage straight from the Men's Underwear Department', shows that not all was well in the costume department and things must have improved at the Wells somewhat when it came to their own production nine years later!

The introductory article mentioned above was, in the event, not written by Sumner Austin but by Geoffrey Corbett, who was to conduct the performances. His account of the production rightly conveyed his pride in this being the first on a British stage: [27]

[27] Geoffrey Corbett, a Communist Party member, is also noteworthy for having conducted the second performance in Britain of Dvořák's *Jakobín* by the Working Men's Association in London in 1947.

Rusalka

Next Week's Production by the Partnership's Opera Group

Last year after our performances of Mozart's 'Marriage of Figaro' one of your correspondents suggested that the Opera Group of the Music Society was well equipped for preparing and performing some of the lesser known operas. I would like to thank that person through your columns for a suggestion which I felt was so stimulating and which made it easier for us to embark on the work which I hope many of your readers will come to see on May 9th, 11th or 12th.

By way of introduction to this work I think the best I can do is to tell you the facts about it — and assure you that if you enjoy the Dvorak of the 'New World Symphony,' the 'Cello Concerto' and the 'Slavonic Dances' — you will find this an enthralling work. 'Rusalka' was composed in 1900, four years before Dvorak died, and so enthusiastic was he over the subject that he completed it in six months. It is the last but one of his ten operas, and the most popular. It was first performed four months after its completion and was immediately successful. It has been revived many times in Czechoslovakia – and other countries, including Poland, Germany and Spain — and it is at present in the repertoire of the Prague National Theatre. Our performances will be the first given on the stage in this country.

The legend on which the libretto is based is an almost universal one, and has been used by many people. Dargomisjki wrote an opera with the same title. Puccini's 'Ondine' is another on the same theme. [28]

The legend is extremely simple — a Water Nymph (Rusalka is Slav for Water Nymph and not the name of any one nymph) sees a Prince come to the lake to bathe, and falling deeply in love with him, begs to be turned into a mortal. Her father, the Water Sprite, tries to prevent this, but she seeks the aid of the witch Jezibaba, who promises to give her a human soul on two conditions. On becoming a mortal she will be dumb, and if the man she loves

[28] There is no such opera as Puccini's *Ondine*; perhaps the reference is a corruption of Puccini's *La Rondine* (The Swallow) of 1917. (ed.) P.H. has suggested the 1843 ballet *Ondine, ou La naïade* by Cesare Pugni.

betrays her, she cannot regain her former status but must become a Will o' the Wisp. The first act deals with Rusalka's transformation and discovery by the Prince, the second with her betrothal and subsequent betrayal by the Prince, who, finding her speechlessness too much of a barrier, deserts her for a Foreign Princess. The last act shows Rusalka begging the witch to give her back her original form of Water Nymph. This can only be done if she will kill the Prince. This she refuses to do, and the Prince, finding too late that he can love only her, chooses death through her kiss rather than life without her. Dvorak has put into this tale a richness of harmonic and melodic music that is as fine as in anything he wrote; the construction of each act is well thought out and in addition to the characters mentioned we have a Gamekeeper and Kitchen Boy — in two lively scenes — and a trio of singing Nymphs. The one big ensemble scene with chorus and ballet is the betrothal party in Act II. The opera was to have been performed at Covent Garden in 1939, but the War prevented this, and the coming performances by the John Lewis Partnership Opera Group give you the first opportunity of seeing it in this country.

A simple programme was produced for the performances giving the outline of each act and a summary of the above history. The cast for the performances was as follows:

Rusalka	Mary Maxwell
The Watersprite	C. Phipps Hunt
Jezibaba (The Witch)	Nancy Strike
A huntsman	D. E. C. Goodman
Prince	R. A. Fisher
Princess	Dorothy Humphreys
A game keeper	W. G. Higbee
A kitchen boy	Muriel Smith
Three Wood Nymphs	Doris Cassé Nelly M. Overend Joan Coleman

John Lewis Music Society Chorus and Orchestra

Conductor	Geoffrey Corbett

The John Lewis Gazette of 13 May 1950 duly reported on the *Rusalka* production. The Editor was very pleased to have secured the services of Mosco Carner for the review. It was spread across three columns and starts by giving the author's qualifications to compare it with other prductions. [29]

> *It is a far cry from the Prague National Theatre, where before the war I first heard 'Rusalka', to the Peter Jones Theatre in Sloane Square, where the Partnership's enterprising Music Society produced this opera last Tuesday night. But comparison would be invidious, and let me say at once that the still vivid memory of that highly polished Prague production in no way lessened my enjoyment of what I heard at Sloane Square. This, I gather, was the first English production of Dvorak's enchanting opera, which may seem strange in view of the composer's close links with this country. He came here several times during his lifetime, on each occasion he was fêted as the great master of Czech music, and for England he specially wrote a number of works. Yet the Dvorak whom the Englishman knows and loves is the composer of chamber music and symphonies. Chamber music players will tell you about the joy they all derive from the sensuous beauty and rhythmic vitality of his trios, quartets, and quintets, and as for the popularity of his last two symphonies, it is no rare occurrence to hear the butcher's boy whistle the lovely melancholy tune from the second movement of the 'New World'.*

---

[29] *The Gazette of the John Lewis Partnership* introduced Mosco Carner as follows: 'Dr. Mosco Carner, Musical Critic of *Time and Tide* and the author of a book on Dvořák. Dr. Carner first made his name in this country in a series of Mozart concerts at the Cambridge Theatre, London, which were given under the auspices of Sir Thomas Beecham. He also conducted the B.B.C. Symphony Orchestra, the London Philharmonic Orchestra, the London Symphony Orchestra, the Philharmonia Orchestra, and the Radio Eireann Symphony Orchestra. Other Orchestras that have played under his direction are the Vienna Concert Orchestra, the Orchestra of the Danzig State Theatre, and the Danzig and Konigsberg Radio Orchestras'.
Two valuable articles by Carner on Dvořák's music were published in his *Of Men & Music* (London: Joseph Williams Ltd. 1944), 'The Great and the Popular in Dvořák' and 'Dvořák's Church Music', the latter reprinted from the Viktor Fischl symposium, *Antonín Dvořák: His Achievement.*

Yet of Dvorak's operas we seem here almost completely ignorant. True, operatic conditions in this country have up to a few years ago not been favourable to the production of lesser-known work, and when in 1939 Covent Garden got as far as undertaking to produce 'Rusalka', the outbreak of war put an end to this praiseworthy venture. Let us hope that this amateur production may serve as a reminder of an unfulfilled promise. Dvorak's great ambition was opera. Perhaps it was an ambition roused in him by circumstances rather than an inner calling. The fact that out of his eight published operas only two, 'Rusalka' and 'The Devil and Kate', have travelled far beyond the frontiers of his native country, is, I feel, a significant commentary upon Dvorak the operatic composer. However, this is not the place to discuss his shortcomings in the sphere of the theatre, and 'Rusalka' is certainly a work in which he succeeded in composing, as he said, 'an opera which, like some of Verdi's work, should live in the people'.

Its production by the Music Society was a most creditable achievement and showed how much could be got out of gifted amateurs by what I presume must have been long and hard work. Considering the severe limitations of the stage, Mr. Sumner Austin did an excellent piece of work, cutting his coat exactly to the cloth available. Fortunately, the opera requires only two different sets, and his solution in the circumstances was the only possible one, i.e., to retain the same background and suggest the change of scenery by a few props. Being a fairy-tale opera, it was an advantage to give it so simple a setting and leave the rest to his spectators' imagination. Perhaps a little incongruous was, hence, the contrast of the rich costumes worn in the second act by the Prince and his entourage. More imagination, however, could have been shown in the costumes of the supernatural creatures, the Nymphs and the Watersprite. There was little in their make-up to suggest their watery abode; the Watersprite looked as if he had walked on to the stage straight from the Men's Underwear Department, and Rusalka's transformation from a nymph to a human being, at the end of the first act, should have been indicated much more visibly in her dress and general appearance.

Musically, 'Rusalka' is, for all the naivety of the plot and the small demand it makes on acting and staging, not an easy work to perform. Yet it was surprising how much of it was realised under the alert and musicianly direction of Mr. Geoffrey Corbett. Mishaps there were, notably in the horns, which seemed of a dyspeptic disposition. And if at times the orchestral playing was ragged and the tempo dragging, — well, Dvorak's score puts a strain even on a professional orchestra. It would be churlish not to praise the valiant effort shown by Mr. Corbett's band, particularly the woodwind, and here I would single out the first flute and clarinet.

Among the singers, Miss Dorothy Humphreys' Princess was the most impressive performance. Vocally and in her acting she left nothing to be desired. She has true dramatic instinct, which made me regret the relative smallness of her part. Her rival, Miss Mary Maxwell's Rusalka, was charming, and she well brought out the childlike innocence of the heroine. But her sweet voice is too small for the part, and except for its high notes it was hardly a match for Dvorak's symphonic orchestra. Miss Nancy Strike as Jezibaba looked and acted every inch a witch, with nutcracker face, hunchback and all. She might have stepped out of Hell that very evening.

Mr. R. A. Fisher as the unfortunate lover showed himself the possessor of a beautiful operatic tenor, but he ought to becareful not to lose support in the high register, where his tone is a little 'pinched'. Mr. C. Phipps Hunt as the Watersprite impressed by his resonance rather than beauty of tone and his enunciation leaves room for improvement. Nor did I feel that his reading of the part did sufficient justice to the paternal, good-natured quality with which the composer tempers this awe-inspiring creature. As Mr. Alec Robertson puts it in his excellent book, 'the Watersprite is a sort of benevolent Alberich, a figure who must have immediately appealed to the nature-loving soul of Dvorak'. In the subsidiary parts the gamekeeper of Mr. W. G. Higbee and Miss Muriel Smith's kitchen boy were a well-matched pair, and uncle and nephew provided, between them, much comic relief. The three nymphs, chorus and ballet performed with adroitness. There was no doubt that the packed audience enjoyed itself greatly.

THE JOHN LEWIS PARTNERSHIP
MUSIC SOCIETY

Presents

RUSALKA

BY

ANTONIN DVOŘÁK

Libretto by Jaroslav Kvapil
English Version by Christopher Hassall

PETER JONES THEATRE

On

9th, 11th and 12th MAY, 1950

at 7 p.m.

Cover of the programme for the John Lewis Partneship Music Society's performance of 'Rusalka'

That Mr. Carner was knowledgeable of Dvořák's life and works is easily divinable from his brief booklet on the composer for the Novello company. [30]

The John Lewis production was reviewed by both *The Times* and *The Daily Telegraph.* These are reproduced in order to demonstrate the mountain of critical opinion that *Rusalka* had to ascend.

Anon, *The Times*, 12 May 1950:

> *Dvorak's 'Rusalka'*
> *First English Performance*
>
> *It is left to amateurs to stage for us those operas by composers howsoever eminent which do not get into the international repertory. Of Dvorak's 10 operas only three have ever been given in this country. 'The Devil and Kate' at Oxford, and 'The Jacobin' under Mr. Geoffrey Corbett, who also conducted last night 'Rusalka' now given for the first time here by the Musical Society of the John Lewis Partnership. It is easy to see why Dvorak's operas do not get into the international repertory, any more than do those of another natural melodist, Schubert. The action is slow and though the set arias are often lovely they build up no dramatic tension. 'Rusalka' also suffers from the composer's reliance on formulae, developmental figuration, and other such stock-in-trade of symphonic-writing. It was indeed curious that the one really dramatic moment in last night's performance at the Peter Jones Theatre, the conventional operatic love-duet, was pure fustian — not even Dvorak. But in all the nature music, the trios (excellently) sung by the water nymphs, much of Rusalka's own solo music, and a great deal of the orchestral commentary, which, if truth be told, was more distinctive than the solo writing, one heard that wood-note wild that is authentic Dvorak. There were also national Czech idioms, reminiscent of 'The Bartered Bride', in the subsidiary episodes of the Kitchen Boy and the Gamekeeper.*
>
> *The cast contained some good voices, and though it is not given to every amateur to get words over an orchestra in*

[30] Carner, M., *Dvořák,* (London: Novello's Biographies of Great Musicians, 1941).

singing a fair and true vocal line – men can do it better than women for acoustical reasons unconnected with voice production — the singing was at a high level of competence. The Watersprite of Mr. C. Phipps Hunt was the most effective sung part, though Mr. R. A. Fisher used his true tenor voice to good purpose as the princely lover who suffers from his fatal fascination by a water nymph (Rusalka). She, the heroine, was prettily sung by Miss Mary Maxwell. There was a little professional help with the orchestra, and Mr. Sumner Austin had produced the opera. An English text by Mr. Christopher Hassall seemed, when it could be heard, to avoid both absurdity and sentimentality, which is much in a romantic opera about fairyland by a simple-minded composer.

Mosco Carner also wrote the review for *The Daily Telegraph* on 12 May 1950.

Dvorak Opera

At the Peter Jones Theatre last night the John Lewis Partnership Music Society gave a spirited performance — apparently the first in this country — of Dvorak's opera, 'Rusalka'. The story is the familiar one of a water-fairy's fatal love for a mortal prince, the musical idiom a blend of Czech folk song with Wagnerian mannerisms and orchestration. Mary Maxwell in the title part could not always assert herself above the orchestra, but R. A. Fisher and Dorothy Humphreys (Prince and Princess) proved themselves robust singers quite capable of holding their own. C. Phipps Hunt and Nancy Strike thoroughly entered into their roles of Watersprite and Witch.

6. Interlude: The recording of 'O silver moon' 23 January 1952

Alec Robertson reviewed a new recording of 'O silver moon' from Act 1 of *Rusalka*, and 'Twill soon be midnight now' from Tchaikovsky's *Queen of Spades* in the April 1952 issue of *Gramophone*. He thought the Dvořák aria 'lovely' and compared it with an old recording he had with Ada Sari singing to piano accompaniment. In the present recording, he felt it a pity that some of the orchestral music had had to be cut but was more than happy with the 'lovely introduction'. The record went on to enormous success and has since been reissued in many formats and compilations to the present day. (See page 225) The recording in question was HMV's 12 inch shellac record, (DB 21451), with Joan Hammond singing and Vilém Tauský conducting the Philharmonia Orchestra. The huge success of this record was acknowledged, again in *Gramophone*, in that magazine's February 1959 issue. This was the occasion for Philip Hope-Wallace to review a new 7 inch, extended play record, (HMV 7ER 5118) including the same 'O silver moon' recording but this time with other items from *Rusalka* again performed by Joan Hammond with the same orchestra but conducted by another Czech exile, Walter Süsskind. Hope-Wallace was never a fan of *Rusalka* or even, possibly, of Dvořák as a composer at all. He acknowledged the 'Song to the moon' to have attained 'great popularity' but severely questioned Miss Hammond's performance of the three pieces on the E.P. He hinted that some of the popularity of the record had meant much to 'those who faintly sensed a resemblance in it to Judy Garland's 'Somewhere over the Rainbow''. In spite of Hope-Wallace's opinions this record also went on to considerable success and resulted in many more requests on BBC radio.

In talking about the genesis of both the 1957 concert performance for the BBC and the Sadler's Wells production of Rusalka in 1959, Tauský reported the stroke of fate that resulted in such success.

> *An interesting story underlies the reason that Joan came to be chosen as Rusalka. Some years before, she was making a recording of operatic arias with me and the Royal Philharmonic Orchestra. One morning the 'Ave Maria' by Max Bruch was scheduled for recording, but the orchestral material did not arrive in time from Germany, so I said to Joan: 'Now is our chance, let's do the 'Moon song' from 'Rusalka',' a hitherto unknown aria in England. Walter Legge, who was in charge, surprisingly agreed, and the 'B-side' became a best selling record which is still in constant demand. As a result of this record the BBC invited us to do a full broadcast of Rusalka with Rowland Jones as the tenor, and it may have been this performance that influenced Norman Tucker to put on the opera at the Wells.* [31]

---

[31] *his story*, p.133; the orchestra was the Philharmonia, not the RPO.

Tauský remained extremely proud of the recording and of his relationship with Joan Hammond. Earlier in the biography he wrote:

> *I enjoyed every show I did with Joan, and am very proud of the records I made with her, especially of the Moon song from 'Rusalka' by Dvořák, which was hitherto unknown, and is now famous throughout the world. It was a sad day for music when Joan's brilliant career was cut short by heart trouble. I fear she had worked too hard and had given too unsparingly of herself.* [32]

The relationship between Vilém Tauský and Joan Hammond was a long, friendly and profitable one for both. They first came together at the Carl Rosa Opera Company in 1945 and she sang many roles under Tauský's baton, a time she remembered with affection:

> *Soon after this, I had the pleasure of working with another Czech-born conductor, Vilem Tausky. He had the same flexible easy style as Walter [Walter Süsskind (ed.)], and a beat that was clear and decisive. His knowledge of opera is the most extensive and profound of any conductor I have ever worked with, before or since. Even apart from his work, he is one of the most interesting men to talk with. He lives for music. Vilem is the greatest asset to any opera company. He'll work and train his orchestra and singers with the minimum of fuss. We were all devoted to him in the Carl Rosa, and he certainly improved the standard of performances. Being reticent and unassertive made his road the harder in this world of 'the louder you shout the sooner you'll get there'. I should like to have him on a quiz session being asked who composed a particular ballet, concerto, symphony or song, and where and when it was first performed. His knowledge of music is limitless and his taste is catholic.* [33]

---

[32] *his story*, p.92.

[33] Hammond, J. , *A Voice, A Life*, (London: Victor Gollancz, 1970), pp.148-149. Quotations from Joan Hammond's autobiography are published by kind permission of The Orion Publishing Group, the current owners of Victor Gollancz. Other attempts at tracing the copyright holder of the book were unsuccessful.

Vilém Tauský fulsomely reciprocated in his own biography:

> *I was fortunate on joining the company to have Joan Hammond to sing Tosca, Madame Butterfly, Marguerite and Violetta. In addition to an exceptionally beautiful voice and distinguished stage presence, she cared deeply about every note of the music. I can honestly say that I have never known a singer who loved the music of the opera so much for its own sake as Joan did. She was the greatest perfectionist and expected the same high standards from all her colleagues as she gave herself. Of course this helped to raise the standard of any performance in which she was concerned.* [34]

7. BBC Home Service 19 May 1954

In 1954, the BBC mounted a small commemorative festival for the 50th anniversary of the death of Dvořák. This was to take the form of a series of concerts in May and June that year. On Wednesday 12 May Sir Malcolm Sargent conducted Dvořák's *Carnival, Cello Concerto No.2* and *Symphony No.2 in d minor* (now known as *No.7*). The soloist was Pierre Fournier. The third concert had Sir Malcolm conducting the *Slavonic Rhapsody No.3 in A flat, Othello, Te Deum* and *Symphony No.4 in G* (now known as *No.8*) plus an aria from *The Spectre's Bride* sung by Elisabeth Schwarzkopf. With Bruce Boyce, Schwarzkopf and the BBC Chorus and Choral Society performed the *Te Deum*, which was always a strong favourite of Sargent's. The fourth and final concert was on 2 June and again had Sir Malcolm Sargent conducting the *Symphonic Variations, Violin Concerto* and the *New World Symphony*. Endré Wolf was the soloist in the concerto.

The second event in the series was a concert performance of *Rusalka*, the fourth broadcast performance of *Rusalka*, and it seemingly had everything about it to make it definitive; unfortunately this was not to be the case. The conductor was to be the newly appointed Music Director of the Royal Opera House, Rafael Kubelík, who was to take up his post the next year. Kubelík was to conduct the June revival of the 1951 Sadler's Wells production of Janáček's *Kaťa Kabanová* (originally conducted by Charles Mackerras) and he was attracting a great deal of attention in view of his imminent arrival at Covent Garden: he was a natural choice for *Rusalka*.

[34] *his story*, p.91.

Negotiations with regard to extra rehearsal time and cuts were considered important enough to be handled by R. J. F. Howgill, Controller, Music at the BBC. He had looked at the timings of each act of the 1949 broadcast and, at 57, 45 and 56 minutes each, 'this is much too long', he wrote to Kubelík's agent in The Hague, Mme. J. Beek. He wanted no more than 55 minutes before the interval and no more than 60 after it. This meant making severe cuts and the parts of the Kitchen Boy and Gamekeeper disappeared. Their two principal scenes, at the start of the second act and scene two of the third act do not amount to 45 minutes, so various other cuts were also made in acts two and three.

James Johnston, Kubelík's personal choice, was pencilled in as the Prince 'albeit with a very shaky top C' but he gave way to Rowland Jones. Kubelík also favoured Sylvia Fisher as the Princess and Martha Lipton as Jezibaba, neither of whom were available. Howgill believed that Christopher Hassall's translation was 'good'. Gré Brouwenstijn was very much a favourite at the BBC in those days and she remained first choice throughout casting. A small flyer for the series was produced by the BBC with a brief introduction by Frank Howes. [35]

> *During the war we celebrated, as best we could, the centenary of Dvořák's birth, for we have always been fond of him here. Just what the affinity between Britain and Bohemia is defies definition, but in Dvořák's case it was obviously a matter of mutual attraction.*

A comprehensive programme was produced for the concert. A synopsis of the opera with an excellent introduction to its genesis was provided by Alec Robertson. Not surprisingly, since this was written for a concert programme, it is in glowing terms about the work and its music. Most interestingly, Robertson, far from calling for the cuts he requests in his *Master Musicians* book, here, in speaking of the parts of the gamekeeper and kitchen boy, he describes their absence from the concert as 'unfortunate'. He most carefully details the missing sections.

---

[35] Frank Howes CBE (1891-1974) was President of the Royal Musical Association from 1947 until 1958. He lectured in music history at the Royal College of Music for over thirty years, and in 1943 he succeeded H. C. Colles as chief music critic of *The Times*. (http://www.rma.ac.uk)

The eventual cast was as follows:

Rusalka, a water-nymph	Gré Brouwenstijn
The Watersprite	Norman Lumsden
The Witch	Noreen Berry
A Huntsman	Francis Loring
Prince	Rowland Jones
The Foreign Princess	Laelia Finneberg
Wood Nymphs	Adrienne Cole Marion Lowe Pamela Bowden
BBC Chorus Chorus Master	 Leslie Woodgate
BBC Symphony Orchestra Conductor	 Rafael Kubelík

Howgill may have believed the translation of *Rusalka* by Christopher Hassall as 'good' but two example couplets serve only too well to illustrate the banality of the text.

The Water Goblin at the end of Act II, Scene 3:

Go where you will to fly that frost,
cold is thy doom and all is lost.

The Princess shortly following the above:

Down to the uttermost bottom of Hell,
follow your bride, and love her well.

There is certainly a case to be made for opera to be performed in English in the British Isles but when doggerel like this is used it is hardly surprising if the work as a whole is not taken seriously. One cries out for the sort of artistry that could have been had from a serious poet such as Brušák. Hassall's version was used for all the English language productions up to David Pountney's production in 1983. Only at that time was a text used (other than the Czech original) which was worthy of the opera.

The house may have been full for the performance, such was the interest in Rafael Kubelík but the radio audience was tiny. The BBC audience survey reported that the listening figure for each part was just 1% and with an appreciation index of 70, which was said to equal the previous broadcast. Individual audience comments, if any, could not be located. [36]

The concert was briefly reviewed by W. R. Anderson for *The Musical Times* in its July 1954 issue. Far from finding the loss of two of the human characters unfortunate, he wanted to cut the whole second act!

> *The Dvořák celebration gave us a hearing of the opera 'Rusalka', the sad tale of a dumb-struck love-losing Undine, whose deprivation of voice in the middle of the work makes that a weak section. Perhaps Act 2 could be cut out? Another little drawback is the composer's rhythmical square-toedness in his arias. His opening displays the sort of conventionality into which Dvořák, never his own keenest critic, could fall. He knew his Wagner, of course, and we do not mind some very Rhinemaidenly strains. At his best he is an exhilarating free-smiter: one thinks of the best kind of village cricket — everyone out for a good game and not caring overmuch about victory or defeat. Rusalka (Gré Brouwenstijn) though not many of her words could be made out, soared and rang and revelled splendidly. The others were mostly chosen from the familiar B.B.C. teams, and wrought as well as could be expected with an unfamiliar style. There are times when Dvořák seems to have taken the first idea that came into his head. Well, his ways curl into the heart, and I could wish for more composers who could be described as Villon was by Swinburne: 'Our sad, bad, glad, mad brother.' For little glad rashness today some of us would risk the mild sadness of the a d-lad.*

This calculatedly patronising attack on Dvořák as a composer, not merely as the writer of *Rusalka*, perpetuates what had become the norm for the critics: that Dvořák was essentially a second-tier composer who wrote some good tunes but wrote carelessly and with a dull rhythmic sense.

---

[36] BBC Archives, Caversham.

With the only readily available book in English being that by Alec Robertson, it is little wonder that what appear in that as generalisations should now appear in this review as specific barbs against his art as a whole. This sort of criticism would do nothing to warm the inclinations of a potential audience towards future performances of *Rusalka*. It would take a further twelve years for John Clapham to start to undermine this sort of received wisdom in his book on the composer. Until then the idea that Dvořák just wrote down the first thing that occurred to him would continue to colour critical opinion adversely. [37]

8. BBC Home Service 25 April 1957

Very little useful information has been discovered about the curious performance of *Rusalka* in 1957 and nothing could be found in the BBC archives about it. This was the first professional production of the opera which involved the services of Vilém Tauský. Tauský himself hints that the probable cause of his being asked to perform *Rusalka* at this time related to the success of the previously described recording of 'O silver moon'. [38]

[37] Clapham, J., *Antonín Dvořák, Musician and Craftsman*, (London: Faber and Faber Ltd., 1966).

[38] By the time of the 1957 production, Vilém Tauský had become a BBC employee. His name first appears in staff lists as Conductor (Concert Orchestra) in the Light Music Entertainment Department in November 1956. In the June 1961 list he is given an assistant in the form of Mrs. E. Cunliffe, who went on in December 1963 to be Clerk to the popular Music While You Work. At the same time, Tauský was listed as a member of the Music Programmes Department, Light Music and still as Conductor (Concert Orchestra). His last mention in the staff list is in June 1966. (Information from the BBC Archives, Caversham)

In the event, this was a very cut performance. *Radio Times* for 19 April called it 'an abridged version' and so it was, fitting much less than an hour of music into a slot between 10.00 p.m. and the late news at 11.00 p.m. This, then was very much a highlights performance, perhaps to test the water after the unenthusiastic response to the 1954 broadcast. It is interesting to note that two of the soloists were to appear in the Sadler's Wells 1959 production as well.

Rusalka	Joan Hammond
Watersprite	Howell Glynne
Prince	Richard Lewis
The Foreign Princess	Laelia Finneberg
BBC Northern Orchestra	
Conductor	Vilém Tauský

The narrator was Randal Herley and once again the dubious qualities of Christopher Hassall's translation were employed.

9. Sadler's Wells Opera, 18, 24, 28 February, 11, 19 March 1959 and BBC Third Programme 19 March 1959

'slim nymphs who dance, plump nymphs who sing' [39]

The first staged, professional production in the United Kingdom fell to Vilém Tauský to conduct. There were to be many unfortunate circumstances to prevent it being a success but this in many ways marks the crucial point in the reception of Dvořák's operas. Janáček had already started to make his (also very late) mark but for the first time the largest audience thus far and the greatest number of influential critics were able to see and hear a Dvořák opera in the manner intended.

In 1959 Sadler's Wells was recovering from a difficult time in the previous year and only presented two new productions, *Die Fledermaus* and *Rusalka*. At the present time, the archives of Sadler's Wells are in the process of being sorted and catalogued by the local historians of the Islington Libraries in London.

---

[39] See Frank Howes' review in *The Times* on page 183, for the origin of this quotation.

Thus the story of their 1959 production can only be told from the available external sources. However, whilst Vilém Tauský is expectedly brief in his coverage of the event in his biography, he nevertheless conveys a good idea of the excitement he felt at the prospect. Prior to this he had notched up various milestones: the first (concert) performance (with piano) of *Rusalka* in 1945 and a 'pilot' performance for the BBC in 1957.

> *On 18 February 1959 a longed-for wish came true — the premiere of Dvořák's 'Rusalka', with Joan Hammond in the title role, Charles Craig as the Prince and Howell Glynne as the Watersprite. As I have told you earlier, I had worked on an outstanding Czech production by Dvořák's own librettist. Our producer at Sadler's Wells was Wendy Toye, who filled the stage with the poetry of movement. Our hopes were high, but the piece was ill-fated. On the first night the opera house filled with fog to such an extent that it was in doubt as to whether a performance could be held; it was held under these depressing circumstances, with the result that our tenor was too ill to go on a couple of nights later for the second performance. The press was lukewarm in its reception of the opera, one well known London critic saying, 'It may be all right for Prague schoolgirls on a Saturday afternoon, but it is not my cup of tea'. Yet later, when the Prague Opera Company brought 'Rusalka' to Edinburgh, he found it: 'An enchanting piece full of magic and poetry'. This time no praise was too high.* [40, 41]

Joan Hammond's memories of the production and its first night are even more vivid than the conductor's. Her account in her autobiography describes the circumstances perfectly. [42]

---

[40] *his story*, pp.132-133.

[41] Vilém Tauský's 'cup of tea' quotation has not been located in any printed criticisms. It was probably part of a conversation reported to him at a later date. The London newspapers were not consulted for this essay with regard to the Edinburgh International Festival performances. The most likely candidate for the quotation, on the strength of his comments in the *Daily Telegraph* (see below) would be Martin Cooper.

[42] *A Voice, A Life*, p.210-211.

Early in 1959 I began rehearsals of 'Rusalka' at Sadler's Wells. The producer was a very talented and competent artist, Wendy Toye, and the designer was James Bailey, a most proficient young man. Vilem Tausky was the conductor. I should say this production was one of the happiest with which I had ever been associated, and it ended in being one of the most disastrous, from the point of view of a London première; but to have collaborated with Wendy, James and Vilem and all the excellent cast was nothing but a pleasure.

At 4 p.m. on the day of the première Norman Tucker telphoned me at the Old Cottage and said: 'Joan, Norman here. We're in a spot. Charles [tenor Charles Craig] is almost voiceless and feels he can't go on. Would you be willing to sing 'Madam Butterfly' instead?' 'Whew!' was all I said. Norman never wasted words or time. 'I can get a cast for Butterfly, and Anna Pollak will be your Suzuki, so no worries there. Vilem is confident that the rest of the cast will be okay.' 'That's fine with me, Norman. I'm sorry for you all up there. 'Thanks, Joan, and by the way, it's getting rather foggy.' 'Don't worry. I'll leave here just as soon as I get my wig and costumes out. See you later.'

With that the Old Cottage rocked with activity. I had not sung Butterfly since December, and then it was in Italian. I thought of it mentally while on the journey to London. By the time we reached Shepherd's Bush the fog was unpleasantly thick, and the streets dark. We arrived at the Wells an hour before the performance was due to begin. I had the English words of Butterfly well into my head and I felt mentally prepared. For any première (and Dvorak's 'Rusalka' was to receive its first performance in Great Britain), rehearsals work up to a certain pitch; during the last two weeks we had all lived, slept and eaten 'Rusalka'. So you can imagine the tremendous let-down one feels when such a première has to be cancelled.

I was met at the stage door by the stage manager. He greeted me: 'Joan, it's to be 'Rusalka' after all. Craig has decided to go through with it.' What a mental switch from Cio Cio San to Rusalka, and all in a few minutes!

Poor Charles, the possessor of a lovely rich tenor voice, was most unhappy, but he managed to get through although his voice showed but a shadow of its usual brilliance. The fog had seeped into the theatre and into our dressing rooms, and we heard that three-quarters of the audience could barely see the stage after the second interval. They gave us a wonderful acclamation at the final curtain, but we all felt rather flat because of the ghastliness of the night. Some of us managed to reach James Bailey's flat in the West End, where we had a delightful supper party. It took us over four hours to get back to the Old Cottage, where we arrived at 5 a.m. with stiff, sooty black hair and clogged noses. One of us had to get out of the car at each roundabout and lead with a torch, as the "cat's eyes" had gaps where the different roads led off. Nevertheless we often found other motorists on the wrong road and on the wrong side of a dual carriageway, and twice we met cars coming at us. It was terrifying. The second performance of 'Rusalka' was due to take place two days later, but this time Charles had to cancel, and we did 'Madam Butterfly' instead.

Tauský's depth of knowledge of both Dvořák and *Rusalka* is amply illustrated by the article he contributed to *Opera* for its February 1959 edition. (See pages 9-17) What to previous writers in English were seen as weaknesses, Tauský shows are actually strengths. For example, the music for the human characters is of necessity a contrast with that for the supernatural ones. The rhythmic nature of the piece is of a part with Dvořák's whole background in music and Tauský was the very man to bring all this out to the best advantage. Indeed, while virtually the whole production was received very critically, time and again it was Tauský's handling of the music that was to receive its just and even extravagant praise. The cast was as follows:

Rusalka	Joan Hammond
The Spirit of the Lake	Howell Glynne
Jezibaba, the Witch	Patricia Kern [43]

[43] The part of Jezibaba was to be sung by Gita Denise. However, following a bad attack of bronchitis, the part was sung on the first night by Patricia Kern. Kern was also listed in *Radio Times* for the broadcast of the final performance of the run, so presumably she appeared in all. Patricia Kern was listed in the theatre programme for the actual third performance on 28 February. (ed.)

Voice of a huntsman	Alberto Remedios
The Prince	Charles Craig
The Foreign Princess	Joan Stuart
The Forester	Joseph Ward
The Kitchen Boy	Anna Pollak
Wood Nymphs	Ava June Joan Clarkson Dilys Davies
Sadler's Wells Chorus Chorus Master	 David Tod Boyd
Sadler's Wells Orchestra Conductor	 Vilém Tauský

The rather cynical atmosphere surrounding the impending broadcast was not conducive to happiness for the future of the work. Arthur Jacobs provided a pre-act narration for the 19 March broadcast and on his letter about his text to Mr. L. D. Harris, Opera Manager at the BBC, someone had scribbled the following:

> *As you will guess, it makes a pretty naïve evening in the theatre. The moral is: if you let a Rusalka kiss you, she will leave lipstick all over your face!!* [44]

This was doubtless coloured by the reviews of the first night performance. Mr. L. Stokes, however, adds, rather more hopefully, but still only faint praise:

> *To me, it seems a better version than the ballet 'Ondine'* [45]

There was, however, an element of doubt about the whole enterprise within the BBC. The physical atmosphere for the first night's performance was even worse: London was enveloped in one of the worst smogs in memory: probably the last, indeed, following the passage of the Clean Air Act 1953. After the disastrous 'Great Smog' of 1952, the

---

[44] BBC Archives, Caversham.

[45] *Ondine,* a ballet choreographed for Dame Margot Fonteyn at Covent Garden by Sir Frederick Ashton to the specially commissioned music of Hanz Werner Henze, had opened to very mixed reviews on 27 October 1958.

air of the capital city had begun to improve but the winter of 1959 brought a return almost to the same level of pollution. It had begun on 29 January, returning on several days and not finally dissipating until a day or two after the première of *Rusalka.* The cast and, doubtless, some of the orchestra too, was already afflicted by bronchitis and Charles Craig was expected to be unable to sing. Such was the concern that the whole staff was warned to prepare, as previously noted, for a repeat of Puccini's *Madam Butterfly* instead. In the event, *Rusalka* went ahead and in spite of the traffic chaos caused by the smog, the auditorium was full. Disastrously, though, such was the insidious power of the smog that it crept into the theatre through every door and invaded the stage. This might have created a suitably mysterious effect for the first act but was hardly conducive to the success of the second. What is more, Charles Craig's already afflicted voice was put into even greater danger. [46]

It is also more than unfortunate that Christopher Hassall's translation was used yet again. Some critics complained about not being able to hear every line, but hearing them all might not have improved their opinion of the plot. All in all, it is not perhaps surprising that of the critics and other reporters present for the first night, most were to treat the event with humour and doubt.

Karel Janovický was present at the first night of the production. As one who knows the work and its origins far better than most, he was perfectly placed to pass judgement on the proceedings. [47]

> *I do remember the 1st night of 'Rusalka' taking place during a typical London pea-souper. For what it is worth, here are some more of my memories of that evening:*

---

[46] The extreme horror of London's air prior to the first Clean Air Act of 1953 is hard to imagine nowadays. London had been afflicted by its notorious 'Pea-soupers' for hundreds of years but the 'Great Smog' of 1952 killed many thousands: estimates of 3,500 to 4,000 have risen in recent research to over 12,000 people. In those days the problem was caused by cold winter fogs combined with the smoke of coal fires and, most dangerously, Sulphur Dioxide.
The Smog of February 1959 was the last peak event of its type in London.

[47] Karel Janovický, (b. Plzeň 1930) came to Britain in 1950 and graduated from The Royal College of Music and also studied with Mátyás Seiber. He worked for many years at the BBC and remains active as a composer, coach, speaker and writer.

As the performance went on, the fog gradually seeped into the auditorium, making the lights appear as bright cones in the darkness. The Prince was developing laryngitis, with Rusalka — keen not to catch it from him — looking away each time he was meant to kiss her. Wendy Toye's staging was fairy-tale-like and therefore 'traditional', but she — well known at the time as a pantomime director — made it easy for the ignorant critics to look upon the piece as a sort of junior 'Ring'. The Ring', of course, is about power, myth, Wotan's fateful political errors, bloodlines etc. 'Rusalka' is about none of those things. It is about things close to every human heart that anybody can understand, the fairy-tale setting being a mere metaphor. That's why the metamorphosis of Rusalka the wraith into Rusalka the girl is done as light-hearted comic turn for the Witch and her tomcat Mourek. Critics fail to point this out when writing about some ghastly recent productions involving bloody surgery — they merely wonder why the music in these scenes should be so 'folksy' — it's just amusing. Vilém's part in the production was splendid: great orchestral sound, tempi, singing, chorus.

Far from a Rusalka 'leaving lipstick all over your face' it would appear that Joan Hammond did all in her power to avoid Charles Craig's face! It must also be debatable as to whether she was the best person for the title role. Her singing of arias from the opera were one thing but hers was already hardly the sort of sylph-like being that is associated with a work such as this. The production, though, seemed to have been fated from the start. James Bailey's costumes were certainly attractive and very much in keeping with the production and sets. Wendy Toye took criticism with regard to her production. The sets were described as 'too busy'. This was not helped by some props being rather dwarfed by the cast and the rather old-fashioned appearance did not assist the production's popularity. [48]

[48] Wendy Toye CBE, (1917-2010), first danced on stage at the age of three. She danced with the Ballets Russes, at the Café de Paris and many other companies and later appeared in several films. Her career as a choreographer and producer started in the 1950s and went on through stage, film and television, only retiring in the 1990s.

If the weather did not affect the attendance on the first night at Sadler's Wells, then subsequent reviews in the press may well have played a part in reducing the radio audience. The Audience Research unit reported that the broadcast of Act I on 19 March was less than 0.1% with that for Acts II and III being too small to be measured.[49]

Questionnaires were completed by just 111 people, who gave an Appreciation Index of only 66%. 'Opinions', says the report, 'varied considerably'. Many had thought the work a 'charming fairy story set to most lovely music' and objected to the opera's neglect and poor criticism in the past. One teacher wrote:

> *Very enjoyable. A delightful plot, easily followed, for which Dvorak composed some very beautiful music. I disagree completely with the critics who say the work is dull. I have waited many years to hear this opera and I am very pleased to have heard it.*

Others, however, used words such as 'did not add up to a dramatic whole', 'uneven in quality', 'much second-rate stuff', 'long boring stretches', 'weak libretto', 'inept translation', 'absurdity of a dumb heroine', 'a foolish story and indifferent music', 'lack of temperament in singers and conductor' and 'poverty of the music'. A Naval Officer wrote:

> *I enjoyed the opera, as it was gay and tuneful. However, one can understand why it is seldom performed nowadays. The music was pleasant but not of lasting quality.*

The report did, however, go on to praise the performances, especially Charles Craig and Joan Hammond, though the latter did not garner universal praise from the radio audience. Opinions in the press were divided but mostly against both work and production.

Edmund Tracey had praise only for Vilém Tauský:

---

[49] BBC Archives, Caversham.

'Rusalka'

It really seems very perverse of Sadler's Wells to stage Dvorak's 'Rusalka'. We hear a great deal these days about the financial difficulties of opera in England, yet the cause of keeping it alive can hardly be served by putting on a new production of so empty a piece.

Dvorak's melodic vitality is usually unquestionable, but in this opera, except for certain lyrical passages like the clarinet motif associated with Rusalka and the famous song to the moon, the music is lifeless and undistinguished and certainly has none of the drama and driving force of, say, the 'D Minor Symphony' or the 'Symphonic Variations'. The real trouble, I think, is that Dvorak has attempted to subject naive and rhythmically symmetrical melodic ideas — a large part of the music falls into two-bar phrases — to a symphonic treatment in the Wagnerian manner: but in such a giant grip these simple regular tunes crumple and die.

It is not really fair to judge the standard of the new production by the performance on Wednesday evening, for the cast was heavily stricken by illness. Charles Craig as the Prince was too ill to give more than a token performance. Patricia Kern was a creditable last-minute deputy as the Witch, and Joan Stuart's Princess, though rather scrawny-toned, was sung with great assurance. As Rusalka Joan Hammond shaped her vocal lines firmly and her top notes had their customary ringing splendour, but her middle and lower registers were inexpressive and lacking in personality. The orchestral performance reached a high level of accomplishment under Vilem Tausky's sensitive direction. [50]

A thus-far unidentified newspaper carried a lengthy review by their correspondent 'A.M.'. He/she appears to have found much to enjoy in the performance but was dubious about Miss Hammond's performance and whilst praising Vilém Tauský for his conducting, seems to have felt that the singers were occasionally 'secondary'. The paper gave a complete cast list but mistakenly listed Gita Denise's replacement in the part of Jezibaba as 'Patricia Kirkwood' rather than Patricia Kern.

[50] Edmund Tracey, *The Observer,* 22 February 1959.

RUSSALKA [51]

First professional performance in this country of the opera by Dvorak, with libretto by S. J. Kvapil, English version by Christopher Hassall.
Presented at Sadler's Wells on February 18.

DVORAK'S fairy-tale opera, 'Russalka', given its first professional performance in this country at Sadler's Wells on Wednesday of last week, has a rather naively constructed libretto about the Spirit of the Lake and his daughter Russalka, who longs to walk the earth and taste the joys of human love. The attempt to link the world of eternal nature with mortality has the inevitable doom, and the faithless prince whom she loves ultimately meets his destiny with her in the bosom of the lake.

It has its enchantments, as well as complexities, longuers and dancing and swaying nymph-conventionalities. It does not quite touch with any force of tragedy or deep emotion. Dvorak was not a composer of unfailing stage-strokes, and it develops into a series of numbers, solos, ensemble and an occasional chorus, without any real build-up to climax and with a long-drawn ending that betrays a lack of dramatic instinct. At the same time it is rich in Dvorak's typical honest, simple and skilful weavings of melody, and if it has Wagnerian echoes, its warmth, sincerity and imaginative touches constantly rescue it from tedium.

CHARLES CRAIG

It did not have a performance that could do it full justice for Charles Craig sang the part of the Prince under the handicap of bronchitis. He did remarkably well in the circumstances. Although his voice scarcely rose above piano, it maintained a surprising beauty and accuracy. Joan Hammond was not altogether happy as Russalka, a difficult role that has to combine the fey and the human and has a longish period of dumbness in the latter state. She produced some fine full high notes, but frequently fell to inaudibility.

---

[51] The double 'ss' in *Russalka* seen here and elsewhere, is reproduced as in the original reviews. This spelling can also be found in pre-première publicity. (ed.)

Nor did her waving movements of hands and arms get quite beyond the mannered stage. Howell Glynne got the note of despair into his voice, without the requisite remoteness, in another difficult role, the wet Lake-Spirit rising like a diver into static helplessness. There were well sung smaller performances by Patricia Kirkwood, deputising for Gita Denise as a witch, Joan Stuart, Russalka's princess rival, Anna Pollak kitchen boy, and Joseph Ward, a forester.

GRACEFUL GROUPING

Wendy Toye's production had a good deal of graceful grouping and fairy atmosphere, without completely convincing as an interaction of two worlds. There were some awkward standings-about in the muddy lake while things were going on around, and on one occasion the Spirit's agony was masked. The settings in general made a brave suspending of disbelief, and there was some enchantingly effective lapping of lake-water. Vilem Tausky brought out the score's many beauties, though there were times when the singers seemed secondary.

Noel Goodwin thought it all too dull and naïve: [52]

Joan Hammond is majestic - but it's naive stuff

JOAN HAMMOND'S return to London opera last night after five years was a mixed delight. Not because the Australian soprano was any less impressive than before, indeed, her singing had that majestic tone sustained on warmth and feeling which is her most endearing quality. But she chose for her come-back Dvorak's fairy tale opera 'Rusalka', given its first professional stage production in Britain. Miss Hammond has spread its name far and wide by her recording of the haunting aria 'O, Silver Moon', sung by the water sprite who gives up her immortality for fickleness of human love.

A DULL TIME

But that is over in the first half-hour. Rusalka gets her human soul in exchange for giving up speech, which makes for a dull time thereafter, until the last act. Wendy Toye's production and James Bailey's sets contrived an attractive stage picture.

[52] *The Daily Express*, 19 February 1959.

Vilem Tausky's conducting often overpowered the singers. Tenor Charles Craig, as the hero, sang gallantly in spite of last-minute bronchitis. But much as I welcome a newcomer to our limited operatic repertory, such naive stuff as Dvorak made of it has long been outstripped by time and taste.

Philip Hope-Wallace was also bored. His tongue was also surely in his cheek in his description of Joan Hammond as 'not perhaps altogether unlike a water nymph'. He lamented an excess of motion on stage whilst at the same time complaining about the 'static story'. [53]

Miss Hammond in another piece of enterprise

What with Miss Sutherland's Lucia at Covent Garden and now Miss Hammond drawing the crowd through the fog to Sadler's Wells for 'Rusalka', our national opera houses might be said to be keeping up with the Joans. This 'Rusalka', by Dvorak is not to be confused with Dargomizhsky's of the same name which Chaliapin used to sing. It is a work with many lovely passages in it not least the song to the moon which Rusalka sings in the first act and which Miss Hammond has lifted — if that is the word — into the top ten of popular taste and to which we may perhaps ascribe this handsome production even in a theatre full of fog but also full of attentive listeners. The imaginative settings are the work of James Bailey.

But why is it that operas about water sprites nearly always end by damping our enthusiasm? In spite of the tumultuous orchestra texture and the charm of the characteristically Bohemian idiom, the opera in dramatic terms is often rather a bore. The nymph-made-human loves a prince but cannot find happiness with him and is always threatening to go home to Daddy, a dank spirit who keeps rising from the lake and making moan. Wendy Toye's production has sought to remedy the static nature of this story, which at times, is spun out to positively Wagnerian length, by keeping the stage alive with motion, where possible and sometimes where not possible, or at least not wise. It makes a plausible fairy tale, rather like 'Swan Lake', but sung.

[53] *The Manchester Guardian,* 19 February 1959. The name *The Guardian,* was adopted on 24 August 1959.

Miss Hammond sings the main part with great assurance. The top of her voice rings like an electric bell with a newly charged battery. She moves gracefully and, herself a champion swimmer, is not perhaps altogether unlike a water nymph. She gave much pleasure. Howell Glynne, enunciating admirably, sang the watery father; Charles Craig, in spite of a bad cold, and Joan Stewart, as the prince and the rival princess, sang bravely on and on. The orchestra played very well under Vilem Tausky. The translation which made sense without always making a very poetical effect, is the work of Christopher Hassall. Our opera houses can hardly be accused this week of lack of enterprise.

Writing in April 1959, Mr. Hope-Wallace was even more trenchant. He criticized the casting of smaller roles, such as the nymphs and was one of several who thought the sets were out of scale. [54]

Sadler's Wells, 'Rusalka' (February 18)

Opinions vary as to 'Rusalka's' value as an opera; that the music is frequently very beautiful indeed is not of course in question, but the timing of the story-telling, the quasi-Wagnerian method allied to the Bohemian idiom elsewhere so pleasingly used does not make the happiest of blends nor serve a story which with the best will in the world does not greatly excite. Rusalka emerges here in the likeness of Miss J Hammond (who was once no mean swimmer herself) draped in water weed. She proceeds, as the police say, on land, sings the lovely 'O silver moon' aria which tells us of her love for a mortal prince and then 'gets changed' by a land witch. But she finds no happiness and is soon wooed back by her melancholy and even more subaqueous father (Howell Glynne). Vilem Tausky conducted finely and secured excellent playing. But it was a night of choking fog and the singing all more or less suffered with some singers off and others apologised for. Miss Hammond with her professionalism and her high notes ringing like bells all over a country house gave a stately and touching performance as far as circumstances allowed. We liked James Bailey's sets for the

[54] *Opera,* April 1959.

enchanted lake-side, which looked wonderful with its flickering lights until two too-solid nymphs and others went capering around in Wendy Toye's rather restless and uncertain production. The middle set, built around a lily pond, with a lift in it, shows the palace gardens: this too is a good picture but looked disproportioned when the figures began to move around in it. Of course Sadler's Wells is not an easy stage to decorate; here the fault seemed the producer's. The translator is Christopher Hassall. The enterprise won a full house even in such weather.

James Bailey's designs for the costumes of the Prince and the Foreign Princess

Robert Wraight was more interested in humour than serious criticism. His foggy journeys and missing the start of the opera may well have caused some of his dyspeptic writing: [55]

Mystery in the stalls

OH what a night it was, my night at the opera. Perhaps I ought to have known the fairy story of Dvorak's 'Rusalka', even though it had never been performed here before. But I didn't and, prevented by the fog from arriving in time to get a programme, the first act baffled me.

[55] *The Star*, nd.

Every time I craned my neck to change a close-up view of the Countess of Harewood's back (she was in the seat in front) for a glimpse of the stage my alarm increased. Apparently three well-fed witches from Macbeth were hurling choral epithets at Shylock, up to his waist in a chilly pool with a Junoesque blonde.

My relief when these characters turned out to be three wood-nymphs, the Spirit of the Lake and Miss Joan Hammond in a wig, masquerading as his daughter, Rusalka, may be imagined. Later, the Shylock character turned up in a fish pond outside a castle where his daughter, in human form, was beguiling a plum prince. In return for her human guise she had been made temporarily dumb — an extraordinary thing to happen to an operatic heroine. The prince was understandably brassed off and sent her back to her father in the fish-pond. A long time later everything ended unhappily when girl and prince dived into the well of the stage together and were never seen again.

This, at any rate, is how it seemed to us in the front stalls for whom the whole thing might as well have been in Czech as English for all the words we could hear above the orchestra. Yet a brief trip to the dress circle showed that up there they were hearing virtually a different opera, in which Joan Hammond was magnificent, Charles Craig (the prince) bravely concealed an attack of bronchitis and the Spirit of the Lake's dirges were beautifully done by Howell Glynne. But none of this was much consolation to me on my two-hour journey home through the fog.

Leslie Ayre was another bored critic, producing a rather typical tabloid-style essay but displaying little fundamental knowledge: [56]

Dvorak And Bronchitis

DVORAK'S opera 'Rusalka' certainly contains much more than the now familiar aria, 'O Silver Moon'. Perhaps too much more, for it is a very long-drawn-out and slow-moving affair.

[56] *The Evening News*, nd.

But complete judgment can hardly be made on last night's new production at Sadler's Wells, for tenor Charles Craig was battling gallantly against severe bronchitis and there were other similar troubles. Joan Hammond, however, making her first appearance at the 'Wells' since 1951, was quite unshaken by the circumstances around her and sang throughout the evening with complete assurance and fine big tone.

'Rusalka' is a fairy story, about a water-maiden who emerges to fall in love with a human Prince. James Bailey has contrived attractive and ingenious forest settings for it and Dvorak's music is very Czech and tuneful — even though it often seems to be going nowhere in particular.

Frank Howes utterly missed both the plot and Dvořák's style, reckoning that he had no dramatic sense and that *Rusalka* lacked romance. It is not known if his claim of knowledge of Dvořák's earlier operas has any basis in fact. He was certainly in agreement with others about the crowded sets: [57]

DRAMA LACKING IN RUSSALKA
ROMANCE MISSED

The flora and fauna are familiar: slim nymphs who dance, plump nymphs who sing, a figure like Old Father Thames, water glinting in the moonlight among the trees. A land witch is an addition to the company, who are concerned with the unlucky love of mortal and mermaid. There are other operas, symphonic poems and ballets which deal with this Undine situation, but Dvorak's version, which was the most successful of his almost uniformly unsuccessful operas, has not had a professional performance on an English stage till last night, when it was put on at Sadler's Wells with decor by James Bailey under the musical direction of Mr. Vilem Tausky, who as a Czech had the legend and the music in his blood. In his operas Dvorak leaned heavily on Wagner: in the earlier ones comically so to our present hearing. But in 'Russalka', though the native music sometimes recalls parallel situations in 'The Ring', the native note which welled up naturally in Dvorak — how often one hears it in his writing for wood wind! — has all his characteristic euphony.

---

[57] *The Times*, 19 February 1959.

His tunes are good, but what is not good is his dramatic pace, which never quickens but is constantly making room for passages that might have come from the development sections of his symphonies. The plot is ill-designed to vary the pace, and it is not conducive to good opera for the heroine to be a mute as soon as she comes on land. In trying to move the opera along, the producer, Miss Wendy Toye, relied too much on choreography — the Witch's four attendants would have been better away.

Miss Gita Denise and Miss Joan Hammond in a scene from 'Russalka' in rehearsal at Sadler's Wells. [58]

The opera went smoothly if slowly in spite of casualties. Mr. Charles Craig as the Prince pleaded for indulgence on account of bronchial trouble, though his singing was, if quiet, always

[58] Gita Denise probably posed for the publicity photograph published by *The Times* but was replaced in the actual performances by Patricia Kern.

clear. Miss Patricia Kern successfully understudied the singer announced to play the witch, Jezibaba. The water sprite was sung by Miss Joan Hammond on the strength of the aria 'O silver moon' being one of her favourite pieces. Mr. Howell Glynne emerged now and then from below the surface to utter admonitions, but they had precious little magic about them.

That was the trouble: here is a romantic opera with all the apparatus of romance from horn calls to wedding processions, but it lacked the magic of romance and it lacked the dramatic sense which was not included among Dvorak's rich gifts.

Desmond Shawe-Taylor had no better an opinion than Mr. Howes in his sister daily paper but he did at least admit to some knowledge of Dvořák's operas. Praise was specially directed to Vilém Tauský's conducting. His comments about the voice of Joan Hammond's singing are to the point and do touch on a fundamental problem with the production as a whole. The accompanying photograph does rather draw attention to the question of Joan Hammond's suitability as a water-nymph in a stage production. [59]

Russalka

AFTER such an evening the long-winded delights of Dvorak's 'Russalka' at Sadler's Wells were bound to seem a little pale. This is the most popular of his operas, but I prefer 'The Jacobin' and 'The Devil and Kate', both of which have lively librettos, as well as more variety and pace in the musical handling. On Wednesday, Vilem Tausky's conducting and James Bailey's fairy-tale decor did all that was possible for the work; and the last act, which contains the loveliest music, rewarded those who had stayed the course. Joan Hammond, an intensely human singer both in her virtues and her faults, was no obvious choice for the fey mermaid; her spasmodic phrasing and fearless, ringing top notes proved rather

[59] *The Sunday Times,* 22 February 1959. It is assumed that the phrase 'AFTER such an evening' referred to the new production of Donizetti's *Lucia di Lammermoor* with Joan Sutherland which had taken place on 17 February at Covent Garden.

too much for Dvorak's dreamy, nostalgic tunes, which require a cooler and smoother deployment of tone. Charles Craig will be a good Prince, no doubt, when he has recovered from his present bronchitis. Howell Glynne moaned away dutifully as the Water-Sprite, Joan Stuart melodiously vamped the Prince from under Miss Hammond's fins, so to speak, and there was a lively pot-boy 'en travesti' from Anna Pollak.

Things were no better, in a brief report in which Percy Cater and Edward Eaton combined to tell about their night at the opera. Eaton detailed tales of bronchitis and panic while Cater was rather nasty about the whole enterprise: 'This was the first British professional theatre production of *Rusalka*. In my view we have suffered no great deprivation in all these years.' [60]

---

[60] *Daily Mail*, 19 February 1959.

One of the more unexpected appearances of *Rusalka* was in the *News of the World.* Brief in the extreme, it was hardly a critical classic but it was, at least, a positive review: [61]

> *RUSSALKA (Sadler's Wells)*
>
> *First appearance on a British professional stage of Dvorak's fairy opera about a water-sprite in love with a mortal. A lovely production in which Joan Hammond sang gloriously.*

Matters had not improved for Martin Cooper. A patronising attitude towards Dvořák and his works was slightly ameliorated by his praise for Tauský's mastery of the score. [62]

> *LAMENTATIONS OF A CZECH WATER-SPIRIT*
> *DVORAK'S 'RUSSALKA'*
>
> *Dvorak's 'Russalka', which had its first professional performance in this country at Sadler's Wells last night, is a favourite children's opera in Czechoslovakia. I have seen a Saturday afternoon house in Prague packed with children who plainly took desperately to heart the adventures of the Water-Spirit's daughter and her mortal lover, the witch Jezibaba and the whole array of attendant fairy fauna. It is not so easy for the rest of us, and Dvorak's music is not always a very powerful stimulant. The succession of long, sweet Czech melodies is apt to cloy and the Wagnerian prophecies of lamentations of the Water-Spirit — a kind of aqueous Wotan in the posture of Erda — fill a disproportionate space in what is a singularly static story.*
>
> *JOAN HAMMOND'S CHARM*
>
> *Joan Hammond in the title role had the best music of the evening, and although she was not very happily cast the familiar charm of her ringing top notes delighted the audience. Charles Craig was suffering from bronchitis but sang gallantly as the Prince. Patricia Kern replaced Gita Denise (another victim of illness) as the witch. Howell Glynne declaimed forcefully, though largely unintelligibly, as the Water-Spirit, and Vilem Tausky communicated to the orchestra his enthusiasm*

[61] *News of the World,* 22 February 1959.

[62] *The Daily Telegraph,* 19 February 1959.

and vigorous belief in Dvorak's score. James Bailey's sets and costumes provided a conventional fairy-story setting.

Two reporters covered *Rusalka* for the *News Chronicle*, one anonymously, presumably Alan Dent, the regular music critic and Charles Reid, whose comments were rather more hopeful for the work. There was much about the first night's problems and it wisely pointed out that this should cause one to reserve judgement: [63]

STAND-IN OPERA WASN'T NEEDED

UNTIL late yesterday afternoon a scratch 'Madame Butterfly' cast which had been hastily rounded up by taxi and telephone calls, stood by at Sadler's Wells opera. Charles Craig, the tenor, was down with bronchitis. He had been billed to sing the Prince in the new production of Dvorak's 'Rusalka'. As he received treatment at the theatre from a throat specialist, 'Butterfly' scenery, costumes, props and band parts were brought in ready for a last-minute switch.

Curtain up

Soprano Joan Hammond was prepared to sing either Butterfly or the name-part in 'Rusalka'. Costumes for both roles were delivered to her dressing-room. At 6 p.m. Mr. Craig's specialist said it would be safe for him to sing after all. Puccini was scrapped. The curtain went up on Dvorak. Mr. Craig sang with a temperature. Charles Reid comments: Mr. Craig sang most of the time in a tentative 'rehearsal' voice and was so clearly handicapped that it would be unfair to judge 'Rusalka' on what we heard last night. One's provisional judgment is that the work lushly combines 'Lohengrin', 'The Immortal Hour' and 'Siegfried'. When Mr. Craig partners Miss Hammond in full voice ones opinion may be modified.

The no longer extant magazine, *London Musical Events* was very much in line with other reviews. Jeremy Noble, in his regular *Musical Survey* column, was scathing about everything apart from Vilém Tauský. He rather curiously describes the production as 'a revival': [64]

---

[63] *News Chronicle,* nd.

[64] *London Musical Events,* April 1959.

Rusalka

In the operatic field everything was overshadowed by Joan Sutherland's triumph in 'Lucia' at Covent Garden, described elsewhere in this issue by Ernest Chapman. Another of our Australian divas, Joan Hammond, appeared in the revival of 'Rusalka', but it was hardly her fault if this failed to set the town on fire again. 'Rusalka', for all its folky charm and the beauty of the mature Dvorak's orchestration, is a pretty damp squib dramatically. The plot hovers between drama and mere picturesquerie, and this indecision is reflected in the music; Dvorak seems occasionally to be attempting a kind of Wagnerian 'symphonic' style, but this is short-breathed. On the other hand the music he gives to the soloists is too lyrical, too little heroic for the theatre. Miss Hammond sang her song to the moon charmingly, but she could do little more with the part. I suspect that it would take a native Czech company to persuade us that this was a really stageworthy opera, although it must be said that Vilem Tausky did succeed in drawing some very persuasive playing from the orchestra.

Andrew Porter was altogether more taken by the opera though he did complain about the staging. His impression of the work as being one of atmosphere is fresh and perceptive. Again the crowded set was seen as an obstacle: [65]

SADLER'S WELLS
RUSALKA

'RUSALKA' is generally deemed the finest of Dvorak's operas. The only other I know is 'Kate and Devil' — and that I think finer. For though 'Rusalka' is filled with tender, leisurely, romantic music, it moves very slowly. The plot, a version of the Undine story, is reduced to a slight framework, and presented undramatically, almost tentatively. It is an opera not so much of character as of atmosphere. Rusalka herself sings two lovely arias. The water nymphs sport to delicate, picturesque music. The wood nymphs sing an attractive trio. But there is certainly a monotony of mood, broken only by the robust Bohemian music of the Kitchen Boy and the

[65] *The Financial Times,* 20 February 1959.

Forester, and to some extent by Witch Jezibaba's incantations. The beauties of the work lie largely in the score, and especially in many magical transformations of the tenderly curving Rusalka motif. Rusalka, the Water Sprite and the Prince are all characterised by firm motifs: the score is in some ways a Wagnerian one, transformed by Dvorak's more intimate and homely poetic sense. But the effect is often that of a symphonic poem, rather than lyric theatre.

Joan Hammond in the title role Dvorak's opera " Russalka " last night.

In the title role, Joan Hammond makes a welcome reappearance on the London stage, with her voice a sweeter, more even, more responsive instrument than ever before. She sang in delicate lyric style last night — sometimes more gently than Vilem Tausky conducted. It was not exactly a gripping performance, but a thoroughly artistic one.

James Bailey's scenes are very pretty at curtain-rise, but when the cast fills them, the scale seems to be wrong; the nymphs and courtiers are giants moving through a toy forest and toy palace-garden. Wendy Toye's production is a little too straightforward for an opera whose weak dramatic construction needs more imaginative handling.

The effect is striking the first time the Water Sprite rises through the swirling waters of the lake; but by the tenth time or so we tire of it. Ava June as first Wood Nymph and Joseph Ward and Anna Pollak as Forester and Kitchen Boy deserve special mention. Tausky conducts a beautifully orchestrated score with evident affection, though some of the playing lacks finesse.

By far the most thorough and thoughtful review was that of Ernest Bradbury. The writer acknowledged a life-long love of Czech music and Dvořák in particular. Perhaps with the added advantage of an extra day prior to publication, Mr. Bradbury could take greater care over what he wrote. His sole error would appear to be ascribing the part of *Jezibaba* to 'Pat Cairns' rather than Patricia Kern. Throughout the article, Mr. Bradbury demonstrates the superiority of much musical criticism emanating in those days from the provinces when compared to the often hurried contributions in the national dailies in London. [66]

A CHARMING BOHEMIAN QUALITY
Dvorak at his most mature in 'Rusalka'
From ERNEST BRADBURY
LONDON, Thursday

We are still in the process of discovering the music of Antonin Dvorak. There are those works of his, like the 'New World' Symphony, that belong to the classical repertory. There are some, like 'St. Ludmilla', written for the 1886 Leeds Festival that have been cast into oblivion, in spite of the fact that the 'Stabat Mater' survives. There are some works, pronounced fit and suitable by the experts, that are not known here at all; and among these are the operas.

---

[66] *The Yorkshire Post and Leeds Merçury*, 20 February 1959. Ernest Bradbury b. Leeds 3 March 1919, d. 18 November 1994. Pianist, organist, quondam composer, (studying under Sir Edward Bairstow at York Minster). He was a lifelong pacifist and worked as a forester and with Jewish refugees during the war. He started at the *Yorkshire Post* in his twenties and became its music critic in 1947, also writing for *Music and Musicians, Musical Times* and *Radio Times.* In 1966 he won the Hannen Swaffer Award for the consistently high standards of his music criticism. For the 1934 Brno production, mentioned in the text, read 1938. (ed.)

Last night's production of 'Rusalka' at Sadler's Wells, of which there are to be five more performances before the current season ends on March 28, was claimed as the first-ever professional theatre production in Britain of a Dvorak opera, though it was first performed in Prague in 1901. It was Dvorak's penultimate opera, and it therefore represents the composer at his most mature, which also means at his most national. Added to the brilliant musical imagination, and a surprisingly attentive intuition for drama, there is also that distinctive and charming Bohemian quality which is not so easily reduced to phrase and formula, a quality that Whistler, for instance, might have denied. 'There is no such thing as English art: one might as well speak of English mathematics'.

Folk nature

And as usual we must allow that Whistler is experimenting in paradox, since at least he does not show us the counterparts of Reynolds and Gainsborough, Morland or Constable. Dvorak's national qualities are not to be denied just because they are not so easily explained. As a fact we find in 'Rusalka' that the basic character of the whole musical conception is related to the folk nature of the opera. For this reason Dvorak seems actually more sure in his relation to the fairy-tale figures in the work than to the human characters, who are less sympathetically and more conventionally portrayed. Wagner proves something of an influence, superficially in the 'green' opening at the lake in the forest, where the three wood nymphs (supported by the dancing water nymphs) sing in trio like the Rhinemaidens, and where the Spirit of the Lake appears as some wiser and more mature Alberich. Less superficially, we find the Wagnerian influence in a wealth of fine musical phrases, solidly weighted with dramatic sense and mood and organically uniting the musical structure of the whole opera.

Beautiful finale

The closing 10 minutes are as moving and beautiful as those of any opera, and it is here that the doomed Rusalka who is none other than de la Motte Fouqué's 'Ondine', personified at the moment in another part of London by Dame Margot Fonteyn, croons her bliss as she sinks to the bottom of the lake with her dead prince.

Dvorak's own compassionate absorption in Rusalka's suffering and everything around her was made very clear in Joan Hammond's interpretation of the part. Miss Hammond here showed a quality we have not normally associated either with her work or with her singing — tenderness. There are some vocal climaxes for Rusalka which Miss Hammond had no difficulty in meeting, when her voice took on that superb, though cold, trumpet-like quality for which she is renowned. Perhaps the coldness was in taste for this watery creature with the 'white blood'. But there was infinite pathos and much warmth in the many more lyrical sections of the part, which Miss Hammond sustained with great conviction. And in that stretch of the second act (a peculiar one for a prima donna) where her mortality renders her a dumb creature — to her lover's dismay and final irritation — she acts with a sweet charm that was, indeed wholly human. Miss Hammond's return to the London operatic stage had therefore a sense of occasion about it.

Doubly heroic work

She was well partnered by Charles Craig as the Prince, in spite of the severe attack of bronchitis from which he was suffering and which, in these circumstances, made his evening's work heroic in a double sense. Gita Denise, who should have sung the part of Jezibaba, the witch who transforms Rusalka from her immortal state, is also a victim of the prevailing affliction. This part was also well done in Miss Denise's absence, by Pat Cairns. And Howell Glynne, suffering from nothing save those artistic endowments of which he is the master made an excellent Spirit of the Lake, the forlorn father of Rusalka who warns her in vain of her inevitable doom. The work was well played, and brightly conducted by Vilem Tausky, who was once associated with the librettist's own production of the opera at Brno in 1934, and is therefore something of an authority.

The production by Wendy Toye was as conventional as her choreography was outstanding. Her dances for the wedding scene in Act II were among the most effective moments of the staging. James Bailey's sets were useful but not very striking, and their effectiveness was occasionally weakened by some rather inept stage lighting.

The house for this first performance was crowded and there is no valid reason why a public that has taken Smetana to its heart should not do the same for Dvorak

The now defunct magazine *Theatre World* also carried a wholly positive and full review. Sadly anonymous, the reviewer clearly loved every aspect of the music and production and drew attention to the part played by Vilém Tauský. Apart from the review itself, *Theatre World* also carried a two page spread with five photographs from the production. These are reproduced overleaf as they appeared in the original publication:

SADLER'S WELLS
'Rusalka'

ALTHOUGH Dvorak wrote eight operas besides The Water-Nymph, none of them is even mentioned in the Earl of Harewood's revised edition of Kobbe's Complete Opera Book, in which Dvorak's name appears once only in a parenthesis. This is most misleading of his talent as an operatic composer, of which I was lucky enough to have a foretaste when singing in the Oxford University Operatic Society's production of 'Kate and the Devil' more years ago than I care to recall.

The libretto, by Jaroslav Kvapil, a whilom director of the National Theatre in Prague, has been Englished by Christopher Hassall, who has retained the Czech title. As a witty colleague has remarked, operas about water-nymphs consist of thin nymphs who dance and fat nymphs who sing, and this devastating observation obtruded and almost spoiled the pleasure which Dvorak's melodious score and Wendy Toye's lovely production combined to evoke. Half the fun came from the ingenious decor (by James Bailey) who not only re-created a shimmering lake's surface on stage but also all but managed to make one believe that the coming and going fairies had access to and from the cellarage without the use of well-oiled stage-traps. The other half was duly assured by the lyricism of the music, the virtuosity of Joan Hammond's lyric-dramatic soprano in the title-role, and the magical orchestral control exercised by the Czech-born conductor, Vilem Tausky.

Let us hope that the enterprise of the directors of Sadler's

Wells — whom ill-judged criticism quite wrongly blamed for staging the first English professional production of Rusalka— will earn them ever more popular audiences for this notable example of a popular art-form.

The critical welcome for *Rusalka* was thus far from friendly. The production can be fairly judged a failure in that it was never revived nor taken on tour. Most recognised much of the beauty of Dvořák's score but blamed the composer for his perceived lack of dramatic ability. A closer reading of all that was written, however, reveals other reasons for the overall failure. Only two critics gave the opera a fulsome welcome but others picked away at the production itself, complaining particularly about the sets and the way it crowded the actors out. The smog creeping into the auditorium was clearly far more than an annoyance and one suspects that many in the audience, including the critics, had had a hard time getting to the theatre. People in those days were thoroughly used to poor translations so that appears not to have been a factor. It would seem that the fairy-tale atmosphere was just not what the critics of the day wanted to see. They were already used to opera with a harder edge and the crowded stage with its watery characters was plainly not to their liking. Perhaps out of politeness, several critics made oblique references to the unsuitability of Joan Hammond in the title role. They knew her recording of 'O silver moon' well but realised that this did not translate directly to the stage itself.

James Bailey's design for the costume of Jezibaba

Above: A lake in the forest. The nymph Rusalka (Joan Hammond) rises out of the water and tells her father, the Spirit of the Lake (Howell Glynne), that she has fallen in love with a mortal Prince and that she longs to be human so as to know his love. *Below*: Rusalka, transformed into a beautiful woman by the witch, Jezibaba, at the price of being dumb, meets the Prince (Charles Craig) in the forest.

"Rusalka" [67]

Scenes from Dvorak's opera which had its first performance at Sadler's Wells on 18th February in an English version by Christopher Hassall, with settings by James Bailey and production and choreography by Wendy Toye. Vilem Tausky conducted. "Rusalka" like "Ondine," is the fairy tale of the water nymph who becomes a mortal but who must return to the depths should her lover deceive her.

[67] These two pages are a recreation of the photo spread from the April 1959 *Theatre World*.

Above: The garden of the Prince's Palace. The Prince and his bride-to-be receive the courtiers' welcome. *Below left*: The Prince is already cooling towards the unhappy dumb Rusalka and finds the charms of the Foreign Princess (Joan Stuart) more to his taste. The Prince proves untrue and the Spirit of the Lake rises out of the fountain to seize back his daughter. *Below right*: The Forester (Joseph Ward) and the Kitchen Boy (Anna Pollak) are terrified when they see the Spirit of the Lake.

10. Interlude: A recording of part of the Sadler's Wells production.

It is to be hoped that somewhere in the archives of either the BBC or of Sadler's Wells there exists a decent quality recording of the performance on 19 March. As it is, there is but a fragment available. This is described as *Rusalka* – Scene and it is available from Dr. Irwin C. Elkins of the Omega Opera Archive. [68]

The catalogue entry for this item is:

> 1612 Dvořák *Rusalka* (Sc.) 3/19/1959 Hammond, Craig, Pollock--Süsskind BBC.

In spite of the error of giving Süsskind as the conductor, the rest of the cast as given on the front of the packaging and the date given is that of the last Sadler's Wells performance. The singing similarly is identifiable with Joan Hammond and Charles Craig. There is only part of the first act on the CD. This runs from the start of the duet between Rusalka and the Watersprite to the end of Act 1, a total of some 42 minutes. It would appear to have been recorded on a rather poor reel-to-reel tape recorder, certainly without the benefit of Dolby filtering and complete with several very short breaks, tape slips, etc.

Joan Hammond is in fine voice and very clear even if rather shrill and with too much vibrato on occasion. Howell Glynne's voice as the Watersprite is rather forced and his diction really is rather unclear at times: his pronunciation of 'daughter' comes across as 'dooter', for example and many of his lines seem rather too low for him. Charles Craig is very sweet-voiced and he had clearly recovered well from his bout of bronchitis.

The sound of the orchestra is compressed but the delicacy with which Tauský guides his players in accompaniment, the care with which each phrase is stated and the timing of the music make it very plain that the conductor was utterly at ease with the music, knew exactly how it should proceed and how to obtain the effect he wanted. There are very occasional lapses of intonation but that is hardly the fault of the conductor in a live performance. It is perfectly clear that the one thing that united the critics is correct: this was a superbly musical account with perfect mastery of the orchestra in all its aspects.

---

[68] P.O. Box 305, Pomona, NY 10970, USA. http://www.omegaoperasite.net/ and e-mail omegatwo@msn.com

11. BBC 3rd Programme. Holland Festival. 20 October 1963.

In view of what had gone before, it is perhaps surprising that the BBC planned yet another broadcast. The BBC's Opera Organiser, Peter Crossley-Holland, had heard about a forthcoming performance of *Rusalka* at the 1963 Holland Festival. Since the Festival's concerts were frequently recorded for broadcast, it is possible that several such recordings would be offered to the BBC. In the middle of April 1963 he had asked the European Liaison Officer to obtain details. In May he was asking for a tape of the performance. Clearance was obtained from Bärenreiter-Verlag in Kassel and the permission granted by Stichtung Nederlandsche Radio-Unie to use it for broadcast. The initial plan had been to broadcast *Rusalka* in February 1964 but this proved impossible for various contractual reasons and the broadcast was brought forward to October 1963. The cast was as follows:

Rusalka, a water nymph	Jadwiga Wysoczanska
Water Spirit	Eduard Haken
Jezibaba, a Witch	Anny Delorie
A huntsman	Gé Genemans
The Prince	Ivo Žídek
The Foreign Princess	Ivana Mixová
A Gamekeeper	Rudolf Kat
A kitchen boy	Els Bolkestein
Three Wood Nymphs	Mizzy van der Lanz Nelly Morpugo Sophia van Sante

Chorus and Orchestra of the Netherlands Opera

Conductor	Jaroslav Krombholc

This was the first Czech language broadcast of *Rusalka* in the United Kingdom taken from an actual stage performance. Arthur Jacobs provided a synopsis and a brief article in *Radio Times* and it was apparent to him, judging from his letter to Lionel Salter, the Head of Opera, that there were problems with the Hassall translation and previous resultant broadcast narrations.

The BBC's Audience Research Report found that the audience for the broadcast was too small to be recorded. The 'dreadful vibrato' of Jadwiga Wysoczanska proved very unpopular and this had ruined the 'Hymn to the Moon'. She was not alone: 'it could have been most enjoyable but I could not stand the singers and switched off', wrote one correspondent. A small number did not like the work itself, reckoning it to be sub-par Dvořák but the quality of the singing was so bad in most opinions that the work was hard to judge.

However, the above appears to have been a minority opinion and many reporters 'thought this a very fine performance of a lovely opera'. The Czech language had been something of a barrier but overall the audience, small though it was, had 'welcomed the opportunity of hearing this relatively unfamiliar opera'.

12. Prague National Theatre, Edinburgh International Festival, 1964.

For anyone already enthusiastic about Czech and Slovak music and, indeed, for any hitherto unfamiliar with either the music or the composers, the 1964 Edinburgh International Festival must have been an extraordinary and tremendously valuable experience. The Prague National Theatre Company came with eighteen performances of five key operas. The advance billing included the following:

Cikker:	*Resurrection* (2 performances)
Dvořák:	*Quartet in A Flat* (Janáček Quartet)
Dvořák:	*Rusalka* (5 performances)
Janáček:	*Sinfonietta* (LSO, Rozhdestvensky)
Janáček:	*Kat'a Kabanová* (3 performances)
Janáček:	*From the House of the Dead* (3 performances)
Janáček:	*Jealousy* (BBC SO, Del Mar)
Janáček:	*Concertino, Capriccio*, 'piano music' (Firkušný *et al*)
Janáček:	Two *String Quartets* (Janáček Quartet)
Janáček:	*Glagolitic Mass* (National Theatre Orchestra, Krombholc)
Janáček:	*Cunning Little Vixen Suite* (National Theatre Orchestra, Krombholc)
Janáček:	*Mládi* (Wind Band of National Theatre Orchestra)
Janáček:	*Pohádka* (Joan and Hester Dickson)
Janáček:	*Diary of One who Disappeared* (Blachut, Mixová, Tichý)
Janáček:	*Violin Sonata* (Manoug Parikian, David Wilde)
Kramář:	*Divertimento* (Wind Band of National Theatre Orchestra)

Mahler:	*Kindertotenlieder* (Fischer-Dieskau, Pittsburg SO, Steinberg)
Mahler:	*Symphony No.2* (Pittsburg SO, Steinberg)
Smetana:	*Dalibor* (5 performances)
Smetana:	*Quartet No.1* (Janáček Quartet)
Smetana:	*Vltava, Tábor, Blaník* (National Theatre Orchestra, Krombholc)

Jeremy Noble of *London Musical Events* could thus have his wish to hear a Czech company performing *Rusalka* as one of the main events in the midst of a heady mixture of some of the best that Czechoslovakia could offer. Not surprisingly, given such a heavy schedule, the company came in full strength with a large cast of principals who could be swapped for different performances. In the table below most of the principals used on the 1st night are marked thus: ❑

Rusalka	Milada Šubrtová ❑ Libuše Domanínská
Water Sprite	Eduard Haken ❑ Karel Berman
Jezibaba, the Witch	Marta Krásová Jaroslava Dobrá Jaroslava Procházková
Voice of a huntsman	Václav Bednář Teodor Šrubař Přemysl Kočí
The Prince	Ivo Žídek ❑ Beno Blachut
The Foreign Princess	Libuše Prylová ❑ Naděžda Kniplová
Gamekeeper	Jiři Joran Antonín Votava
Palace Cook	Helena Tattermuschová
Wood Nymphs	Sylvia Kodetová Miloslava Fidlerová Ivana Mixová

Opera of the National Theatre, Prague

Conductor	Jan Hus Tichý

In his review for *The Scotsman* on Thursday 20 August, Conrad Wilson had gone to the performance without any positive expectations whatsoever. Closely mirroring all the criticism that had gone before, he had clearly made up his mind before he even got to the theatre and was certain that the opera was a bad one.

> *Few opera guides make any mention of Dvorak's 'Rusalka' — not even the thorough Kobbe. Nor do Brockway and Weinstock include it among the 253 operas annotated in their "World of Opera." Its one professional performance in London was a fiasco, though the blame was attributed to the performance than to the opera. No other Dvorak opera has been professionally staged here, and a senior London critic has claimed that none is likely to be.*

His review was an exercise in wish fulfilment. He had listened to Supraphon's 'vivid new recording' and thought the Prague National Theatre might produce 'great things'. [69]

> *In the event, it was rather disappointing. The opera failed to work, to move forward, to hang together so effectively as the records led one to hope. Sight added little of value to sound, and indeed sometimes detracted from it ... On records, it all flows along most winningly. On stage, the music still flows but the drama does not.*

The only aspect of the whole opera that Wilson liked was Libuše Prylová as the Princess. 'B.N.', writing for the *Glasgow Herald* on 20 August, was similarly pessimistic about Rusalka:

> *Folk-ballad and fairy-tale held a special fascination for Dvorak. A consensus of opinion to-day would probably rate his earlier essays on folk and fairy subjects (which include four symphonic poems) rather low.*

By the end of the opera, he had been fully converted. Perhaps there was some benefit in not going to the first night and it is entirely possible that the Czech production had settled down in its new venue at the King's Theatre.

---

[69] Supraphon SUA ST 50440/3. Šubrtová, Žídek, Haken, Mixová, Joran, cond. Chalabala.

Last night's good-sized audience in the King's Theatre clearly found it to their liking. Tickets for later performances should become scarce, for the Opera of the National Theatre, Prague, make a splendid job of it and the work contains some of the most immediately attractive music to be heard at the Festival.

...

Rusalka and the Prince are especially well cast in this production. Milada Subrtova has a pleasing voice capable of strength and tenderness, of sustained legato, and crisp definition. Ivo Zidek combines ardour and sensitivity. The remaining cast work together as a well-drilled team, and some individual talent is to be spotted too.

...

Intentionally, one supposes, the unreal fairy world emerges as more real and close than the real one. In the opera house, where the most absurd things often (vainly) claim our belief, this mildly improbable tale can have an extraordinarily moving effect.

Differences of opinion between the Glasgow and Edinburgh newspapers have been far from uncommon over the years but with the *Herald*'s review, the impression is made that the whole intent of *Rusalka* has been appreciated. Even Ján Cikker's opera *Resurrection* created a favourable impression on critics who had never heard of the composer before this Festival. Together with the rest of the Czech music presented, one can easily detect a sea change in attitude; one that could reap rich dividends in the future.

A few years later, Rudolf Firkušný, a pupil and protégé of Janáček, provided some introductory words for a book on the Janáček-Newmarch correspondence and, talking about the gradual recognition of Janáček, said 'In a way, Edinburgh '64 was an apotheosis'. He was certainly correct in saying that the Festival was very much about Janáček and it was also the very first chance for large numbers of British opera-goers to hear so wide a range of Czech and Slovak music. *Rusalka* in Czech and by a Czech company was a landmark performance in many ways. [70]

[70] Fischmann, Z. E., (ed.), *Janáček-Newmarch Correspondence,* (Rockville MD: Kabel Publishers, 1986).

13. BBC Radio 3, 20 October 1968 and 6 November 1969.

The final production of *Rusalka* in the period under study is rather a curiosity. This was to be Vilém Tauský's fourth and final production in the British Isles, albeit as a studio concert performance. The opera was recorded before an invited audience in the Camden Theatre on 11 May 1968 after four rehearsals from 6 to 10 May. The principals were coached by John Bacon and the smaller roles by George Badesonyi.

Yet again, Christopher Hassall's English translation was used, though on this occasion, the broadcast was to be the first to go out uncut. In the issue of *Radio Times* for 17 October, a brief note was provided by Alec Robertson and the introduction and narration during the broadcast were again the ones prepared by Arthur Jacobs.

Even Alec Robertson seems to have come round to appreciating the opera more fully, though not yet as an item for the stage: 'The opera is rich in melody and colourful orchestration, and having little action is well suited to a studio performance'.

The following made up the cast:

Rusalka, a water nymph	Joan Carlyle
The Spirit of the Lake	Michael Langdon
Jezibaba, a Witch	Ann Howard
The voice of a huntsman	Rodney Macann
The Prince	Rowland Jones
The Foreign Princess	Pauline Tinsley
The Gamekeeper	Joseph Ward
The kitchen boy	Soo-Bee Lee
Three Wood Nymphs	Cynthia Glover Patricia Clark Jean Allister

BBC Chorus and BBC Concert Orchestra

Conductor	Vilém Tauský

Radio Times indicated nothing between the acts for the 1968 broadcast but in 1969 the first interval was occupied by the singers talking and the second by Gabriel Woolf reading Matthew Arnold's *The Forsaken Merman*. The publicity notes end with two most appropriate sentences, also repeated in the introduction to the broadcasts:

> *The opera is conducted by Vilém Tauský, who as a Czech expatriate has known and lived it since his childhood. It could have no better advocate.*

The usual post-broadcast survey of opinion was conducted by the Audience Research Unit and it estimated that the 1968 broadcast was heard by 0.1% of the population of the United Kingdom. The reaction was easily the most positive that Rusalka had received for any BBC broadcast, with 68% giving it A+ or A as a grade. Many were still hearing the work for the first time and welcomed the opportunity. Both singers and orchestra were praised. Joan Carlyle and Michael Langdon were especially picked out as praiseworthy.

14. Interlude: A recording of the BBC's 1968 production.

During the preparation of this essay, a recording was discovered of the whole of the 1968 concert performance. This was found on the website run by Joan Carlyle, who sang the part of Rusalka. A two-CD set on Miss Carlyle's From the Old House label, catalogue number VFOH 51/52, taken off-air is available. [71]

[71] Joan Carlyle, Laundry Cottage, Hanmer, North Wales, ST13 3DQ
www.joancarlyle.co.uk joan@joancarlyle.co.uk

The singing is rather superior to that of 1959, with Joan Carlyle and Michael Langdon making very strong contributions indeed. Ann Howard, as Jezibaba, did not sing her as some sort of villainous figure but a more humorous and sympathetic character. Rowland Jones, returning to the role he first performed in 1954 with Rafael Kubelík, was well suited for the part.

By its very nature, the recording is far from perfect, though the sound is much superior to that from the 1959 Sadler's Wells performance. There are sudden breaks and the sound is rather compressed. In places the sound has obviously rather overwhelmed the machine on which it was recorded and voices then lose definition. However, the essence of the performance can be clearly heard. Once again, Vilém Tauský's musical direction grips the imagination and the singers are perfectly and even delicately assisted through the work. This is not to speak of the orchestra being underpowered, indeed far from it; when the power is needed it is immediately to hand. In spite of the imperfections of the recording, this ranks as one of the finest readings of the score. Should the BBC wish once again to broadcast an English language version of *Rusalka,* then it should look on its shelves and blow the dust off one of the finest there has been.

15. Rusalka since 1969

Following the 1969 broadcast of Vilém Tauský's final production of *Rusalka*, the opera was not to be heard again until 1983, when, with a new English translation by Rodney Blumer it was given by the English National Opera on 16 March 1983 in a production by David Pountney and conducted by Mark Elder. This production broke entirely new ground for Dvořák as an opera composer. An altogether darker and more deeply psychological insight was presented to huge critical and public success. It could be argued that Dvořák's own attitude to the work was a very literal one and that he had not realised the full psychological insight within Jaroslav Kvapil's libretto. What David Pountney achieved was to reveal that hidden content and make of the work something far more in keeping with the zeitgeist of the mid 1980s. The success of the production meant that, when a video recording of it was issued in 1989, it could rightly claim in the sleeve note: [72]

[72] Virgin Classics Opera, VVD 392 and since then on DVD also.

Now, more than 80 years later, the reputation and popularity of 'Rusalka' have never been higher. Dvořák's ambition, unsatisfied in his lifetime, has at long last come near to realisation; the watersprite has achieved immortality.

Some still regard the 1983 production as the first example of what was called by Michael Kennedy *Pountneyfication*, or the clothing of operas in new psychological garb and giving them a totally new style of production value; this did not by any means suit all opera-goers. In fact the opera was only performed because an anonymous benefactor had given £40,000 to the English National Opera in the strict understanding that the work to be given should be *Rusalka*. Posterity is fortunate indeed for this benificence. [73]

Whilst doubts may have lingered elsewhere, the opera had entered the consciousness of a world-wide audience. New productions since 1983 have grown almost exponentially, from Minnesota to Moscow and from Paris to Adelaide as well as several new productions in the British Isles. *Rusalka* has become established as a central and essential part of the international operatic repertoire.

Exactly fifty years after Vilém Tauský led the first professional staged version of *Rusalka* in London, the Czech conductor, Jiří Bělohlávek was invited to conduct a new production at the Glyndbourne Festival Opera in Sussex. The opera was performed in Czech with English surtitles and the Cast included:

Rusalka	Ana Maria Martinez
Prince	Brandon Jovanovich
Foreign Princess	Tatiana Pavlovskaya
Vodník	Mikhail Schelomianski
Jezibaba	Larissa Diadkova
Gamekeeper	Alasdair Elliott
Kitchen Boy	Diana Axentii
Wood Nymphs	Natasha Jouhl, Barbara Senator and Elodie Mechain

The Director, Melly Still, and Designer, Rae Smith, garnered high praise and the music met with critical reaction that was almost the polar opposite to the reception at Sadler's Wells. Every critic was delighted with the manner and musicality of Bělohlávek's conducting.

[73] Gilbert, S., *Opera for Everybody. The Story of the English National Opera*, (London: Faber and Faber, 2009), pp.340 and 460.

It helps to have a masterpiece as your starting point – and Dvořák's 'Rusalka' is certainly that – but when you've a director as painfully honest and unpretentious as Melly Still and a conductor, in Jiří Bělohlávek, whose intent is not merely to conduct the piece but to honour it as a treasured part of his heritage, then we're talking a very special alchemy around what we hear, see, and feel. [74]

If those of us who came to opera long after David Pountney's 1983 ENO production find it hard to imagine a time when 'Rusalka' was not accepted as one of the greatest operas, Jiří Bělohlávek clearly remembers the years when it was denigrated as an exotic oddity and conducts as though calmly dissecting the long decades of prejudice. [75]

This is the first Glyndebourne production of a work that has become increasingly familiar to British audiences since David Pountney's epoch-making ENO staging opened in 1983. And deservedly so, for it is one of the richest of late-Romantic scores,... [76]

That the production still makes an impact is due on one hand to the conducting of Jiří Bělohlávek, who gives Dvořák's prodigious symphonic motifs their due as surely as he paints the score's Wagnerian colours,... [77]

This new production at Glyndebourne is really marvellous, both for its musical quality (of which I am no judge at all, but even I can hear something of how good it is) and because it captures how to tell a fairy tale on the stage. [78]

With this magnificent ... production, Dvořák's 'Rusalka' moves closer towards belated international recognition as one of the great masterpieces of the Romantic repertory. It is strangely moving, deeply weird and hauntingly beautiful. [79]

---

[74] Edward Seckerson, *The Independent*, 8 July 2009. To bring consistency, diacriticals have been added, as necessary, to the reviews covered by f.n. 74-88 (ed.).

[75] Anna Picard, *The Independent*, 12 July 2009.

[76] George Hall, *The Stage*, 6 July 2009.

[77] Andrew Clark, *The Financial Times*, 6 July 2009.

[78] Charles Moore, *The Daily Telegraph*, 20 July 2009.

[79] Rupert Christiansen, *The Daily Telegraph*, 6 July 2009.

Dvořák's 1901 fairytale opera has found its place on UK stages only relatively recently. If all directors approached it with the zestful imagination Melly Still employs, it would be a firm fixture by now. [80]

Jiří Bělohlávek ... relished the rich textures of Dvořák's orchestration, exploring the widest range of dynamics and giving every musical line its own identity and direction ... With first-rate support from the Glyndebourne chorus and the usual festival atmosphere, this was a staging not to be missed: a magical evening. [81]

Over the past century 'Rusalka' has slowly emerged not only as the greatest of Dvořák's ten operas, but also as one of the finest works in the Romantic operatic oeuvre. Yet, this surfacing continues to be a lingering and onerous process. [82]

'Rusalka' is deeply, deeply moving. [83]

Still's vision is first and foremost a fairytale. And one with a warm, if tragic, heart, in the form of Dvořák's sumptuous score and soprano Ana Maria Martinez. [84]

Best piece of operatic casting this year? He doesn't even appear on stage, except to take a bow at the end. It's Glyndebourne's decision to hire Jiří Bělohlávek to conduct its first production of a Dvořák opera ... the dark, swirling undercurrents of Dvořák's magnificent music. [85]

The beauty of the score was underpinned by conductor Jiří Bělohlávek's innate understanding of his fellow Czech's emotional complexity. [86]

Some critics had to hate it, if only to ensure a balance in comparison with the reviews in 1959.

---

[80] Erica Jeal, *The Guardian* 6 July 2009.
[81] Ditlev Rindom, mundoclassico.com 21 August 2009.
[82] William Norris, musicalcriticism.com 24 July 2009.
[83] Kieron Quirke, *Evening Standard,* 6 July 2009.
[84] Talitha Bromwich, *The Argus,* 6 July 2009.
[85] Richard Morrison, *The Times,* 7 July 2009.
[86] Susan King, *West Sussex County Times,* 24 July 2009.

> *It is a horrible mess. It escapes write-off status — and only just — thanks to a sublime musical performance under the Czech conductor Jiří Bělohlávek,...*[87]

> *Many regard this work as a heart-breaking masterpiece. The rest of us - though amid the cheers last Sunday I would have had to amend that to 'one or two of us' - find it charmingly melodic and frankly rather creepy, preferring the jubilant intensity of the tighter forms at which Dvořák excelled: his Slavonic Dances or string quartets.* [88]

The contrast in the reception of *Rusalka* in 2009 in comparison with that in 1959 could not be more stark. The opera was now so central to the main core of the operatic canon that many critics did not even comment on the quality of the music, concentrating instead on the production. After 1964 and especially after 1983, *Rusalka* can hold her head high in the world of opera. Prior to those key dates the situation had been radically different.

Vilém Tauský was the very first conductor to raise a British banner in the cause of Dvořák's *Rusalka*. In four productions of varying quality and content, he maintained an extraordinary sensitivity and passion for the music. For almost half a century Tauský held that banner high and it is not too much to say that those that came after him were indeed standing on the shoulders of a giant.

Addendum: Covent Garden's proposed 1939 *Rusalka* (ed.)

The London Philharmonic Concert Society Ltd promoted an International Opera Season at Covent Garden between 1 May and 16 June 1939. Within this season the Czech National Opera Company had been invited to give operas by Dvořák (*Rusalka*) and Smetana (*The Secret*) under the direction of Václav Talich. This proposal was announced before Germany marched into the remains of western Czechoslovakia on 15 March 1939. In April it was noted that the visit had been postponed 'probably till next [summer 1940] season'. By then it was too late. [89]

---

[87] Hugh Canning, *The Times*, 12 July 2009.

[88] Fiona Maddocks, *The Observer*, 11 July 2009.

[89] Julia Creed, Archivist, ROH Collections, 2010, citing: Rosenthal, H., *Two Centuries of Opera at Covent Garden*, (London: Putnam, 1958), pp.544-545 (ed.).

10

2005: A YEAR OF COMMEMORATION

by Brenda Rayson

west london sinfonia

www.westlondonsinfonia.org

Conductor Philip Hesketh
Leader Philippa Barton

An evening inspired by our late president, the distinguished Czech conductor Vilem Tausky.

Eric Coates
The Merrymakers

Bohuslav Martinu
Intermezzo

Leo Fall
Suite from 'The Dollar Princess'

Leo Janacek
Prelude, Jenufa (Jealousy)

Vilem Tausky
Movement From Serenade for Strings

Bedrich Smetana
Vlatava from Ma Vlast

Interval

Antonin Dvorak
Symphony No.8

5 February 2005
The West London Sinfonia programme

2005: A YEAR OF COMMEMORATION

by Brenda Rayson

Two commemorative concerts were given in early 2005. The first such concert was given by the West London Sinfonia on 5 February. Vilém Tauský was the Sinfonia's President and the concert was conducted by Philip Hesketh. The programme is shown on the previous page.

The second concert on 12 March was organised in Bromley and was attended by the Mayor of Bromley and the Cultural Attaché of the Czech Embassy in London. This concert was very much a community effort reflecting the fact that Vilém Tauský had spent his final years in that location. The programme was presented by the tenor Nigel Douglas and contained items given by local amateur groups and by established performers alike, including Chris Dee, Fan Chang Kong, Linda Watts and David Martin. Other participants included the Bromley Oecumenical Singers conducted by Fraser Goulding and a Brass Quintet from the Bromley Youth Music Trust. Matthew Farthing and Carol Wells played Tauský's *Suite for violin and piano*, and Matthew Farthing, accompanied by Fraser Goulding, played Janáček's *Romance*. Patricia Rozario, accompanied by her husband Mark Troop, contributed a group of Mahler songs. Following arias and duets by Smetana, Dvořák, Lehár and Kálmán, soprano Marilyn Hill Smith concluded the tributes singing *Du mein Schönbrunn* from Leo Fall's *Die Kaiserin*. One feature was the number of messages of remembrance sent by artists who could not be at the concert in person. These reveal the depth of affection felt for Vilém Tauský by his fellow artists and I am happy to reproduce them at the end of this chapter.

Vilém Tauský's well attended funeral service had been held on 25 March, 2004 at Beckenham Crematorium. Graham Melville-Mason read a lesson and David Frous, a Secretary from the Czech Embassy read a speech written by H. E. the Czech Ambassador. The congregation were welcomed by a movement from Tauský's *From our village* and departed to his march *Men of Tomorrow*.

As a final act of commemoration, it was due to the warm help offered by His Excellency Štefan Fühle that it was possible to achieve the ambition 'to return Vilém to the land of his birth'. His Excellency made the initial approaches to the Czech authorities and obtained permission for the burial in the City of Brno Cemetery. Alena Němcová from the Janáček Foundation in Brno provided the help and expertise that we lacked in commissioning the headstone; as non-Czech speakers or residents we could not have managed without her. Liaison between London and Brno was in the capable hands of Monika Studená, another Secretary at the Czech Embassy in London.

Eventually the Ambassador arranged for the urn to be collected and despatched to Brno where a place had been allocated in the musicians' section near to Janáček's grave; very fitting as he was believed to be the last man who had been one of his pupils. A short time later Adrian Pontin, his other executor, and myself, were on our way to Brno for a ceremony at the Janáček Museum and a visit to the grave on 20 July 2005. Sadly, Alena Němcová was ill and unable to attend, but her assistant Eva Drlíková who made all the arrangements ably took her place. Several members of Brno Council were in attendance plus a representative of the Czech Government from Prague.

Our thanks go, not only to those mentioned above, but to the City of Brno Council who covered all the cemetery expenses incurred at the time and who continue to maintain the grave at their expense.

Tauský's grave in the Brno Central Cemetery

[Photo: Tim Marshall]

Tributes received at the Bromley concert:

From Levon Chilingirian OBE:

In Prague on 8 June 2003, I had the happy privilege of leading the Pharos Soloists in a performance of 'Coventry'. We were honoured to have Vilém in the audience, looking so happy to be at home. This deeply felt composition got a much-deserved ovation and deserves to be heard by a much wider public.

From Peter Fisher:

The name Vilém Tauský was familiar to me through 'Friday Night is Music Night' since my childhood, however it wasn't for another thirty years or so that I was to have the good fortune to meet this true gentleman of maestri through my dear friends Vera and Ariel Evan. As a pupil of Kveta and Jaroslav Vaněček, themselves protégés of the great Bohemian school of violinists, I have always felt a great affinity for Czech music - indeed, Jaroslav Vaněček and Vilém were to collaborate in a performance of the Dvořák Concerto in Dublin, decades before I was to meet either.

I had no idea that Vilém was a composer and was thrilled when he approached me to perform his 'Suite for Violin and Piano', which he had composed upon return from his first visit to his native country since the Second World War in the 1970s. A finely crafted work, the second movement, 'in Memoriam', is particularly heart rending and based on an ancient Czech chorale. It commemorates Vilém's many friends who were no longer to be found on his return to Czechoslovakia. I feel very privileged to have the opportunity to perform the 'Suite' and to have received such encouragement from the benevolent and kindly gentleman that was Vilém.

From Sir James Galway CBE:

As a young man of 21 playing at Sadler's Wells, I never thought I would be asked to write about my illustrious and admired colleague Vilém Tauský. I first saw him when I was sharing a flat with Robert Dawes who was the piccolo player in the BBC Concert Orchestra. I would go from time to time to a concert which Tauský was conducting and listen to the world's greatest melodies in a series called 'Friday Night is Music Night'. It certainly was that and we were introduced to some of the world's finest music sung and played by some of the best talent available.

It was at the Wells that I first played with him and I can remember the first thing we did there together. It was the famous 'Die Fledermaus' of Strauss. He conducted this so well as he had this music in his blood. The charm and clarity he brought to this most difficult and amusing opera was as if someone let the sun in through the roof of the opera house. It was in this opera that I first became aware of his very solid technique. He made everything look so easy and as a result the orchestra and singers played as if it was all in their blood as well. Several years later I had the pleasure to play in Belfast in a special concert for the BBC. Here he conducted me in the Mozart 'Concerto in D major, K.314'. He knew every little nuance of the score and provided me with a wonderful accompaniment.

Vilém was a natural born musician and a gentleman of great charm which showed in everything he did. His understanding of the scores was a marvel. This led to great interpretations and these were nowhere more apparent than in the opera house. It was here that I got to know him best. There is a story that I once changed the score and that he never batted an eyelid but just took charge from memory as he did with most things. It has indeed been a great pleasure to have been around when he was at his very best in my early days in the opera and his mature days as a conductor in the United Kingdom. I know his league of friends, of which I would like to count myself as one, will miss him.

From Emma Johnson MBE:

I was sorry to hear of the death of Vilém Tauský because not only was he a fine musician but he was also a lovely man. I worked with him once on my birthday and at the beginning of the rehersal he got the BBC Concert Orchestra to play, not the opening of the concerto I was expecting, but 'Happy Birthday to You' instead. It was a nice birthday present. My best wishes to everyone at this celebration of a fine conductor and a kind man.

From Peter Katin:

My association with Vilém goes back to 1954 when I played the Rachmaninov 'Paganini Rhapsody' for the BBC at short notice, for the first time. He was most helpful and co-operative, as he was in the many subsequent occasions on which we worked together.

From Howard Shelley:

I remember Vilém with the greatest of affection. My first encounters with him were on London platforms in the seventies when we would perform the so-called warhorse piano concertos, the Grieg, Tchaikovsky and Rachmaninov's Second. There was never much time for rehearsals, but with Vilém this was anyway not necessary because of his natural and concummate mastery of his art, inextricably and naturally linked to his sensitivity to the music - its heart and soul.

Many years later he generously helped me with advice on conducting, warmly and modestly given. I regard myself as very priviliged to have known and worked with him and I treasure the memory of his smiling, open face and his innate musical being. May God rest his sweet and inspired soul.

From Dame Joan Sutherland OM AC DBE:

I was indeed saddened to learn of Maestro Tauský's death last year. Although I did not do many performances with the Maestro I remember them as being very happy occasions. He always seemed to be very good humoured and helpful with any problems that arose. I looked forward to working with him each time I was asked, as I felt he really enjoyed working with singers.

From Haig Utidjian:

I shall always be deeply grateful to Vilém Tauský, who was extremely generous to me with his guidance, encouragement and assistance. He remains an inspiring example to many of us, not only as a conductor of exceptional warmth and musicality, but also as a man of immense generosity of spirit and kindness. I also believe that his oeuvre as a composer will gain increasing recognition - and I feel enormously privileged to have had the honour of conducting the Czech première of 'Coventry'. [1]

[1] The Czech première took place on 26 November 2000 and was given with the North Bohemian Chamber Orchestra. (ed.)

11

A VILÉM TAUSKÝ DISCOGRAPHY

by Richard Beith

Selections from Die Fledermaus

HMV GES 5786

A VILÉM TAUSKÝ DISCOGRAPHY

by Richard Beith

This discography indicates that although Vilém Tauský made many commercial recordings, sadly, there were remarkably few devoted to the music of Czech composers. For a long time, Dvořák was represented by only one recording: Joan Hammond's much-loved (and now much-copied) 'O silver moon' from 1952. Smetana was not much luckier; a live performance of *Vltava* from 1976 and two extracts from *The Bartered Bride*, one recorded in 1946. However we now have two complete Czech operas culled from BBC sources, a complete *Dalibor* taken from a live performance in 1969 and a complete *Rusalka* from 1968.

The 'Polka and Fugue' from Weinberger's *Schwanda the Bagpiper* can be found from the same 1976 concert as *Vltava*, but of Janáček and Martinů there is absolutely nothing. At least his conducting of operetta at Sadler's Wells Theatre and at the London Coliseum can be sampled in generous highlights of works by Lehár and Johann Strauss II, still available in CD transfers.

This listing is divided into sections for Vilém Tauský as composer, as arranger and as conductor. The final section includes the many compilations of popular classics listed by record label, not forgetting his participation in brass band concerts recorded in the Royal Albert Hall.

The 'off-air' recordings listed towards the end of this discography contain a number of CDs which exhibit short breaks in the music, suggesting that they were produced from non-commercial sources.

The HMV prefixes DB and C and the Columbia prefix DB, indicate 78 rpm recordings. 7P, 7EP and 7ER numbers relate to 7 inch, 45 rpm, recordings. Record numbers in **bold** are CDs or CD reissues. Where known, the place and date of each recording are given at the end of each entry. Known live performances are so indicated. The sole 'off-air' DVD is shown in ***bold italic***.

The invaluable assistance of Peter Herbert in compiling this discography is warmly acknowledged.

Abbreviations used are:

AbR	Abbey Road
arr.	Arranged
BBCCO	BBC Concert Orchestra
BBCSO	BBC Symphony Orchestra
CFP	Classics for Pleasure
KH	Kingsway Hall
LSO	London Symphony Orchestra
NALSO	New Abbey Light Symphony Orchestra
nd.	No date
P	Published
PhilO	Philharmonia Orchestra
RAH	Royal Albert Hall
RPO	Royal Philharmonic Orchestra
SWOO	Sadler's Wells Opera Orchestra
STSO	Studio 2 Symphony Orchestra
VTHO	Vilém Tauský & His Orchestra

Overtures by Auber and Méhul

HMV 7EP 7097

Vilém Tauský as composer

Commercial recordings:

Bohemian Carnival, in 'Music for Two Harmonicas', Tommy Reilly and Sigmund Groven w. Armon String Quartet, etc, Polydor LP 2922 008, 3240 008 (audio cassette). (London, 23 and 25 August 1976).

Concertino for Harmonica and Orchestra, in 'Works for harmonica', Tommy Reilly, Academy of St. Martin in the Fields, Sir Neville Marriner, Argo LP ZRG 856, KZRC 856 (audio cassette), Chandos **CHAN 8617**. (London, St. John's, Smith Square, 1 and 2 June 1976).

Concert Overture for Brass Band, in 'Pride of the North', Besses O' th' Barn Band, Polydor Carnival LP 2928 011. (New Community Hall, Whitefield, Lancashire). (P 1972).

Coventry, A Meditation for String Quartet, (1941), in 'Continental Britons, The Émigré Composers', Ensemble Modern, Frankfurt, Nimbus **NI 5730/1**. (London, Wigmore Hall, 2002).

Private or restricted recordings:

March - Trellisick Gardens, in 'Concert of a Choir of 1000 Cornish Male Voices and the Cambourne Town Band', conducted by Vilém Tauský, LP VHF 19383. (London, RAH, 5 November 1983, live recording).

Men of Tomorrow (March), J W Media, (1958), & Audio BMP 119A.

Serenade for Strings, West London Sinfonia, Philip Hesketh (audio cassette) (22 October 1994); Whitgift School Chamber Orchestra, **CD**. (Japan, October 2001).

Sinfonietta, Bromley Youth Symphony Orchestra, Audio Digital 2 x CD **CTRS 301 & 156CD** (+ Dvořák). (Ravensbourne School, Bromley, 27 March 2004, live recording).

Suite for Violin and Piano, (1978), in 'British Czech Celebration', Peter Fisher (violin) and Alvin Moisey (piano), David Birt Recordings. Available on single CD **WGHC01** and 2 CD set **PFAM02.** (London, Wigmore Hall, 6 November 2000, live recording; available from sales@dvorak-society.org).

Vilém Tauský as arranger

Commercial recordings:

BACH: *Jesu Joy of Man's Desiring*, in 'Glorious Melodies', Reginald Kilbey & His Strings, EMI **CC228 790652 2**. (1967).

HANDEL: *Berenice, Minuet*, in 'The Music of England', The Bournmouth Symphony Orchestra, Sir Vivian Dunn. Chalfont C77.001. (1977).

VAŇHAL: *Concerto for Oboe and Strings* in F major, 'Freely adapted by Vilhelm [!] Tausky and dedicated to Evelyn Rothwell', [Lady Barbirolli], Piet van Bockstal, The Prussian Chamber Orchestra, Hans Rotman. Talent **DOM 2910 75.** (2003).

WALTON: *The Quest - ballet suite*, 'Rediscovered score put together with the help of Vilém Tauský in 1961', LSO, Sir William Walton, Lyrita **SRCD 224.** (1961).

WALTON: *The Quest - ballet suite,* further transcribed for wind orchestra by Steven J. Capaldo, UNLV (University of Nevada Las Vegas) Wind Orchestra / Thomas G. Leslie, Klavier **K 11169.** (2007).

Traditional: *Greensleeves*, in 'Glorious Melodies', Reginald Kilbey & His Strings, EMI **CC228 790652 2**. (1967)

Folk Songs: *Whittingham Fair* and *The Laidley Worm O' Spindleston Heugh*, in 'Owen Brannigan Drives Home', Wilfred Parry (piano), Solsgirth LP SHOO1. (1971).

Folk Songs: *One Autumn Morning* and *A Little Hour Before Day*; *Henry my Love* and *The Little White Cat*, Presto, unnumbered 78s.

Vilém Tauský as conductor

Commercial recordings:

ADAM: *La Poupée de Nuremberg*, Overture, RPO, HMV PES 5271/ 7EP 7116, Odeon P-7EP 7116, SXLP 30117, 'Sparkling Overtures'. (1961).

ALWYN: *Miss Julie* (Complete), Jill Gomez, Benjamin Luxon, Della Jones, John Mitchinson, PhilO, Lyrita LP SRCS 121/2, **SRCD 2218** (2CD). (London, KH, 23-26 January 1979).

AUBER: *Fra Diavolo*, Overture, RPO, HMV PES 5258/7EP 7097, SXLP 30117, 'Sparkling Overtures'. (1960).

BIZET: *Le Docteur Miracle,* Overture, RPO, HMV PES 5271/7EP 7116, Odeon P-7EP 7116, SXLP 30117, 'Sparkling Overtures'. (1961).

BORODIN: *Prince Igor*, 'Polovtsian Dances', Goldsmith's Choral Union, BBCSO, BBC Radio Classics **BBCRD 9103**. (London, RAH, 24 July 1976, live recording).

DONIZETTI: *L'Elisir d'Amore*, 'Una furtiva lagrima', Walter Midgley, PhilO, HMV DB 21501, Dutton **CDLX 7040**. (8 April 1952).

DONIZETTI: *L'Elisir d'Amore*, 'Una furtiva lagrima' and *Lucia di Lammermoor*, 'Tombe degli avi miei, Fra poco a me ricovero' and 'Tu che a Dio spiegasti l'ali', Brychen Powell, Delyse Symphony Orchestra, Delyse EC 3136. (nd.)

DOSTAL: *Clivia*, 'Ich bin verliebt', Elizabeth Harwood, BBCSO, BBC Radio Classics **BBCRD 9103**. (London, RAH, 24 July 1976, livo).

DVOŘÁK: *Rusalka*, 'O silver moon', Joan Hammond, PhilO, HMV DB 21451, 7P 243, 7ER 5118, HQM 1186, Odeon P-7ER 5118, Capitol W 6016, Testament **SBT 1013**, Regis **RRC 1197**, Regis **RRC 1231**, Prism Leisure **PLATCD 1347** and **PLATBX 507,** Yesteryear **GLM/Y-3B-09,** Rajon **CDR 0669A/B/C/D**, destraEntertainment **591002/1/2/3**, Hot Record Society **HRS 014**. (London, KH, 23 January 1952).

GIORDANO: *Andrea Chenier*, 'Un di all'azzurro spazio guardai profondo', 'Come un bel di di Maggio' and Fedora, 'Amor ti vieta', Brychen Powell, Delyse Symphony Orchestra, Delyse EC 3136. (nd.).

GOUNOD: *Faust*, 'The hour is late', Charles Craig, Joan Hammond, HMV ALP 1805/ASD 384, EMI (Australia) SOELP 10059, Testament **SBT 1153**. (London, AbR, 28 October 1959).

GRAINGER: *Molly on the Shore*, BBCCO, BBC Radio Classics **BBCRD 9103**. (London, RAH, 25 September 1965, live recording).

GRIEG: *Solveigs Lied*, arr. Semprini, NALSO, in 'Spotlights: Klassik-Hits aus der TV-Werbung', EMI Electrola GmbH, **7243 5 55521 2 9**. (P 1967).

LEHÁR: *The Land of Smiles*, (Highlights), June Bronhill, Charles Craig, Elizabeth Fretwell, SWOO, HMV CLP 1286/CSD 1267, GES 5814/7ER 8361 & GES 5819/7EG 8643, **CFP 57599627**, Price-Less (USA) **D18886**. (London, AbR, 22, 23 and 25 June 1959).

LEHÁR: *The Land of Smiles*, 'The Prophet of the Blue Pagoda', June Bronhill, SWOO, EMI Australia, **0946 3891632**. (In: 'June Bronhill, The Platinum Collection').

LEHÁR: *The Land of Smiles*, 'This was a wonderful day', 'Smiling' and 'Love, let me dream again', Charles Craig, Elizabeth Fretwell, SWOO, in 'Operetta at the Wells', HMV Greensleeve ESDW 712 (2 LP). (P 1981).

LEHÁR: *The Land of Smiles*, Overture, SWOO, HMV SXLP 30117, 'Sparkling Overtures'. (1959).

LEHÁR: *The Merry Widow*, (Highlights), June Bronhill, Ann Howard, Jeremy Brett, David Hughes, John McCarthy Singers, VTHO, EMI TWO 234, **CFP 094633598126,** Price-Less (USA) **D16514.** (London, AbR, 28 June and 8 July 1968).

LEHÁR: *The Merry Widow*, 'Vilia' and 'Love unspoken', June Bronhill, VTHO, EMI Australia, **0946 3891632**. (In: 'June Bronhill, The Platinum Collection').

LEHÁR: *The Merry Widow*, 'Jogging in a one-horse gig', VTHO, **CFP 335 9922.** (In 'Highlights from Musicals and Operettas').

LEHÁR: *The Count of Luxembourg*, (Highlights), June Bronhill, John McCarthy Singers, STSO, EMI TWO 246, **CFP 57599627**. (London, AbR, September 1968).

LEHÁR: *The Count of Luxembourg*, 'Someone's here to marry me', 'Love, goodbye', June Bronhill, STSO. EMI Australia, **0946 3891632**. (In: 'June Bronhill, The Platinum Collection').

LISZT: (arr. Semprini), *Rákóczy March*, Semprini, NALSO, MFP 50004. (P 1970).

MACKEBEN: *Münchner G'Schichten*, BBCSO, BBC Radio Classics, **BBCRD 9103**. (London, RAH, 24 July 1976, live recording).

MÉHUL: *Les Deux Aveugles de Tolède*, Overture, RPO, HMV PES 5258/7EP 7097, SXLP 30117, 'Sparkling Overtures'. (1960).

MEYERBEER: *L'Africaine*, 'O Paradis', Walter Midgley, PhilO, HMV DB 21501. (8 April 1952).

MILLÖCKER: *The Dubarry*, 'Ich schenk mein Herz', Elizabeth Harwood, BBCSO, BBC Radio Classics **BBCRD 9103**. (London, RAH, 24 July 1976, live recording).

MONCKTON: *The Arcadians*, (Highlights), June Bronhill, Andy Cole, Peter Regan, John McCarthy Singers, VTHO, EMI TWO 233, **CFP 3598225**, EMI (Broadway Angel, USA) **ZDM 65068.** Overture only in Ultimate Stereo Presentation, STWO 3 and **981592**, also in The Magical World of Operetta, Readers Digest 6CD set, **RDCD 1191-6**. (London, AbR, 12 July and 27 September 1968). [NB: a second version of *The Arcadians* was recorded by EMI on CFP conducted by Gilbert Vinter. The USA CD fills in the gaps in the original Studio Two recording using the CFP version. The CFP CD reverses this process.]

MONCKTON: *The Arcadians*, 'The Pipes of Pan', 'Arcady is ever young', June Bronhill, John McCarthy Singers, VTHO, EMI Australia, **0946 3891632**. (In: 'June Bronhill, The Platinum Collection').

NOVELLO: *King's Rhapsody*, (Highlights), Cynthia Glover, Patricia Kern, Marjorie Westbury, Robert Bowman, BBCCO and Chorus, EMI TWO 270, Odeon PTWO 270. (BBC Radio, 14 December 1968).

OFFENBACH: *Les contes d'Hoffmann*, 'Elle a fui, la tourterelle', Joan Hammond, PhilO, HMV HLM 7042, Testament **SBT 1013**. (London, KH, 17 January 1952).

OFFENBACH: *La Vie Parisienne*, Overture, RPO, HMV 7EP 7116/ PES 5271, Odeon P-7EP 7116, SXLP 30117, 'Sparkling Overtures'. (1961).

PUCCINI: *Tosca*, 'Mario!, Mario!', Charles Craig, Joan Hammond, RPO, HMV ALP 1805/ASD 384, EMI (Australia) SOELP 10059, Testament **SBT 1153**. (London, AbR, 28 October 1959 and 2 February 1960).

PUCCINI: La Bohème, 'Your tiny hand is frozen', 'They call me Mimi', 'Lovely maid in the moonlight', Charles Craig, Joan Hammond, RPO, HMV ALP 1805/ASD 384, EMI (Australia) SOELP 10059, Testament **SBT 1153**. (London AbR, 31 October 1959 and 4 February 1960).

PUCCINI: *Madam Butterfly*, 'Ah! Love me a little', Charles Craig, Joan Hammond, RPO, HMV ALP 1805/ASD 384, EMI (Australia) SOELP 10059, Testament **SBT 1153**. (London, AbR, 4 February 1960).

ROSSINI: *Guillaume Tell*, 'Ils s'eloignent enfin: Sombre foret', Joan Hammond, PhilO, HMV DB 21549. (London, KH, 23 January 1952).

SMETANA: *Má vlast: Vltava*, BBCSO, BBC Radio Classics **BBCRD 9103**, BBC **MM137**. (London, RAH, 24 July 1976, live recording). [MM137 issued with BBC Music Magazine Vol.IV, No.1].

SMETANA: *The Bartered Bride*, 'Why should he think', James Johnston, SWOO, Columbia DB 2217, Dutton **CDLX 7018**. (17 May 1946).

SMETANA: *Dalibor* (Complete), April Cantelo, Gordon Farrall, Don Garrard, Gwyn Griffiths, Robert [Rowland?] Jones, Pauline Tinsley,

Joseph Ward, BBCCO and Chorus, Gala **GL 100.785**. (2CD). (31 August 1969, live recording).

STRAUSS, J. II: *Die Fledermaus*, (Highlights), Victoria Elliott, John Heddle Nash, Marion Studholme, Alexander Young, SWOO and Chorus, HMV CLP 1272/CSD 1266, EMI ESD 7083 and TC-ESD 7083 (audio cassette), GES 5786/7EG 8543, Act 1: 'I'll be at the Ball tonight'; 'Drown the truth in wine'; Act 2 'What a feast', GES 5807/ 7EG861?, CFP **58500226.** (London, AbR, 20 and 30 April, 1 May 1959).

STRAUSS, J. II: *Die Fledermaus*, Overture, 'Ah, woe that it should be', 'Chacun à son goût; 'Laughing Song' and 'Champagne Song and Finale', Victoria Elliott, Marion Studholme, Alexander Young, SWOO and Chorus, in 'Operetta at the Wells', HMV Greensleeve ESDW 712 (2 LP). (P 1981).

STRAUSS, J. II: *Die Fledermaus*, Overture, SWOO, HMV SXLP 30117 'Sparkling Overtures'. (1959).

STRAUSS, J. II: *The Gypsy Baron*, (Highlights), June Bronhill, Nigel Douglas, Derek Hammond-Stroud, Ann Howard, SWOO and Chorus, HMV CLP 1912/CSD 1629, CFP **58500226**, Price-Less (USA), XY-2234 (audio cassette), **D18304**. (London, AbR, 16 and 18 June 1965).

STRAUSS, J. II: *The Gypsy Baron*, 'Gypsy Song', 'Who made us one?', 'Act 2 Finale' and 'Act 3 March', June Bronhill, Ann Howard and Nigel Douglas, SWOO and Chorus, in 'Operetta at the Wells', HMV Greensleeve ESDW 712 (2 LP). (P 1981).

STRAUSS, J. II: *The Gypsy Baron*, 'Gypsy Song', 'Hear in this dear land', Who made us one?', June Bronhill, Ann Howard, Nigel Douglas, SWOO and Chorus, EMI Australia, **0946 3891632**. (In: 'June Bronhill, The Platinum Collection').

STRAUSS, J. II: *The Gypsy Baron*, Overture, SWOO, HMV SXLP 30117, 'Sparkling Overtures', EMI TV, **VTDCD 951**, 'melodies for you', (P 2007).

STRAUSS, J. II: *Tritsch-Tratsch Polka*, STSO, **CFP 58500226**. (London, AbR, 10 February 1969).

TCHAIKOVSKY: *Queen of Spades*, 'Twill soon be midnight now', Joan Hammond, PhilO, HMV DB 21451, 7P 243. (London, KH, 21 March 1952).

TCHAIKOVSKY: *Twelve Pieces,* No.6, *Chant sans paroles*, orch. Stokowski, LSO, Orchid **OR CD 11042**. (1977).

VERDI: *Aida*, 'I see thee again, sweet Aida', Charles Craig, Joan Hammond, RPO, HMV ALP 1805/ASD 384, EMI (Australia) SOELP 10059, Testament **SBT 1153**. (London, AbR, 4 February 1960).

VERDI: *Don Carlos*, 'Francia nobile', Joan Hammond, PhilO, HMV DB 21510. (London, KH, 15 January 1952); 'Tu che la vanita', Joan Hammond, PhilO, HMV DB 21510, Testament **SBT 1013,** Hamburger Archiv für Gesangskunst **10099**. (London, KH, 17 January 1952).

VERDI: *Otello*, 'Salce, salce: Ave Maria', Joan Hammond, PhilO, HMV DB 21558, Testament **SBT 1160**. (London, KH, 15 January 1952).

VERDI: *Rigoletto*, 'La donna è mobile', James Johnston, SWOO, Columbia DB 2217, Dutton **CDLX 7030**. (17 May 1946).

VINTNER: *Hunter's Moon*, Dennis Brain, BBCCO, BBC Legends **BBCL 4164-2**. (London, BBC Studios, 16 June 1957).

WEBER: *Der Freischütz*, 'Softly sighs', Joan Hammond, PhilO, HMV C 3510. (London, AbR, 15 April 1946).

WEBER: *Oberon*, 'Ocean though mighty monster', Joan Hammond, PhilO, HMV C 3493, Dutton **CDLX 7020,** Hamburger Archiv für Gesangskunst **10099**. (London, AbR, 15 April 1946).

WEINBERGER: *Schwanda the Bagpiper*, 'Polka and Fugue', BBCSO, BBC Radio Classics, **BBCRD 9103**. (London, RAH, 24 July 1976, live recording).

Commercially recorded popular collections by record label:

EMI

EMTVD 45 (2LP), TCEMTVD 45 (audio cassette), **7 90353 2**, *The Classic Experience*, includes Offenbach: 'Barcarolle' and Mascagni: *Cavalleria Rusticana*, 'Intermezzo', both STSO, plus items not conducted by Tauský. (P 1988).

UNCUT EMI 1, *Reel Music, the coolest sounds from the greatest movies*, includes: Mascagni: *Cavalleria Rusticana, Intermezzo*, STSO. [Linked to the film Raging Bull]. (P 1997).

OCLP 3512/OCSD 3512, Semprini in Concert, Semprini and unspecified orchestra, EMI Australia. (nd.).

Weber: *Perpetuum Mobile*
Schubert: *Impromptu* No.4, Op.90
Mendelssohn: *The Bee's Wedding*
Liszt: *Hungarian Rhapsody* No.13
Rachmaninov: *Melodie* Op.3, No.3
Chopin: *Grand Fantasie* Op.13, *Lento*
Greig: *Lyric Suite* Op.54 - *Scherzo*
Albeniz: *Triana*
Plus piano solos

EMI COLUMBIA STUDIO 2:

TWO 176, EMI (Australia) SOEX 9677: *Semprini plays the marvellous music of Grieg*, VTHO. (P 1967).

March of the Dwarfs, Peer Gynt - Solveig's Song, Berceuse, The Last Spring, Wedding Day at Troldhaugen, Holberg Suite - Air, Nocturne, Arietta - Souvenirs and piano solos

TWO 198: *Semprini plays the marvellous music of Tchaikovsky*, NALSO. (1968).

Swan Lake Waltz, Troika, Serenade for Strings, Andante Cantabile, Sleeping Beauty Waltz, Barcarolle, Concerto No.2 (Third Movement), None but the Lonely Heart, and piano solos.

TWO 258: *The best of the world's great melodies*, STSO. (P 1969).

Bizet: *Carmen*, Prelude to Act I, *Habanera*, Entracte to Act 4, Gypsy song
Smetana: *The Bartered Bride*, Dance of the Comedians
Verdi: *La Traviata*, Prelude to Act 1
Puccini: *La Bohème,* 'Your tiny hand is frozen'
Mascagni: *Cavalleria Rusticana*, Intermezzo
Offenbach: *The Tales of Hoffmann*, Barcarolle
De Falla: *La Vida Breve*, Spanish Dance No.1

TWO 274: *Semprini plays Chopin*, NALSO. (P 1970).

Waltz Op.64 No.2, *Nocturne* Op.32 No.2, *Polonaise* Op.40 No.1, *Prelude* Op.28 No.15, *Grande Polonaise Brilliante* Op.22, and piano solos.

TWO 288: *Starlight Concert*, STSO (P 1970), also 8X-TWO 288 (eight track cartridge).

Chabrier: *Espana*
Debussy arr. Moulton: *Clair de Lune*
Ponchielli: *La Gioconda*, 'Dance of the Hours'
Albeniz arr. Arnold: *Tango*
Puccini: *Madame Butterfly*, 'Love Duet'
Wolf-Ferrari: *School for Fathers*, Intermezzo
Rimsky-Korsakov: *The Snowmaiden*, 'Dance of the tumblers'
Strauss, J. II: *Tritsch-Tratsch Polka*
Gounod: *Faust*, 'Waltz'
Offenbach arr. Binder: *Orpheus in the Underworld*, 'Can-Can'

TWO 317: *Semprini plays Liszt*, NALSO. (P 1970).

Rákóczy March, Devotion, Tarantella, Hungarian Fantasy, Le Rossignol, Consolation, and piano solos.

TWO 394: *Semprini plays Schubert, Mendelssohn, Mozart*, NALSO. (P 1972).

Schubert: *Schubertiana, Serenade, Waltz of Longing*
Mendelssohn: *Concerto No.1, 3rd movement, On Wings of*

Song
Mozart: *Don Giovanni*, selection arr. Liszt and piano solos.

TC-EMS 1298 (audio cassette), *Semprini Golden Classics*, NALSO. (P 1988). A compilation taken from earlier Studio Two LPs, containing:

Chopin: *Polonaise* Op.40 No.1, *Waltz* Op.64 No.2
Grieg: *Solveig's Song, March of the Dwarfs*
Lehár: *Gold and Silver Waltz*
Liszt: *Rákóczy March, Hungarian Fantasy*
Massenet: *Thais*, 'Meditation'
Mendelssohn: *On Wings of Song*
Schubert: *Serenade*
Tchaikovsky: *Barcarolle, Trepak, Swan Lake*, 'Waltz',
Waldteufel: *Skaters Waltz*
Seville/Serradel: *La Golondrina*

ENCORE

ONCR 528, Semprini, At Your Request, with Orchestra or NALSO, plus piano solos and items not conducted by Tauský. (1967-1969, P 1979).

Chopin, *Polonaise* Op.40 No.1
Greig, *The Last Spring* Op.34, *Holberg Suite* Op.40 - Air, *Nocturne*, Op.54
Tchaikovsky, *Andante Cantabile, Sleeping Beauty* - Waltz, *Serenade for Strings* - Waltz, *Trepak*

PICKWICK

PDA 036 (2LP), PCD 839: *The London Symphony Orchestra present music you have loved*, LSO. (London, St. Giles, Cripplegate, 23, 26 and 27 September 1977).

Verdi: *La Traviata*, 'Prelude Act I'
Grieg: *Norwegian Dance* No.2
Binge: *Elizabethan Serenade*
Mendelssohn: *Wedding March*
Massenet: *Meditation from Thais*, with John Georgiadis

Waldteufel: *The Skater's Waltz*
Mascagni: *Cavalleria Rusticana*, 'Intermezzo'
Hummel: *Trumpet Concerto*, finale with Maurice Murphy
Delibes: *Sylvia*, 'Pizzicato'
Debussy: *Clair de Lune*
Tchaikovsky: *Chant sans paroles*
Elgar: *Salut d'Amour*
Gounod: *Faust*, 'Waltz'
Strauss, J. I: *Radetzky March*
Bach arr. Walton: *Sheep may safely graze*
Walton: *Façade*, 'Popular song'
Granados: *Goyescas*, 'Intermezzo'
Sibelius: *Valse triste*
Grainger: *Handel in the Strand*
Wolf-Ferrari: *I Quattro Rusteghi*, 'Intermezzo'
Handel arr. Guiraud: *Xerxes*, 'Largo'
Strauss, J. II: *Pizzicato Polka*
Benjamin: *Jamaican Rhumba*
Mozart: *Horn Concerto No.4*, finale with David Cripps
Thomas: *Mignon*, 'Entracte'
Reznicek: *Dona Diana*, 'Overture'

PLE 7007, PLC 7007 (audio cassette), *20 Classical masterpieces*, 'Limited Edition'. Includes the works by Debussy, Delibes, Granados, Grieg, Mozart, J. Strauss II, Thomas and Verdi listed in PDA 036 above, plus piano solos by Peter Katin. (1978).

PLD 8007, (2LP), PDLC 8007, (double audio cassette), 'Limited Edition', *40 Classical Masterpieces*, LSO, includes the works by Mascagni, Benjamin, Hummel, Elgar, Walton, Binge and J. Strauss I, as in PDA 036 above, plus items not conducted by Tauský. (P 1977 and 1978).

CD (?), *The Collection*, Volume 1, includes works by Verdi, Grieg, Mendelssohn, Massenet, Waldteufel, Hummel, Delibes, Elgar, Gounod, Granados, Handel, J. Strauss II, Mozart and Thomas as in PDA 036 above, plus items not conducted by Tauský. (P 1994?).

CD (?), *The Collection*, Volume 4, includes Verdi: *La Traviata*, 'Prelude Act 1', plus items not conducted by Tauský. (P 1994?).

ORCD 11017, *Golden Melodies from Opera*, includes Verdi: *La Traviata*, 'Prelude Act 1', LSO, plus 11 items not conducted by Tauský. [Issued in 'The Orchid Series', by Innovative Music Productions Ltd, part of the Pickwick Group.] (P 1993) [Also in 3CD album **1070** (?), *Invitation to the Opera.* (P 1998)].

HALLMARK

CD, *More Opera Favourites*, includes Verdi: *La Traviata*, 'Prelude Act 1', conducted by Tauský. (P 1999?).

CD 350342, *Themes you have loved*, LSO. Includes the works by Binge, Mascagni, Tchaikovsky, Strauss, J. I, Bach/Walton, Walton, Sibelius, Grainger, Wolf-Ferrari, Benjamin and Reznicek, listed in PDA 036 above, plus items not conducted by Tauský. (P 1995).

PYE

NPL 18260/NSPL 18260, *National Brass Band Festival at the RAH 1968*, Grimethorpe Colliery, Wingates Temperance, CWS (Manchester), Luton and Shaftesbury Crusade (Bristol) Bands. Works conducted by Tauský:

Wagner, arr. Frank Wright: Prelude, *The Mastersingers*,
Osterling, arr. Frank Wright: Concert March, *Thundercrest*
Handel, arr. Denis Wright: *Music for the Royal Fireworks*,
J. Strauss II, arr. Frank Wright: *Thunder and Lightning Polka*
Tomlinson: *This Scepter'd Isle* (March)
Elgar: March, *Pomp and Circumstance No.1*

GSGL 10445, *National Brass Band Festival at the RAH 1969*, Brighouse and Rastrick, Black Dyke Mills, GUS (Footwear) and CWS (Manchester) Bands. Works conducted by Tauský:

Frank Wright: *Preludio Marziale*
Sibelius: *Finlandia*
J. Cacavas-Hazelgrove: *Burnished Brass*
Toselli, arr. J. Ord Hume: *Serenata*
German, arr. D. Wright: *Men of Harlech*
Tchaikovsky, arr. D. Wright: *Overture 1812*

CHANDOS BRASS BAND SERIES

BBR 1003, *National Brass Band Festival 1979*, Besses O' Th' Barn Band, Hammonds Sauce Works Band, Parc and Dare Band, Sun Life Stanshawe Band, Bristol and Wingates Temperance Band. (London, RAH, 6 October 1979, live recording). Apart from individual bands under their own conductors, Tauský conducted the massed bands in:

Grieg arr. Banks: *Homage March*
Jacob: *Symphonic Study*
Strauss, R., arr. Banks: *Festmusik der Stadt Wien*
Langford: March, *Carnival Day*
Langford: *Strauss Fantasy*

CBRD 1009, *The Chandos Sound of Brass*, includes, Langford, *Carnival Day*, from the 1979 Festival above. (P 1982).

Private or off-air recordings:

BOUGHTON: *The Immortal Hour*, (Complete), Eidwen Harry, John Mitchinson, BBC Singers, BBCCO, Oriel Music Society, **OMS 052** (2 CD). (Broadcast 6 May 1979).

DVOŘÁK: *Rusalka*, Joan Carlyle, Rowland Jones, Ann Howard, Michael Langdon, Pauline Tinsley, BBC Chorus, BBCCO, A Voice from the Old House, **VFOH 51 & 52**. (Camden Theatre, May 1968). (www.joancarlyle.co.uk)

DVOŘÁK: *Rusalka,* 42 minutes from Act 1, Joan Hammond, Patricia Kern, Charles Craig, Howell Glynne, Alberto Remedios, SWOO, Omega Opera Archive, **CD** no number. (London, Sadlers Wells Theatre, 19 March 1959, live recording).

ELGAR: *The Music Makers*, Gwyneth Griffiths, Central London Orchestra, Acorn CF 219. (60th anniversary Princes Risborough Music Society).

MOZART: *The Impresario (Der Schauspieldirektor)*, Patricia Wise, Nan Christie, Giuseppe Di Stefano, Patrick Cargil, English Chamber Orchestra, Encore ***DVD 2609***, House of Opera, ***DVD530***, BBC TV. (1980).

OFFENBACH: *Daphnis et Chloé*, singers and orchestra of Guildhall School of Music, London, House of Opera **CD8278.** (live performance, 21 December 1977). (www.houseofopera.com).

SUPPÉ: *Requiem*, Wendy Eathorne, Penelope Walker, Ramon Remedios, David Thomas, BBCCO, Royal Choral Society, Voce-89 (2 LP). (nd.).

SUPPÉ: *The Finishing School (Das Pensionat)*, singers and orchestra of Guildhall School of Music, London, House of Opera **CD11219**. (live performance, BBC, 1977).

Documentary

Graham Melville-Mason in conversation with Vilém Tauský and Karel Janovický, Dvořák Society Video cassette (no number), Bechstein Room, Wigmore Hall, London, 6 November 2000.
(Available from sales@dvorak-society.org)

12

REFERENCES TO VILÉM TAUSKÝ IN THE BRITISH LIBRARY NATIONAL SOUND ARCHIVE (NSA)

REFERENCES TO VILÉM TAUSKÝ IN THE BRITISH LIBRARY NATIONAL SOUND ARCHIVE (NSA)

Abbreviations used are

BBCCO	BBC Concert Orchestra
AHTW	Assembly Hall, Tunbridge Wells
CTL	Camden Theatre, London
RAH	Royal Albert Hall, London
RFH	Royal Festival Hall, London
nmd	no more data given
RCN	NSA Recording Call Number

The following references were taken from the NSA web site (www.bl.uk) during the development of this volume and were rechecked in 2010. Items already listed in the Discography are not repeated here. Each listing finishes with the Archive's allocated RCN. The amount of information given by NSA for each entry varies; a few items which cannot be correctly identified have not been listed.

Tauský as composer and conductor:

From our village, BBCCO. nmd. [RCN: M7367BW BD1]

Coventry (String Orchestra version), London Studio Strings, BBC Radio 3, 1971 (?). [RCN: M4253W TR1]

Tauský as composer:

Soho, Scherzo for orchestra, BBCCO, Christopher Adey. nmd. [RCN: NP8226BW BD 1]

Tauský as conductor:

ALWYN: *Concerti grossi, No.1*, BBCCO. (BBC radio, 6 May 1968) [RCN: M1298W C1]

ALWYN: *Miss Julie*, Jill Gomez (soprano), Della Jones (mezzo-soprano), Benjamin Luxon (baritone), Anthony Rolfe Johnson (tenor), BBCCO. nmd.
[RCN: 29E BBC Transcription 142325/30-S BD1]

ANSELL: *Plymouth Point*, BBCCO. (CTL, BBC radio, 15 February 1964) [RCN: 1CDR0011652 BD9 NSA]

APIVOR, DENIS: *Piano concerto*, Op.13, Gordon Watson, BBC Northern Orchestra. (recorded 1952, nmd) [RCN: NP2827W TR1]

ARENSKY: *Suite*, Op.7, BBCCO. (BBC radio, 2 January 1962) [RCN: 1CDR0007115 BD5 NSA]

ARNOLD: *Concerto for mouth-organ*, Op.4, Tommy Reilly, BBCCO. nmd. [RCN: 023R2 BD1]

BANTOCK: *Old English Suite, (Suite - English Scenes)*, BBCCO. BBC radio, 27 March 1962) [RCN: 1CDR0007129 BD2-5 NSA]

BEETHOVEN: *Piano Concerto No.5*, Sir Clifford Curzon, BBCCO. (BBC radio, 13 May 1961) [RCN: 1CDR0011567 BD1 NSA]

BERLIOZ: *The Damnation of Faust, Hungarian March*, BBCCO. (BBC radio, 15 February 1964) [RCN: 1CDR0011632 BD7 NSA]

BINGE: *The Watermill*, BBCCO. (RFH, BBC Light Music Festival, BBC radio, 30 June 1962) [RCN: 1CDR0011569 BD2 NSA]

BRIDGE: *Summer*, BBCCO. nmd. [RCN: M1222W BD 1]

BRITTEN: *Rape of Lucretia*, Paul Harry, Dawn Symes, Linda Strachan and Andrew Hambley-Smith, Guildhall School of Music and Drama (London). (Broadcast on Radio London, 22 March 1983) [RCN: T5509-T5510BW C1]

BRUCH: *Violin Concerto No.1*, Beryl Kimber, BBCCO. (AHTW, BBC radio, 14 April 1962) [RCN: 1CDR0011663 BD5-7 NSA]

BUSH, GEOFFREY: *'Twelfth Night' An entertainment*, David Galliver (tenor), BBC Chorus, BBCCO. nmd. [RCN: M572W BD 1]

CHAGRIN: *Album for Nicholas*, London Studio Strings. nmd. [RCN: M4252W]

CLARKE: *Trumpet voluntary*, BBCCO. (RFH, BBC Light Music Festival, BBC radio, 30 June 1962) [RCN: 1CDR0011569 BD1 NSA]

COATES: *Three Bears*, BBCCO. (CTL, BBC Light Programme, 16 May 1959 [RCN: 1CDR0002177 S1 BD19 NSA]

CRUFT: *Meditation on the Passion*, BBCCO. nmd. [RCN: M7366BW BD 1]

DICKINSON, PETER: *Diversions, for orchestra*, BBC Midland Light Orchestra. nmd. [RCN: M5114BW BD1]

DVOŘÁK: *Nocturne for strings* [B.47], BBCCO. (BBC radio, 2 December 1961) [RCN: 1CDR0007071 BD6 NSA]

DVOŘÁK: *A Hero's song (Píseň bohatýrská)* [B.199]. nmd. [RCN: NP1886W BD1]

DVOŘÁK: *The Water Goblin (Vodník)* [B.195], BBCCO. (BBC radio, 22 November 1962) [RCN: 1CDR0007112 BD15 NSA]

ELGAR: *Spanish Serenade*, Op.23, Bexhill Choral Society, BBCCO. (BBC Radio 3 broadcast from De La Warr Pavillion, Bexhill, 13 January 1962) [RCN: 1CDR0007087 BD9 NSA]

FALL, LEO: *Madame Pompadour*, Elizabeth Robinson, Rowland Jones, Leslie Fryson, BBC Singers, BBCCO. nmd. [RCN: B1277/1 0.04'23"]

GRAINGER: *The Warriors*, Cyril Gell, Martin Goldstein and Edward Rubach (pianos), BBCCO. nmd. [RCN: M4590W BD 1]

GRIEG: *Peer Gynt, Suite No.1*, BBCCO. (BBC radio, 22 September 1962) [RCN: 1CDR0011632 BD8 NSA]

HARTY: *In Ireland,* William Bartlett (flute), BBCCO. (BBC radio, 13 September 1962) [RCN: 1CDR0007140 BD6 NSA]

HARTY: *Fantasy Scenes*, Midland Light Orchestra. nmd. [RCN: M5116BW]

HAYDN: *Trumpet Concerto*, Norman Burgess, BBCCO. (CTL, BBC radio, 15 February 1964) [RCN: 1CDR0011683 BD4-6 NSA]

IRELAND, JOHN: *A London Overture*, BBCCO. Two versions. (Recording dates 19 July 1963 and 17 December 1964) [RCN: 25A1682 and 25A1686]

JACOB: *Uncle Remus*, BBCCO. nmd. [RCN: M678R C1]

JANÁČEK: *Osud*, BBC Chorus, BBCCO. (CTL, 16 October 1971) [RCN: C961/72 BD4]

KELLY, BRYAN: *Cantilena* and *rondo*, BBCCO. nmd. [RCN: M166R BD1]

KHACHATURIAN: *Gayaneh, Dance of the Young Maidens* and *Lullaby*, BBCCO. (CTL, BBC radio, 5 April 1963) [RCN: 1CDR0011590 BD5-6 NSA]

KHACHATURIAN: *Gayaneh Suite*, BBCCO. (CTL, BBC radio, 15 February 1964) [RCN: 1CDR0011652 BD10 NSA]

KHACHATURIAN: *Masquerade Suite*, BBCCO. (CTL, BBC radio, 15 February 1964) [RCN: 1CDR0011652 BD10 NSA]

LAMBERT: *Horoscope*, selected movements, BBCCO. (AHTW, BBC radio, 14 March 1964) [RCN: 1CDR0011736 BD8 NSA]

LEHÁR: *Merry Widow,* Waltz, Hallé Orchestra. (RAH Proms, 1 September 1956) [RCN: 1CD0071449 D2 BD5]

LISZT: *Piano Concerto No.2*, John Ogdon, BBCCO. (BBC radio, 11 November 1961) [RCN: 1CDR0011617 BD4 NSA]

MASSENET: *Phèdre*, Overture, BBCCO. (BBC radio, 27 January 1962) [RCN: 1CDR0007081 BD12 NSA]

MORGAN, DAVID: *Overture for a Festive Occasion*, BBCCO. nmd. [RCN: M7365BW BD1]

MOZART: *Serenade in D major* K.239, Hallé Orchestra. (RAH Proms, 1 September 1956) [RCN: 1CD0071449 D1 BD4]

MOZART: *Symphony No.36 Linz*, K.425, Hallé Orchestra. (RAH Proms, 1 September 1956) [RCN: 1CD0071449 D1 BD5]

MOZART: *The Impresario*, Patricia Wise (soprano), Nan Christie (soprano), English Chamber Orchestra. (BBC TV recording, broadcast BBC2, 7 December 1980. Audio only) [RCN: T3547W C1]

MOZART: *Piano Concerto* K.466, Denis Matthews, BBCCO. (CTL, BBC radio, 15 April 1961) [RCN: 1CDR0011547 BD2-4 Playback]

MOZART: *Piano Concerto* K.491, Denis Matthews, BBCCO. (CTL, BBC radio, 5 April 1963) [RCN: 1CDR0011590 BD2-4 NSA]

MYASKOVSKY: *Sinfonietta, for strings,* Op.32, No.2 (?), Langham Chamber Orchestra. [RCN: B388/1 0:00'34"]

OFFENBACH: *Tales of Hoffmann, Barcarolle*, BBCCO. (AHTW, BBC radio, 14 March 1964) [RCN: 1CDR0011736 BD10 NSA]

PHILLIPS, MONTAGUE: *Sinfonietta* Op.70, Ulster Orchestra. nmd. [RCN: NP7672BW C 2]

PHILLIPS, MONTAGUE: *Surrey Suite*, Ulster Orchestra. nmd. [RCN: NP7643BW BD 1]

PROKOFIEV: *Peter and the Wolf*, Frank Phillips (narrator), BBCCO. (RFH, BBC Light Music Festival, BBC radio, 30 June 1962) [RCN: 1CDR0011569 BD3 NSA]

RACHMANINOFF: *Aleko, Intermezzo* and *Men's Dance*, BBCCO. (BBC radio, 2 January 1962) [RCN: 1CDR0007115 BD2 NSA, and 1CDR0007115 BD4 NSA]

RACHMANINOFF: *Piano Concerto No.2*, Peter Katin, BBCCO. (BBC radio, 3 October 1958) [RCN: 1CDR0011606 BD2-4 NSA]

ROSSINI: *La Gazza Ladra,* Overture, BBCCO. (AHTW, BBC radio, 14 April 1962) [RCN: 1CDR0011524 BD3 Playback]. Also CTL, 29 December 1962. [RCN: 1CDR0011670 BD7 NSA]

ROSSINI: *Italiana in Algeri*, Overture, BBCCO. (BBC radio, 11 November 1961) [RCN: 1CDR0011617 BD2 NDA]

SAINT-SAËNS: *Carnival of the Animals*, Mary and Geraldine Peppin (pianos), BBCCO. (CTL, BBC Light programme, 16 May 1959) [RCN: 1CDR0002177 S1 BD5-BD18 NSA]

SAINT-SAËNS: *Introduction and rondo capriccioso*, Alan Loveday (violin), BBCCO. (BBC radio, 30 March 1963) [RCN: 1CDR0011668 BD5 NSA]

SAUNDERS: (?) *Diversions*, for strings, Langham Chamber Orchestra. nmd. [RCN: B5991/06 0:48'52"]

SCHUBERT: *German Dances*, D.820, arr. Webern. Hallé Orchestra. (RAH Proms, 1 September 1956) [RCN: 1CD0071449 D1 BD2 and 1CD0071449 D3 BD1]

SMETANA: *Dalibor*, Act 3, April Cantelo, Pauline Tinsley, Gwyn Griffiths, Rowland Jones, Joseph Ward and Don Garrard, BBCCO and Chorus. (BBC radio 17 April 1970.) [RCN: 1CDR0007176 BD2 NSA] (Earlier incomplete short excerpts with Joan Hammond and Richard Lewis, BBCSO from 8 May 1955. nmd. [RCN: 1CDR0004390 BD2-BD4 and 1CDR0006474 BD7 NS])

SMETANA: *Má vlast - Vltava*, BBCCO. (CTL, BBC radio, 15 February 1964) [RCN: 1CDR0011683 BD3 NSA]

STANFORD: *Irish Rhapsody No.5*, BBCCO. (BBC radio, 1 February 1962) [RCN: 1CDR0007110 BD6 NSA]

STRAUSS, JOHANN I: *Radetzky March*, Op.228, Hallé Orchestra. (RAH Proms, 1 September 1956) [RCN: 1CD0071449 D2 BD4]

STRAUSS, JOHANN II: *Roses from the South*, Hallé Orchestra. (RAH Proms, 1 September 1956) [RCN: 1CD0071449 D2 BD2 and 1CD0071449 D2 BD3]

STRAUSS, JOHANN II: *Tales from the Vienna Woods*, BBCCO. (BBC radio, 11 November 1961) [RCN: 1CDROO11617 BD3 NSA]

STRAUSS, JOHANN II: *Kaiserwalzer*, Op.437, BBCCO. (AHTW, BBC Light programme) nmd. [RCN: 1CDR0011612 BD2 NSA]

STRAUSS, RICHARD: *Rosenkavalier* - Suite, Hallé Orchestra. (RAH Proms, 1 September 1956) [RCN: 1CD0071449 D2 BD6]

STRAVINSKY: *The Firebird,* Suite, BBCCO. (RFH, BBC radio, 29 June 1963) [RCN: 1CDROO11713 BD3 NSA]

SULLIVAN - MACKERRAS: *Pineapple Poll*, BBCCO. (AHTW, BBC radio, 14 March 1964) [RCN: 1CDR0011736 BD9 NSA]

SUPPÉ: *Morning, noon and night in Vienna*, Overture, Hallé Orchestra. (RAH Proms, 1 September 1956) [RCN: 1CD0071449 D2 BD1]

SUPPÉ: *Zehn Mädchen und kein Mann*, Collette McGahon, Kim Begley, Guildhall School of Music and Drama Symphony Orchestra. (London). (BBC recording, BBC Radio 3, 3 September 1981.) [RCN: T4413BW C1]

TATE, PHYLLIS: *London fields*, BBCCO. nmd. [RCN: M298W TR1]

TCHAIKOVSKY: *Piano Concerto No.1*, Peter Katin, BBCCO. (AHTW) nmd. [RCN: 1CDROO11612]

TCHAIKOVSKY: *Sleeping Beauty*, Suite, BBCCO. (BBC radio, 29 June 1963) [RCN: 1CDR0011713 BD2 NSA]

TCHAIKOVSKY: *Suite No.3*, BBCCO. (CTL, BBC radio, 15 February 1964) [RCN: 1CDR0011683 BD7 NSA]

VERDI: *Forza del Destino*, Overture, BBCCO. (AHTW, BBC radio, 14 March 1964) [RCN: 1CDR0011736 BD6 NSA]

WALTON: *Crown Imperial*, BBCCO. (RFH, BBC radio, 29 June 1963) [RCN: 1CDR0011713 BD4 NSA]

WEBER: *Oberon*, Overture, BBCCO. (CTL, BBC radio, 10 January 1963) [RCN:1CDR0011573 BD1 Playback, and 2CDROO10173 BD1 Archive]

WIENIAWSKI: *Violin Concerto No.2*, Elizabeth Balmas, BBCCO. (BBC radio, 22 April 1965) [RCN: 1CDR0009534 BD11-12 NSA]

WOLF-FERRARI: *I Quattro rusteghi*, Intermezzo (?), BBCCO. (AHTW, BBC radio, 14 March 1964) [RCN: 1CDR0011736 BD7 NSA]

Four English Composers, Alan Frank reminisces about his association with Rawsthorne, Lambert, Vaughan Williams and Walton. Includes Rawsthorne: Overture: *Street Corner* and extracts from the ballet *Madame Chrysanthème*; Walton: film music from Henry V and *Hamlet*, and the *Johannesburg Festival* Overture, BBCCO. (BBC recording, broadcast (repeat) on BBC Radio 3, 21 June 1973.) [RCN: P1330BW BD1]

Tauský as arranger and conductor:

SCHUBERT: *Grazer Galopp*, Hallé Orchestra. (RAH Proms, 1 September 1956) [RCN: 1CD0071449 D1 BD3]

WALTON: *The Quest*, Suite, BBCCO. nmd. [RCN: M785W TR1]

Tauský as arranger:

HANDEL: *Berenice*, Overture, Reginald Kilby and his strings. nmd. [RCN: 1LP0184235 6 Columbia, and 2LP0030627 6 Columbia]

TCHAIKOVSKY: *Marche militaire*, BBCCO, Ashley Lawrence. nmd. [RCN: NP8919BW C4]

WALTON: *The Quest*, BBCCO, Ashey Lawrence. nmd. [RCN: 1CDR0023390 BD15 NSA]

Tauský in conversation:

I was there, as vocal coach for the première of 'The House of the Dead'. (recorded 1995) [RCN: H5871/2 2:30'42"]

Interview with Vilém Tauský, recorded for Radio Medway. (3 March 1974) [RCN: CDR0022829 BD5 NSA]

Music Now, *Vilém Tauský celebrates 50 years of opera conducting*. (BBC Radio 3, 11 May 1979) [RCN: NP3552W C1]

Out Of The Mist, on Janáček, with Patrick Lambert, Jan Smaczny and John Tyrrell. nmd. [RCN: B7232/ 01 0:10'50"]

On Janáček, interval talk. nmd. [RCN: M1498R C1]

Leo Fall, my uncle. nmd. [RCN: M4157R BD1]

Music Weekly, extract includes *a visit to Janáček's home in Hukvaldy* and *a conversation with Vilém Tauský*. nmd. [RCN: T8244W]

In addition to the above, Greg Terian has noted the following Tauský references in the Sound Archive:

TAUSKÝ: *Waltzing through Czechoslovakia*, BBC Midland Light Orchestra, conducted Rae Jenkins, record No. 6955-6, 2 March 1944.

TAUSKÝ: *Under Czech Skies*, BBC Midland Light Orchestra, conducted Rae Jenkins, record No. 18093-9, 10 January 1945.

TAUSKÝ: *This is Northern Ireland*, Northern Ireland Light Orchestra, record No. MX/14589-91, 2 March 195?.

TAUSKÝ: *Harken Good Sir*, Manchester Children's Choir, record No. 11555, 22 December 1947.

TAUSKÝ: March: *Men of Tomorrow*, BBC Concert Orchestra, 29 June 1957.

Terian also discovered that recordings made by the Czechoslovak Army Choir have been preserved from 25 December, 1942, 27 October 1943 and 15 December 1943, in which Tauský may well have been involved, though not named. [1]

[1] Greg Terian, personal communication, 2010.

13

AN ANNOTATED LIST OF COMPOSITIONS BY VILÉM TAUSKÝ

2nd Concert, 20 August 2009

Introduction — Joseph Horovitz: »Emigration in England«

Joseph Horovitz (* 1926)

String quartet no. 5 (1969)

Kurt Weill (1900 – 1950)

String quartet no. 1 op.8 (1923)

Introduktion. Sostenuto, con molta espressione

Scherzo. Vivace

Choralphantasie. Andante ma non troppo

●

Vilém Tauský (1910 – 2004)

»Coventry« (1941)

Meditation for String Quartet

Joseph Haydn (1732 – 1809)

String quartet F-major, op. 77/2, Hob. III: 2

Allegro moderato

Menuet. Presto

Andante

Finale. Vivace assai

aron quartett

Ludwig Müller, Violine

Bama Kobori, Violine

Georg Hamann, Viola

Christophe Pantillon, Violoncello

Tauský's 'Coventry' was played at the 2009 Kammermusikfestival, Schloss Laudon, Austria

First performance in Austria

[Courtesy G. Hamann]

AN ANNOTATED LIST OF COMPOSITIONS BY VILÉM TAUSKÝ

Stage works:

Operettas: *Marcella, Smile!, The Little Girl in Blue*
All given at the Brno Opera House from 1932 to 1938.
Speaking in 2001, Tauský doubted if the scores had survived. [1]

Orchestral works:

Sinfonietta for full orchestra (1930)
Awarded State Prize

Divertimento for Strings (1968)

From our village, three movement suite for orchestra based on Czech Folk Songs (1978)

Soho, Scherzo for Orchestra (1980)

Serenade for Strings (1994)

Solo instrument with Orchestra:

Rhapsody for Piano and Orchestra on themes by Smetana (1945)
(premièred by Louis Kentner)

Fantasia da burlesca for Violin and Orchestra (1951)
(premièred by Frederic Grinke)

Tauský's thoughts on this work have been recorded:

> *Tauský had noted that when stationed in East Anglia with the Czechoslovak Brigade, air raids were frequent and caused tension among the soldiers. In Tauský's billet, however, the wail of the siren was the invariable signal for one of the soldiers to pick up his violin and begin practicising his scales and arpeggios - a*

[1] Interview with Michael Haas, October 2001, see p.55. However, one original m/s page from an operetta was received by Tauský by post from Brno c.2003. No sender's details were given; personal communication Brenda Rayson, 2010.

self-imposed distraction which was received with very mixed feelings by the other occupants. 'Fantasia da burlesca' is in two movements, played without a break. In the first movement, the-composer reflects on the serious side of life; but at the point where his meditations are interrupted by memories of the air raid, he sees the lighter side even of so grim an occasion, and with recollections of the fiddling soldier, the mood changes to one of burlesque. The work finishes with the 'All Clear' and the throwing down of the player's violin. [2]

Concertino for Harmonica, Strings, Harp and Percussion (1973)
Allegro moderato, Nocturne and Scherzo.

Written for Tommy Reilly; also used as a ballet score in New York.

Military and Brass Band music:

The Czechs are Marching, Call to Arms, Pour la Patrie and *Dans le Combat,* military marches (1940)

Cakes and Ale - Fantasy for Brass Band (1950)

Men of Tomorrow (1958) For the BBC Concert Orchestra

Concert Overture for Brass Band (1972)

This was commissioned for the Championship Section of the 1972 Regional Finals for the National Brass Band Championships of Great Britain. Tauský wrote at the time:

> *The music was inspired by the events of the Russian occupation of Czechoslovakia in 1968. The sombre opening expresses the feelings of subjugated people, and their hopelessness under oppression, which ultimately leads to a rebellious mood. The second part, the Allegro, starts in this mood with trumpet calls inciting the oppressed to resistance. In the following section hope and desire for freedom are expressed in a tune of folk character. Now the revolutionary mood grows, quietly and secretly the forces gather, until a great climax proclaims ultimate victory. The lyrical tune returns as [a] triumphal chorale with which the overture ends.* [3]

---

[2] 'Arpeggios in an Air Raid', *Radio Times* 16 November 1951, cited in *Dvořák Society Newsletter,* No. 70, January 2005.
[3] Sleeve note of Polydor LP 2928 011, see page 223.

Incidental Music for radio plays:

Marcela (1932)

Christopher Columbus (Cristobal Colón) (1934)

Film Scores

The Lost World - a documentary (1935)

The Picture of the 'White Lady' is missing (1938)

Interim Balance - a documentary about the Czechoslovak Army in Great Britain (1943)

Miscellaneous Vocal Works:

Three Songs for Soprano and Piano (1930)

Nursery Rhymes - a cycle of songs with piano accompaniment to Slovak folk poetry (mid 1930s)

Songs of Slovácko (mid 1930s)

Four Songs for Soprano and Piano (1934)

Songs of an Infantry Man (1937)

God Great and Mighty God - male voice chorus (c.1937)

Czech Christmas Carols - English language settings for the Czechoslovak Red Cross (1944)

Up and down the River Danube - Collection of Czechoslovak Folk Songs (1975)

Chamber Music:

Cello Sonata No.1 (1925)

Tauský recounted in 2003 that Leo Fall's younger brother Siegfried, a professor at the Berlin Conservatoire, saw a single movement for cello and piano which he, young Tauský, had written. 'You must study music' said the professor and this single movement was later expanded to become the Sonata which Tauský presented for his entrance to the Brno Conservatoire. [4]

Wind Quintet (mid 1930s)

Little Piano Suite (mid 1930s)

Variations for piano on an original theme (1939)

Coventry: A Meditation for String Quartet (1941)
Later arranged for string orchestra

Variations on a Welsh tune, for piano (1942)

Cello Sonata No.2 (1964)

String Quartet (1965)

Essay for solo viola (1965)

Ballade for Cello and Piano (1975)

Suite for Violin and Piano, (1980)
(premièred by Peter Fisher)

Arrangements:

Walton: *The Quest*, ballet suite, (1961)

Vaňhal: *Concerto for Oboe and Strings* (1968)
(arranged for Evelyn Rothwell - Lady Barbirolli)

Vaňhal: *Divertimento for String Orchestra*

Schubert-Liszt: *Soirée de Vienne* - version for piano and orchestra

---

[4] Interview with Martin Anderson, December 2003, see p.55.

Smetana: *Bartered Bride - Polka,*

(arranged for Rudolf Firkušný)

Several other popular arrangments exist, see also the discography and the National Sound Archive listings.

Orchestrations:

Friml: *Katuška*, operetta (1939)

Weinberger: *Na růžích ustláno (A Bed of Roses)*, operetta (1933) [5]

Weinberger: *Císař na třešních (The Emperor Picking Cherries)*. operetta (c.1934) [5]

Weinberger, *Apropos co dělá Andula? (by the Way, What's Andula doing?)*, operetta (c.1934)

....

Sources: Developed from *Music on the Web* [online], at: http://www.musicweb-international.com/Tausky/index.htm [Downloaded July 2007] with additional listings from Karel Janovický's account of Tauský's early years in Brno.

---

[5] The scores of both these operettas with music by Weinberger and orchestrated by Tauský were described as 'lost' in Sadie, S., *New Grove Dictionary of Music and Musicians*, (London: Macmillan, 1980).

INDEX [1]

[1] This Index does not cover Appendices I and 2 to Chapter 8, the discography and the NSA listings, which are all listed alphabetically.
Footnotes have not been indexed.

"The Conservatoire of Europe"

This title was bestowed on Bohemia because of the astonishing quality and number of its musicians and composers. It is a title no less deserved today than it was 200 years ago.

To most music enthusiasts, "Czech music" means the distinguished line of Smetana - Dvořák - Janáček - Martinů, but there always was - and still is - so much more to explore.

The Dvořák Society of Great Britain was founded in 1974 and is devoted to all the music and musicians of the Czech and Slovak Republics. Our journal *Czech Music* is published at intervals under the distinguished editorship of Graham Melville-Mason and we also have a *Newsletter* which is issued every quarter. Our Record Service enables economical access to all the record labels of both countries and our growing Library is a study resource containing many useful books, scores, pamphlets and recordings.

Our activities depend very much on the wishes of our members. We hold social and musical events, talks and courses, often in conjunction with other bodies. We have organised several musical holidays in both the Czech Republic and Slovakia. Only rarely do we promote concerts ourselves, but we are frequently and closely involved in supporting the promotional work of others.

For further information please see our website: dvorak-society.org or if you would like further details and samples of our newsletter, please contact: membership@dvorak-society.org

The Dvořák Society is a Registered Charity no. 267336

Patrons: Josef Suk; Graham Melville-Mason

Previous Occasional Publications

No 1: Rudolf Firkušný 1912-1994
(1999)
ISBN 0-9532769-0-2 (paperback only)

No 2: A Tribute to Petr Eben
(2000)
ISBN 0-9532769-1-0 (paperback)
ISBN 0 9532769-1-0 (hardback)

No 3: Václav Talich 1883-1961
(2003)
ISBN 0-9532769-2-9 (paperback)
ISBN 0-9532769-3-7 (hardback)

No 4 Antonín Dvořák
Complete Catalogue of Works
(2004)
ISBN 0-9532769-4-5 (paperback)
ISBN 0-9532769-5-3 (hardback)

No 5: Bohumil Fidler: "My Life and Memories"
(2008)
ISBN 978-9532769-6-7 (paperback)
ISBN 978-9532769-7-4 (hardback)

The Society is delighted to acknowledge the continued support of its Corporate Members

Commercial members:

Supraphon
John Whibley
HNH International
Talacko Sheet Music
Editio Bärenreiter Praha
The Prague Concert Company
Maestro Tour Management Ltd
London Express (Coach Link) Ltd

Non-commercial members:

MusicEnterprise
Royal Academy of Music
Indian Summer in Levoča
The Ján Cikker Foundation
The Royal College of Music
The City of London Libraries
St Lucia Campus, Queensland
University of California, Santa Barbara
The Friedheim Library, Peabody Institute, Baltimore
Harold B Lee Library, Brigham Young University, Utah

For full details of the benefits that Corporate Membership can bring, please contact the Corporate Membership Administrator, Richard Beith: richard@mbeith.demon.co.uk